Management Accounting: Pathways to Progress

Professor Michael Bromwich

CIMA Professor of Accounting and

Financial Management

and

Dr. Alnoor Bhimani

Lecturer in Accounting and Finance

The Chartered Institute of
Management Accountants
63 Portland Place
London W1N 4AB

Copyright © CIMA 1994
First published in 1994
Reprinted 1995, 1996
The Chartered Institute of Management Accountants
ISBN 1 874784 27 2

The publishers of this book consider that it is a worthwhile contribution to discussion, without necessarily sharing the views expressed, which are those of the authors.

For Sofiya Nur

Acknowledgements

Our appreciation is again extended to the business executives, consultants and researchers who generously gave their time to assist in this project and to the anonymous reviewers drawn from a variety of backgrounds. We also wish to express our gratitude to Paul Plowman, the chairman of CIMA's Research and Technical Committee, to Andrea Jeffries, the Director of Research at CIMA and her staff, especially Mai Lai who helped us in collecting and analysing the large amount of relevant literature, and to CIMA Publishing, who coped very well with an impossible timetable. We are also very grateful to the CIMA Research Foundation for funding this and other projects. The secretarial and typing skills of Ann Cratchley and Dorothy Richards have been especially appreciated as always. We are also grateful for the assistance of Claudine Finnegan in typing the bibliography.

Contents

Preface

This book represents the successor to *Management Accounting: Evolution Not Revolution* (*Bromwich and Bhimani*, 1989) and was also commissioned by the Chartered Institute of Management Accountants.

The external and manufacturing environments in many countries, both mature and newly industrialised, are undergoing a large variety of rapid changes in an increasingly competitive context. Many firms are adopting innovative production systems, advanced manufacturing technology and many new organisational and managerial techniques. Some commentators believe that management accounting is experiencing a prolonged 'crisis' because it has lagged behind these changes. Indeed, a large number of calls are still being made for altering management accounting practices in the name of such changes.

In the UK, no one school of opinion yet dominates views on the nature of reforms which might be appropriate for management accounting. The case for wholesale reform has not been accepted in practice. However, in this report we evaluate many suggested changes to management accounting and are able recommend a number of approaches and practices which seem to provide practical promise in helping accountants to respond to the challenges identified in this study.

The first edition of this study was sponsored by the Chartered Institute of Management Accountants in October 1988 to identify '. . . the criticisms being made, the way in which management accounting techniques already exist to meet them, the findings of research in this field and any gaps that might initiate further research'.

This study retains much of the substantive material of the earlier report and continues to address the original brief. It thus examines the implications for management accounting of the changes which are taking place within British firms which are adopting different forms of advanced manufacturing techniques and managerial processes. It reviews information concerning changing managerial perceptions of information requirements, the use of new communication forms and channels, and the implications of changing organisational structures so as to help the management accounting profession to react to this new environment.

The report supports its conclusions by exploring the findings of empirical investigations of United Kingdom, North American and Japanese firms undertaken by various independent researchers and concentrates on documenting changes in management accounting processes in these countries. This study thus seeks to explain the implications for management accounting of recent changes in technology, and in organisational procedures and in management.

The report focuses more than the previous edition on a wider array of opportunities facing the management accountant. The passage of time since the first edition allows us to spotlight a number of approaches which provide the promise of strengthening the roles that accountants can be expected to play in organisations, some of which are relatively novel whilst others have been more tested in practice. The title of *Management Accounting: Pathways to Progress* reflects this wish to also present approaches which may help expand the accountant's role in a dynamic and turbulent environment embodying increasing global competition in a growing number of industries.

All the chapters in this book have been rewritten. This was the only way to adequately capture some of the opportunities and challenges arising since the earlier report. The chapter on Japan (Chapter 6) has been substantially expanded to cover the environment and management practices of Japanese firms without which it is difficult to fully appreciate their accounting systems and any lessons they contain for the West. The chapter (Chapter 2) reviewing new technologies and innovations in management practices in order to understand their possible implications for management accounting has been expanded.

A new chapter (Chapter 3) has been added which seeks to examine these implications and to discuss the full menu of new accounting approaches available for tackling changes in the industrial environment. This allows the two chapters focusing on North America and the UK (Chapters 7 and 8) now to concentrate more on analysing how far the empirical findings document that changes are being made to accounting methods and models in the face of the challenges and opportunities identified in this report and their characteristics.

Brief references to especially innovative French and German accounting practices have been added to appropriate chapters. Space and time constraints and the lack of an English language literature mean that the full richness of management accounting in these countries cannot be fully explored in this study. Further research is urgently needed in these areas.

A completely new chapter on the strategic dimension of management accounting (Chapter 5) explains the relatively new ideas of strategic management accounting. A second new chapter (Chapter 4) dealing with new approaches to fixed overheads includes some of the results of the CIMA-sponsored study entitled: *Fixed Overhead Allocation in High-Tech Industries* (*Bromwich and Wang*, 1993)[1].

The aim of this book is to give a fairly detailed exposition of a relatively comprehensive range of recently suggested accounting techniques in an accessible fashion. The book also examines the reasons for their existence and their strengths and weaknesses employing organisational and economic perspectives. The relative promise of these approaches for the future, considered in terms of their ability to enhance further the role accountants can play in organisations, is also assessed. We believe many of these approaches do represent pathways to progress in the management of firms. Some of the approaches explored here represent relatively well trodden pathways, others merely the beginning of promising tracks to progress.

There is an increasing number of case studies documenting changes in actual management accounting systems in the UK and elsewhere focusing especially on activity based approaches. Many of these case studies have been sponsored by the Chartered Institute of Management Accountants as part of their research policy which, among other things, encourages attempts to examine how

---

[1] The term 'cost allocation' is used in the book as a general term referring to absorption and apportionment. CIMA's official terminology defines absorbed overhead as overhead charged to products or services by means of absorption rates. Cost apportionment is defined as that part of cost attribution which shares costs among two or more cost centres or cost units in proportion to the estimated benefit received, using a proxy.

management accounting is affected by changes in product markets and the new manufacturing environment.

This report complements these studies by integrating their findings within the broader perspective of novel management accounting techniques being adopted by firms both in Britain and in other parts of the world. It is very commendable that the CIMA should devote resources to exploring new frontiers for the practice of management accounting, thereby helping to ensure that practitioners continue to play a full role in enterprise management. It is hoped that this report will contribute towards meeting the challenges facing the profession as the manufacturing and market environments undergo rapid changes by delineating the multitude of possibilities open for management accounting change and recommending desirable courses of action.

Michael Bromwich and ALnoor Bhimani

February 1994

1
Introduction and Executive Summary

1.1 Introduction

This book is a second edition of a report sponsored by the Chartered Institute of Management Accountants (CIMA) entitled *Management Accounting: Evolution Not Revolution (Bromwich and Bhimani*, 1989). The original brief was to investigate the major changes taking place within industry and to evaluate the arguments that these required major revisions to management accounting.

Since the 1980s, industry in Western countries has had to respond to a number of major challenges. These include the need to increase spending on R & D and the requirement to make major investment in new technology and in supply processes. International competitors have also posed the challenge of delayering cumbersome managerial structures and downsizing to become leaner and thereby increase productivity to withstand competition from 'world' class firms in a recessionary world environment.

Competitive challenges are also to be met by product diversity, high quality, better delivery and increased flexibility to satisfy new consumer demands and enhanced global competition.

There is no doubt that the performance of British industry is presently improving. Although throughout the 1980s, output grew by a modest 2 percent, productivity increased by nearly 5 percent per year mainly through decreasing employment. Using manufacturing employment as the measure of the manufacturing base of the UK, this base has declined by almost 40 percent during this time. Other measures, such as net assets, suggest a substantially lower decline but figures of well over 20 percent are common. Over 1992/93, output increased by over 2 percent and productivity increased by 7.25 percent whilst wage costs fell by 2 percent.

Since 1992, productivity has increased faster than wage costs thereby improving manufacturing cost competitiveness relative to the labour costs of competitors (*Lind*, 1993). Much of this improvement is relatively recent and disguises very poor figures for both investment and commercial R & D relative to competitors and a long-term declining share of world trade. A recent study using some 371 variables to measure the overall competitiveness of countries ranked the UK sixteenth in a world league of competitive countries. More startlingly, measuring competitiveness on a scale which gives Japan a score of 200 and the USA a score of 125, the UK scored minus 40 (*World Competitiveness Report*, 1993).

Similarly, in the mid to late 1980s management accounting was subject to major challenges. An outstanding critic is *Kaplan* who accuses accountants of using the wrong measures, which he says:

> move the company in the wrong direction, reward managers for damaging the business and provide no incentive for improvement (1988b, p.40).

Similarly, he accuses accountants of lagging behind the time and

> living off innovations in management accounting that were made 60, 80 and 100 years ago. (*Kaplan*, 1986a, p.7).

These challenges to management accounting are now becoming well known and were reviewed initially in the earlier report. They are also considered in Chapter 3 of this book (see also *Drury*, 1992, pp. 1-13 and *Ashton et al.*, 1991, pp. 1-16). They include:

(1) The subservience of management accounting to financial accounting where the use in management accounting of the arbitrary allocations permissible in financial accounting must fail to reflect the cost drivers encountered in modern manufacturing industry.

(2) Traditional product costing is therefore argued not to reflect the pattern of cost causation in firms using modern technologies including JIT and modern supply systems. Thus, traditional management accounting may distort costs and profits. Additionally, managerial bonuses may be based on these figures thereby encouraging incorrect decisions. It is claimed that these problems may be overcome by using activity based costing.

(3) These challenges have more recently been broadened to include the internal orientation of existing accounting systems and their inability to report on the business environment (see Chapter 5).

In response to these and other similar challenges, CIMA sponsored the first edition of this report to consider:

> the criticisms being made, the way in which management accounting techniques exist to meet them, the findings of research in this field and any gaps that might initiate further research.

The original report *Management Accounting: Evolution Not Revolution* suggested that experiments with new techniques be encouraged, and identified a set of problems for accounting and a significant number of opportunities for management accountants to further aid firms in decision making and control. The report counselled caution in responding to the most heavily publicised challenge ever faced by management accounting. Many authoritative commentators agreed with the report's view that 'the emphasis in accounting change should be on evolution rather than revolution'.

These challenges have not gone away but their continual nature and their increasingly vociferous and stark character has diminished. An important task of this report is to help in assessing how far accounting reforms are necessary and whether suitable accounting and other techniques exist to meet any identified need.

In the present report, the suggested changes in accounting in the last five years are charted and evaluated for their sustainable promise to industry and to management accounting. The limitations and difficulties of these, and other suggested new accounting approaches, are also considered.

The focus of the report is on manufacturing industry, reflecting that the bulk of the literature and documented experience address this area. However, there seems no reason to believe that many of the techniques discussed here are not at least equally valuable to the retail and services areas and provide considerable promise for both the not-for-profit sector and the public sector. Indeed, some evidence is given in this report to suggest that the service sector, at least, is beginning to be more innovative in accounting than the manufacturing sector.

Similarly, our selection of the challenges and opportunities to accounting and accounting techniques to be reviewed is dictated by their believed contemporary relevance and their perceived importance. Time and space constraints have meant we have not been able to give as much emphasis as we might have liked to some challenges to accounting and to potential implications. Some areas we have been unable to tackle at all.

Thus whilst maintaining the original brief, this book also searches for innovative methods which can be proposed as likely to lead to progress (broadly defined) in accounting. The title of this second edition *Management Accounting: Pathways to Progress* reflects this wish. It should, however, be recalled that progress along pathways can involve hard work, along circuitous and undulating routes which may sometimes become impassable or dwindle away however promising the original outlook.

1.2 Executive Summary

Identified challenges to management accounting

Considerable progress has been made in assessing and coping with some of the challenges identified in the first report.

(1) Some evidence has been found to support the view, drawn from USA history, that management accounting has, at least in some firms and countries, been subservient to financial accounting requirements (*Drury et al.*, 1993). Certainly, many accountants in Britain, at least, are aware of what might be called the 'black book' syndrome. Their time is spent following the requirements of the monthly reporting manual (generally black), generating reports that often obtain little attention at executive or board meetings, and the requirements of budgeting and capital appraisal manuals; the latter often function merely to legitimate already settled decisions.

Given these regular burdens, it is not surprising that many practising accountants have little time for working closely with managers, devising new systems, reforming existing systems or even thinking critically about accounting issues.

However, many British senior practitioners have denied that this problem ever applied in the British environment, arguing that management accounting considerations dominated integrated accounting systems with financial accounting requirements being met by end of period adjustments. This hypothetical subservience of management accounting to financial accounting implies a major deficiency in management in its willingness to continue to use redundant systems for relatively trivial reasons.

This book does however provide strong evidence that fundamental changes to accounting systems are difficult to initiate and carry through (see Chapters 7 and 8). Indeed, this problem often applies to suggestions made many years ago, such as using departmental and machine hour overhead rates. The reasons for this are not clear. It is difficult to believe that almost all suggested innovations in accounting fail the cost/benefit test by failing to provide benefits which outweigh their cost of implementation for the great majority of firms (as has been suggested by many USA commentators as an explanation of the relatively low take up of such innovations).

There is a very strong need for further research to explore this problem; especially important will be investigations as to whether managers and accountants understand the weaknesses of conventional management accounting systems sufficiently to be able to make subjective and other adjustments to reported results to reflect the enterprise's actual manufacturing and market environment, and whether *ad hoc* accounting studies allow any defects in the formal management accounting system to be overcome.

Many reformers have sought wholesale changes to the entire accounting system, thereby generating very large costs in terms of widespread consultation and bargaining and in major reprogramming, system reconfiguration and hardware costs.

Empirical evidence on the use of activity based costing (ABC) and its variants confirms that firms tend to be very timid in introducing new accounting systems and restrict their innovations to 'putting their toes in the water', often for a long period. One way of overcoming the possible need for large-scale revision of accounting and information systems is to seek to set up new free standing decision and/or control information systems. Some Japanese companies are establishing such systems for decision-making information. Another is to structure accounting reports so that they may be flexibly and routinely analysed in different ways depending on the decision in mind. This approach is followed in Germany where different sections of accounting reports routinely yield information on the 'profitability' of a variety of decisions concerning production and products, and of organisational segments (see Chapter 4).

Accounting systems have properties which extend beyond their conventional roles and which may inhibit easy change. They give structure and support to the formal and informal pattern of managerial responsibilities; they provide information configured in a way that supports the existing organisational structure. Moreover, accounting systems may well reflect the managerial power structure both formal and informal within the organisation. Further influences inducing conservatism towards accounting change may be generated by the frequently observed relation between managerial bonuses and accounting profits and the oft believed relationship between short-term accounting profits and securities prices.

(2) This book, other recent work and much consultancy activity has been geared to remedying 'the lack of strategic considerations in management accounting and project appraisal', noted in the first report, both by indicating essential elements that need to be included in strategic orientated management accounting systems and implementing such systems (Chapter 5).

One recent British survey (*Bright et al.*, 1992) indicated that over 40 percent of the firms surveyed were considering the introduction of at least elements of strategic management accounting. This result may turn out to be too optimistic, but many commentators favour an extension of the role of management accounting to encompass the costing of strategy and estimating the cost structures of competitors. This may seem something of a 'blue skies' idea to many accountants but it is not clear how otherwise firms can become or remain global competitors.

Harnessing an awareness by finance departments to strategy may encourage a more corporate-wide view of strategy and the co-ordination of information from all parts of the organisation, and aid in forming a team orientation towards corporate strategy. Here, information 'owned' by other departments is used in accounting reports to give an overall picture of corporate strategy and (via new performance measures including non-financial and even non-quantitative measures) to force strategy down the organisation so that all employees understand what their jobs contribute to achieving the organisation's strategy (an objective which is accomplished in Japan in very different ways: see Chapter 6).

Critics of this approach worry about its information needs, especially in terms of estimating competitors' cost structures. Chapter 5 seeks to show that obtaining sufficient information is possible but requires more resources to be devoted to monitoring a much wider set of information than seems to be currently collected (see Chapter 5). A report from the *Harris Centre* (1990) confirms the view that relatively little external information is routinely and regularly used in strategy formulation. Informed evidence is that much more is going on in this area than is presently publically visible because of its commercial sensitivity.

(3) Parts of Chapter 3 of this book review the strong argument, cited in the earlier report, that management accounting is based on redundant assumptions which may be overcome by adopting activity based costing (ABC) based on more realistic drivers than volume related bases, such as either labour or machine hours. Parts of Chapters 7 and 8 look at the empirical evidence concerning activity based accounting approaches.

There is no doubt that the use of ABC can produce a better understanding of those overheads which vary with clear and unique cost drivers other than the volume of production units. However, the conditions required to legitimately apply activity based approaches are restrictive and confine their use to a relatively small set of overhead costs: those which derive from a specific cost driver and which exhibit no jointness with other products or organisational units (see Chapters 3 and 4). Statistical studies cited in Chapter 7 do suggest that non-volume related activities may explain at least part of the cost functions of firms.

The effect of using activity based cost functions on optimal profits is not yet clear. To demonstrate a clear relation between profitability and the introduction of ABC may be very difficult given the other factors simultaneously acting on profits at any time. The very large number of case and field studies of ABC, discussed in Chapters 7 and 8, indicate that many firms have found ABC and its variants very useful. ABC seems especially helpful in understanding costs in service industries; the Royal Bank of Scotland, for instance, perceived traditional management accounting as having been less than satisfactory when justifying its support of ABC information.

One impression from these case and field studies is that often the discipline enforced by the introduction of ABC is at least as useful as the suggested precision of results in terms of activity costs and new product costs. The process of using ABC systems often seems to inform management of problems which they might have discovered already. More recent studies (see *Johnson*, 1992, for instance), discussing using non-accounting information, reiterate the point made in the earlier report that

> Some of the reasons adduced for introducing activity costing seem to be, in fact, examples of deficient management practices as much as poor accounting (*Bromwich and Bhimani*, 1989, p.3).

Reflecting a wish for ABC to extend its role in management, the practical emphasis on ABC has switched from product costing to activity based cost management and activity based budgeting (ABCM and ABB) (see Chapters 7 and 8) where the emphasis is on reducing costs by seeking to eliminate non-value added activities and on managing and planning the organisation using activity analysis. These processes convert activity based approaches from being a contribution to accounting to being more general management tools.

Although the required assumptions may limit the role that ABC can play within a firm, ABC and its variants should be welcomed as a new and important tool for accountants and for management for certain types of overhead costs. Current evidence and experience suggest that those who urged the use of ABC as a revolutionary approach to accounting likely to cause a wholesale change in extant accounting systems have not yet provided a sufficiently strong case or the necessary empirical evidence to convince practitioners. The application of ABC is, effectively, still in its infancy.

The slow take up of ABC in the UK and USA and, indeed a number of documented cases of either decisions not to use ABC or to abandon its use, suggest that these doubts about ABC are still shared by practitioners. There are a number of firms mainly in the service industries which have successfully reoriented their entire accounting systems to ABC. However, the great majority of documented uses are in what might be called pilot studies. In both the UK and USA only an important but small minority of firms are using ABC in any major way (perhaps, some 10 percent) though it is only fair to say that a much larger number of firms are still considering the use of ABC and its variants (see Chapters 7 and 8).

(4) The final challenge to accounting listed in the earlier report was:

the maintenance of traditional assumptions in performance appraisal and the continued short term orientation of this process (*Bromwich and Bhimani*, 1989, p.2).

Surveying the more recent evidence suggests that little has changed here, though CIMA has recently published an important work on performance measurement in the manufacturing sector in conjunction with a number of universities (*CIMA*, 1993). This report provided guidelines on important financial and non-financial indicators which reflect new manufacturing processes. One significant finding was that:

No optimal set of measures has yet emerged either in practice or theory to monitor the performance of manufacturing companies. A manufacturing enterprise, however, may use a general 'road map' approach to establish a range of performance measures relevant to its own operations. For instance, monitors could focus on quality, delivery, process times and flexibility as well as working capital, capital market, financial return and lender security (p.35).

Generally, a broad approach to performance measurement in both the short and long term was recommended. Another CIMA report examines performance measurement in service businesses (*Fitzgerald et al.*, 1992) and identifies six dimensions of service business including financial and competitive performance, service quality, innovation, flexibility and resource utilisation. It also emphasises the need to monitor those intangible aspects which contribute to success.

Life cycle costing has been urged as a way of overcoming some short-termism problems. However, there is little evidence that such methods are used in practice other than by very few firms (see Chapter 7). The detailed frameworks of such systems still need considerable further development prior to wide practical use.

Surveying the empirical evidence, it is difficult to avoid the conclusion that accounting control measures do sometimes induce short-termism by managers. The concern with monthly variances, many of which are beyond the control of managers, provides one example. The dependency of managerial bonuses on annual financial performance provides another as does, perhaps, the increasing use of the payback method of investment appraisal incorporating very short payback periods.

Discovered opportunities for accountants

This study considers in some detail the progress with regard to what the earlier report identified as opportunities for accountants to play a more useful role in management.

(1) In a representative firm, some 60 percent of costs are accounted for by the purchase of materials and components. In response to the view in the earlier report, Chapter 6 suggests that firms might consider abandoning the rather legally orientated purchasing systems still predominantly used in the West. The benefits of the Japanese system of entering into supplier/purchaser partnerships need to be considered. Such systems allow the purchaser and supplier to work together to improve the supplier's systems and to benefit jointly from intra-organisational economies. It also allows the purchasing firm a much clearer view of possibilities for economies and better design. Accountants and engineers work in cooperation with the supplying firm. A number of large UK firms have recently switched to this system which encourages the accountant to play a strong and reforming role in purchasing and in improving the supply chain.

(2) The promise identified in the earlier report as offered by strategic management accounting is, as has been said, explored in Chapter 5.

(3) The earlier report identified as one of the most fruitful areas for reform in accounting the control of overheads, especially discretionary or decision driven overheads. Chapter 4 considers these urgent matters where there is still relatively little theory to help practitioners who wish to abandon the use of notoriously arbitrary allocations in favour of methods which reflect the economic reality of overhead costs. Decision driven or discretionary overheads are those which are not generated by the technology being used but rather by managerial decisions.

It is suggested that one possible key to dealing with these costs both in planning and control is to seek to ascertain how far such costs contribute to generating benefits for which customers are willing to pay. That is, such costs might be considered in terms of their expected contributions to specific organisational and market strategies. With this approach, training, a cost notoriously difficult to handle, should be evaluated in terms of its expected broad contribution to attracting new customers or retaining existing ones.

With regard to overheads more generally, it is first suggested that many common costs do not need to be allocated but can be traced (often using activity based approaches) to the product or organisational component which employs them. Joint costs arise where the benefits of an installed resource can be used simultaneously by more than one part of the firm; for example, an existing data bank. These costs are much more difficult to handle. It is suggested in Chapter 4 that any allocation of such costs to organisational units or products should be regarded as a target contribution required to pay for the joint cost.

Alternatively, it is suggested that a new type of accounting report should be used, similar to that utilised in Germany. Such reports assign joint costs to that element of the product or organisational hierarchies at which they become avoidable with the closure of that segment of the organisation's activity. These reports present the contribution to profits and higher level overheads made by each product level element or organisational segment after meeting all their avoidable costs including joint overheads.

Throughout this book attention is paid to the possible unanticipated results of management accounting systems and the roles, both formal and informal, which accountants may play in the management teams which are growing up in more informally managed organisations. Many commentators have noted the breakdown of rigorously functionalised management and its replacement by cross-functional informal teams positioned as near as possible to the market place emphasising frequent and rapid informal communication. This may yield many new opportunities to the management accountant and allow responsibility for many of the accountant's planning and control functions to be shared more widely amongst the whole management team (see *Lewis and McFadyen* (1993), *Keating and Jablowsky* (1990) and *Innes and Mitchell* (1989)).

1.3 Pathways to Progress

This study has identified a number of especially important opportunities for management accountants which are believed to offer the potential of enhanced decision making and control within firms. A selection of these are discussed briefly below. Some associated problems for accountants are also presented. A number of these approaches are fairly new and are recommended for consideration and experimentation. The chapter(s) in which they are discussed in the body of the text are indicated.

(1) The use of activity based approaches is recommended where clear cost drivers for individual activities can be identified and where each activity can be demonstrated or assumed to be relatively unaffected by the levels of the firm's other activities (Chapter 3). The use of ABC in suitable circumstances is seen as helping to make understandable the behaviour of some costs which are presently collected in overhead pools and then allocated. It also helps to make the behaviour of some costs far more visible, and therefore more controllable, than under traditional accounting methods (Chapter 3).

It should be understood that some activities are likely to be affected in a variety of ways by output volume changes, at least over the time period where output and scheduling decisions may be revised substantially. The literature suggests that a major advantage of activity based approaches, just as with many techniques, is not found in the precise results generated but rather in unexpected effects generated because of the different focus entertained by ABC relative to traditional accounting methods.

A further important benefit frequently documented in the literature is the extra insights yielded by the information collected and the general discipline required to undertake ABC studies (Chapters 7 and 8). Activity based cost management also shares these promises but greater strength would be given to the approach if the search for non-value added activities was more clearly linked with strategy and more clearly encompassed the views of customers as to the benefits of each activity under consideration.

(2) In many chapters of this study, it is suggested that monitoring performance and indeed the planning of performance may be improved if non-financial information is utilised together with financial information. This is especially helpful where some costs may be difficult to define and to measure though a wide array of real

time non-financial information is available (Chapter 2). Some commentators, for example, believe that the performance of JIT systems is best measured in terms of items like elapsed time, distance moved, space occupied and product complexity (Chapter 3).

The use of what is called the *tableau de bord* in France, literally the 'dashboard' in English, represents, perhaps, the pinnacle of the combined use of non-financial and financial information. The dashboard of a car allows a driver to regularly monitor the function of various activities of the car and highlights substandard or dangerous performance. In the same way, a manager's dashboard information system regularly presents key performance measures and highlights any problematic performances. Key control information, tailored specially to the requirements of each manager, irrespective of whether it is financial or non-financial, is presented regularly. The essence of the system is that information presented to subordinate managers is aggregated for more senior management levels in a way which assures it does not lose its meaning in order to provide a hierarchy of control information (Chapter 3).

Other chapters of this study suggest that the use of non-financial information might go far beyond its use in routine monitoring. Chapter 4, for example, suggests that it may be the only way to deal with 'difficult to manage' costs such as R&D and corporate costs which are not easily traced to the objectives of the firm. Similarly, using this type of information may be helpful in planning and controlling discretionary or decision driven costs (Chapter 4). There are, however, costs to using non-financial information. Different sources of such information may be given conflicting advice. Aggregating non-financial information may require very subjective decisions to be made concerning the trade offs between the conflicting signals from different performance measures.

(3) The literature reviewed in this book suggests there is a strong argument for firms to introduce a strategic dimension to accounting (Chapter 5). It is believed that there is a need to determine the costs associated with strategies employed by the firm and to monitor the cost structures of competitors. Presently, the costs of many operations which offer added value to the consumer, such as flexibility in manufacture, quality, distribution and after sales service, are rendered invisible by submerging them in the overheads pool and then adding 'noise' by allocating them.

Strategic management accounting (SMA) seeks to make such costs visible to management. A major problem possibly inhibiting the use of SMA is the perception that it makes impossible information demands. However, against this, it can be argued that much of the information needed for strategic management accounting must already be collected by 'well managed' companies.

(4) The adoption of any accounting or related technique from a foreign context is not straightforward. However, a number of Japanese accounting approaches have successfully been considered and adopted by UK firms (Chapters 6 and 8). Cost Tables which allow the costs of changing the specification of the product to be easily estimated provide one example. Target costing takes prices from the market (in contrast to the general Western practice of pricing by reference to costs). The aim is then to drive down costs to permit the charging of the desired target price. Such an approach does imply a market driven organisation.

Similarly, the clear use of accounting to motivate specific behaviour (by, for example, levying additional charges over costs on what are deemed unnecessary operations or expensive parts), and its more general use to motivate continuous cost reduction may work better in a Japanese context. However, these and other elements of Japanese accounting practices are worthy of consideration by British firms seeking to survive against global, including Japanese, competition (Chapter 6).

(5) The review of the USA experience in this report (Chapter 7) suggests that firms are divided in their take up of new accounting techniques, such as ABC. Many firms are continuing to hold to the traditional ways. This suggests that the likelihood of the acceptance of new accounting techniques will differ from firm to firm. New techniques may therefore not be of universal interest. It is not yet clear whether any unwillingness to change systems is confined to accounting or encompasses all suggested modern managerial and organisational techniques.

(6) Thus, one rather disturbing finding from the study is of a great reluctance in the West to change accounting systems even in the face of strong advocacy in the accounting area for such changes (see Chapters 7 and 8). This wish to retain traditional accounting systems in a fundamentally unaltered state is not shared by the Japanese,

though in Japan such systems are less central to management than in the West. Further research is essential in this area.

(7) One interesting observation both from the US studies reviewed and coming through even more clearly from the British studies is that management and accountants are perhaps most open to change where informally organised management operates as a friendly team only weakly organised on a functional basis in the face of a dynamic and challenging market and business environment (Chapters 7 and 8).

(8) A new method of handling discretionary or decision driven costs is suggested (Chapter 4). This involves the linking of these costs with the benefits which customers perceive as offered to them by decision driven activities. Similarly, new accounting methods are suggested for treating joint costs which are growing rapidly with the introduction of new manufacturing and information technologies and which are probably the most difficult costs for accountants to handle.

(9) One major theme that runs throughout this report is that in evaluating the effects of new technology and new accounting systems, attention has to be paid to the context of the organisation in which they are introduced, and similarly such innovations can only be understood by exploring how they impinge, interact and build on each other. Effectively, an understanding of the many potential roles of accounting in organisations is desirable (*Burchell et al.*, 1980).

As suggested above, the findings of this study indicate that at least some parts of the profession have responded well to many of the challenges to management accountants presented in the previous report. Continuing challenges and newly identified challenges include:

(1) revising accounting methods in the new environment facing the service sector, and especially the financial sector, and seeking to suggest how promising accounting techniques can be applied in the not-for-profit and government sectors.

(2) further developing more market orientated management accounting building on work already done in this area, such as customer profitability analysis.

(3) recognising the wide organisational changes generated by innovations in technology, information systems and management accounting.

(4) positioning management accounting so that it can play its full role in informally managed organisations and in the chains of organisations formed by the adoption of supplier and customer partnerships.

(5) considering how to account for 'green' issues and for the regulatory requirements faced by firms.

(6) continuing to address the still major problem of integrating non-financial and financial information.

(7) addressing the reasons why there seems great reluctance to change accounting systems in the face of dynamic technological changes and increasingly uncertain business environments.

(8) one of the major challenges to management and to management accountants, that of the impact of globalisation, need not be explicitly articulated in this report as the theme runs throughout this study. This is the need for management accounting to react to the increasing globalisation of business. Pressures towards globalisation identified in this study include the perceived need to use leading edge methods utilised by competitors wherever they are located, the reduction in trade barriers which requires an increasing number of commodities to be seen as being traded in a global market with competitors located far away, and overseas direct investment in order to maximise low cost production by operating across frontiers.

Companies which seek to compete globally are continually seeking the right balance between the advantages of economies of scope and encouraging worthwhile interrelations between often widespread elements of the organisation governed by different local regulations and demands and operating in very different cultural contexts and local autonomy. This and other processes require the accountant to revise both corporate accounting information systems and local systems to reflect these changes.

The very different management accounting systems which this report indicates are used in different countries have to be expressed in a common and universally understood corporate language so that managerial performance in very different locations can be compared and so that planning throughout the organisation can be linked to corporate strategy. Little documented experience of these problems and possible solutions has yet appeared. This is an area where further fact finding and research is needed.

1.4 *Structure of the Report*

Two themes run through the chapters of this study. One is that of the original edition. The study therefore examines the challenges to management accounting from the new manufacturing environment and the methods and techniques used by competitive nations and leading edge firms, and discusses possible solutions. Secondly, the study identifies and recommends a number of promising solutions to some of the challenges facing management accounting. Chapters 2 to 5 examine the challenges to accounting in detail. Chapter 2 briefly and non-technically examines certain organisational and managerial innovations and technological improvements including JIT, computerised manufacturing, flexible manufacturing and TQM. These innovations give rise to a major set of challenges which many commentators believe that management accounting practice has failed to answer or has sometimes answered only with an undue lag.

Some implications of these challenges for management accounting are taken up in Chapter 3 which also looks critically at suggested solutions. The empirical evidence concerning existing practice from Japan, North America, and the UK, the take up of the suggested solutions and the lessons that can be learnt, are discussed in three separate country specific chapters (Chapter 6, 7 and 8). Chapters 4 and 5 are more focused and look in detail at specific challenges to management accounting. Chapter 4 addresses some of the greatest problems faced by organisations, those concerned with mainly fixed overheads. Chapter 5 looks at the case for strategic management accounting. There is a strong demand for accounting to take on a much more external focus.

As has been said Chapters 6, 7 and 8 adopt a country and empirical focus to assess how far management accounting has responded to the challenges perceived in these countries, to assess how far these challenges and their solutions can be documented by the empirical evidence, to indicate differences in approaches in these countries and to indicate what lessons can be learnt for improving both management and management accounting. One strong theme that comes through in this part of the study is the almost universal reluctance to change accounting systems, and the wish, where changes are to be introduced, to experiment initially within the organisation on a very restrictive basis. Few wholesale or corporate wide changes to accounting systems have yet been documented. Similarly, few empirical studies looking at a reasonable sample of firms have yet demonstrated major benefits or disadvantages flowing from such changes.

Chapter content

We now highlight the contents of individual chapters in a little more detail, emphasising those aspects of each chapter which have not yet been discussed in this summary.

Chapter 2 examines the changing manufacturing environment and introduces its possible implications and problems for management accounting. Some understanding of these areas is necessary as these alleged implications and problems for management accounting lie at the heart of the criticisms which have been levelled at existing management accounting. One major problem identified is the need to integrate the very large amount of real time non-financial information with the financial information mainly used in top management decisions.

Chapter 3 looks at suggested innovations in management accounting which are being proposed to answer the challenges identified in Chapter 2 and other criticisms aimed at current management accounting practices. It is suggested that the full promise of both quality management, JIT and similar processes cannot be achieved while using traditional accounting systems which may yield different signals to those generated by quality and JIT processes. It is argued that these processes, especially JIT type methods, allow the use of 'leaner' accounting systems. Suggestions are made how the information from the accounting system can be made consistent and supportive of the information systems associated with these processes.

The other major focus of Chapter 3 is on the promise and difficulties of activity based approaches including activity based costing. The rationale for these processes and their merits are examined, a detailed example of ABC is provided and some criticisms which may be made of the approach are evaluated.

Incorporating the empirical studies of later chapters, two conclusions already mentioned in this summary are presented about activity based accounting approaches:

(1) that activity based approaches do yield a promising way of dealing with overheads for which a clear cost driver can be deduced, though the costs to which these approaches can be applied are limited by the assumptions which underlie activity based systems; and

(2) that the take up of these accounting systems seems slow and tentative as is the case for most if not all accounting innovations (see Chapters 7 and 8).

Chapter 4 continues the study's review of problems facing management accountants by looking at innovative methods for dealing with fixed overheads. Here, existing practices seem to have shown little change to cope with the growing importance of fixed overheads and with their many difficult characteristics. The relatively few suggestions in the literature are reviewed. Some solutions are offered for dealing with decision driven overheads and with processes which manifest jointness, that is offer benefits simultaneously to various sectors of the organisation. It is suggested that, in contrast to the majority of the literature and practice, overheads that are seen as common costs are often able to be dealt with in ways which reflect their causality. Activity based approaches often have promise here.

Chapter 5 looks at another element of the challenges to management accounting; that it is too introverted and should report on the cost of enterprise strategies and on the cost structures of existing and likely competitors using the tools of strategic management accounting.

The chapter on Japanese management and management accounting (Chapter 6) commences that part of the study which looks at trends in accounting in a number of countries. This chapter goes beyond this and seeks to indicate the importance of the economic and commercial environments and management practices in understanding Japanese management accounting and which may inhibit easy transfers of innovative accounting methods to other countries. Two possibly important lessons are the close link generated between accounting and strategy and the integration of financial and non-financial information. A number of the accounting methods used in Japan seem to be fairly context free and should be investigated for possible importation.

Chapter 7 explores the challenges raised in North America as facing management accounting and discusses the documented evidence of change in American management accounting systems. Included in the findings are:

(1) That one of the major reasons for the lack of accounting innovations is the strong primacy placed on short-term results accruing on the stock market and the results portrayed by financial accounting statements.

(2) As indicated earlier, clear evidence is found of a reluctance to change accounting systems for a large variety of reasons, not all of which reflect concerns that such changes will not bring net benefits to the firm.

(3) No universal changes to accounting systems have been observed. Rather the likelihood of accounting change seems to rest not only on foreseen technical benefits but also on firm-specific considerations extending well beyond accounting. Such changes often have unexpected and sometimes beneficial consequences.

Chapter 8 is the last of the country based studies. This reviews a wide variety of the increasing number of studies, including case studies, which have been undertaken in the United Kingdom. One clear conclusion is the need for management accountants to understand operational processes and the need to embed management accounting systems within operational activities often via informal channels of communications and possibly to suggest a more significant role for using non-financial measurements. Another conclusion from the studies reviewed and from our research is that many firms are unhappy with the results of traditional management accounting and traditional investment appraisal techniques and a non-negligible number of firms have taken on board innovative techniques. Many such firms have found both unexpected difficulties in the implementation phase, often of a behavioural nature, and unanticipated benefits where, for example, new systems generate changes in strategy.

The three chapters focusing on different countries indicate the importance of organisational matters to accounting. The concluding chapter (Chapter 9) firstly looks further at the interfaces between accounting and organisational concerns and then seeks to integrate and structure the many findings, approaches, perspectives and calls for alterations in accounting systems in the name of change which have been reviewed in this report by seeking to indicate some potential pathways to progress and concerns which it seems necessary to keep in mind if accounting innovations are to be seen as holding promise. General findings here include:

(1) Many companies are experimenting with novel accounting approaches and others have ventured well beyond this stage, often in response to changes in the manufacturing environment. This chapter indicates that a number of these innovations show considerable promise but that success in implementation seems to depend upon how well accounting innovations reflect the manufacturing systems and the organisational and behavioural contexts of organisations.

(2) The role of accounting is expanding as the enterprise and its network of suppliers, customers, information sources and government grows. For example, new supplier/customer partnerships are generating new and different demands for accounting information as is the existence of extensive non-financial information. The successful implementation of ABC has also expanded the accountant's role.

(3) The challenges to management accounting cannot be overcome just by seeking to implement one or more techniques, nor has any one suggested accounting innovation been shown to be dominant. Practical innovations in accounting are likely to be successfully undertaken by accountants well grounded in the technological base of their enterprise with a good understanding of its organisational context and behavioural stances.

The final chapter of this report also indicates many relatively new challenges, some of which have already been referred to earlier in this summary. Additional challenges include:

(1) The need for more consideration of accounting change in process industries, in the retail and service sectors, in not-for-profit organisations and in the public sector.

(2) There is a need to consider accounting for all aspects of the value chain especially those prior to production; decisions made in these activities determine the great majority of manufacturing costs, the

quality level that can be attained in manufacturing and the ease of manufacture of products.

(3) Management accounting for service and retail sectors, and for the not-for-profit and the public sector, especially with regard to public sector agencies and market testing.

(4) The need for research into the traditional areas of accounting such as budgeting and standard costing to investigate whether the most successful elements of traditional management accounting require changes to cope with new manufacturing techniques and the changing market environment.

The often very vociferous and stark challenges to management accounting identified here and in the first report have not gone away but they have diminished. These challenges are now being considered with time for mature judgement whilst their proponents are attempting to make their reasoning more compelling and to assemble strong empirical evidence to support their desired solutions. Management accounting has undergone a period of trials and tribulations. It is important that the careful consideration of the roles and methods of management accounting engendered by these difficulties should be continued.

In conclusion, we do not wish to change our previous view that:

> the evidence and arguments advanced by the advocates of wholesale changes are not yet sufficient to justify wholesale revision of management accounting.

However, we have presented many challenges for accounting, identified some very promising pathways and suggested a number of opportunities for strengthening the role accountants play within firms. Developing these opportunities and facing up to existing, emerging and future challenges using the rich experiential base of management accounting should place management accountants on pathways towards further enhancing the roles they play in firms.

2
Automated Technologies and Management Innovations

2.1 Introduction

The fast pace of change which has affected manufacturing industries over the past two decades and whose effects continue to alter not just approaches to production but also organisational structures, business strategies and managerial philosophies has been viewed as a new industrial revolution. *Ayres* (1991, p.viii) suggests that:

> If the first industrial revolution was the substitution of steam power for human and animal muscles, the present revolution is the substitution of electronic sensors for human eyes and ears, and computers for human brains.

Operational changes arising from technological advances are not limited to manufacturing processes but extend to post-production back-up activities and particularly to the service sector.

The impact of these changes has not gone unnoticed by management accountants (*Spicer*, 1992). Calls for revolutionary transformations in management accounting have emanated from many quarters including academics, practitioners, and consultants for at least a decade (*Brimson*, 1991; *Kaplan*, 1983; 1984; 1985; 1986a; 1988a; 1990; *Johnson and Kaplan*, 1987; *Morrow*, 1992). An understanding of the operational nature of the new technologies and hardware being developed and installed in manufacturing settings and service industries is essential for gaining an appreciation of the perceived management accounting implications of these changes. Furthermore, alterations in manufacturing and other sectors of the economy include not just the application of automated equipment and flexible technologies, but also the implementation of radically different work organisation techniques and novel approaches to the coordination, integration, control and management of organisational activities. These transformations in turn have also raised concerns about accounting amongst scholars and practitioners in the field and need to be examined before their significance for accounting activities can be assessed.

Accordingly, this chapter seeks to describe the types of production techniques, automation systems, manufacturing technologies and novel work organisation practices which are currently affecting production and service sector environments and to highlight certain accounting concerns and issues which they raise. The specific types of accounting mechanisms, procedures and strategies advanced by accounting commentators are examined in the following chapter.

2.2 Automated Technologies

Computer numerical control of machine tools

The first step taken in the mid-1950s toward programmability in the factory was the development of numerical controls (NCs) for individual stand-alone production machines. A NC machine is a manufacturing tool which may be programmed with a set of instructions for guiding desired processes within predefined performance criteria. The increased availability of computer power in the 1970s permitted enhanced flexibility of machine controls by computerising numerical controls. Thus computer numerical controls (CNCs) that are locally controlled by a computer and the simultaneous coordination of independent stand-alone NC machines from a central point is readily permitted (via a single computer known as direct numerical control (DNC)). A DNC makes it possible for a machining cell to be instructed for instance to 'make 15 sets of model X'. The DNC consults an on-line database to determine which sub-components are required and examines a file of existing programs to decide the sequence of production steps. It then calls for the stock needed, downloads the instruction program for each desired part and activates the machinery cell. A new job operation may be effected by changing the programmed instructions enabling specialised manufacturing operations such as milling, drilling, boring and grinding to be performed in different ways and in varied sequences.

The principal aim of a NC machine is to shorten production times by reducing set-up activities which do not add value to the processing function. Other benefits which may accrue from NC technologies include improved quality and reduced variability of output, decreased scrap and rework levels, substantial reductions in the number of direct labour workers required to achieve a desired output level and overall productivity gains of up to 300 percent (*McNair, Mosconi and Norris*, 1988, p.13).

The application of NC machines is widespread (see table 2.1) although in performing investment appraisals, the decision to acquire NC technology can be problematic in that benefits such as decreases in direct labour costs, lead times, inventory levels and increases in quality, capacity and manufacturing flexibility are difficult to evaluate quantitatively. This and the problem of separating cash flows from different machines used together in the production process also make performance measurement a difficult exercise.

Table 2.1 Population of NC machine tools in the USA, Japan, UK, FRG and France

Country	Year	NC Machine Tools
USA	1989	222,356
Japan	1987	70,255
UK	1987	53,000
FRG	1985	50,000
France	1985	35,000

Adapted from *Tchijov* (1992) and *Tani* (1992)

Undertaking cost control poses a challenge in that NC machines replace direct labour costs with depreciation and machine-related costs which are not readily captured and controlled by conventional cost accounting systems. Moreover, delineations of controllable versus uncontrollable costs are not easy and may be impossible. For instance, cost tracing and performance evaluation can become complex where the manager making the decision to purchase a NC device is not in charge of scheduling labour usage since labour cost savings assumed in the acquisition decision may not be realised if labour is not subsequently discharged or reallocated. Additionally, the use of NC machines can make product costing increasingly arbitrary as the cost behaviour of machine operator wages is altered but does not become categorically direct or indirect. Further, overhead rates which continue to be based on direct labour costs or hours become volatile and distort product costs to the extent that product line profitability figures may mislead decision-makers when judging the returns from individual product lines. Using machine hours to overcome the problem can be costly, requiring machine time monitoring, personnel retraining, altered information collection practices and difficult organisational problems to be solved, yet still leaving certain cost incursion problems unaddressed (this is further discussed in the next chapter).

Other management accounting issues which must be confronted within a production environment using NC machines include volatility in cost behaviour patterns which can be seen as variable in certain circumstances and fixed in others. Also, the focus on short-run costs as opposed to long-run costs affects NC machines specifically. Efficiency measures, for instance, which stress the former may take precedence over total productivity which views efficiency as one of many factors contributing to long-term performance.

Computer aided design and computer aided manufacturing

Computer aided design (CAD) refers to a computerised system for design purposes consisting of a computer with a high-resolution display screen, a plotter, and sophisticated software for creating graphics and for combining and recombining graphic elements. CAD allows multidimensional images to be manipulated and redesigned. Benefits which may accrue from installing CAD include:

- Improved productivity of designers and product design.

- Reduction in design times.

- The ability to design products that are too complex to be designed manually.

- Gains from integrating design and production.

CAD systems have produced productivity increases of up to four times for design (*Primrose, Creamer and Leonard,* 1985), with one study revealing CAD as providing the highest productivity increases of any automated manufacturing technology (*Astebro,* 1992).

Computer aided manufacturing (CAM) systems are high-level computer supervisory systems that may carry out planning and scheduling functions for a production plant and generate programs for individual machine tools and cells. CAM in effect uses computerised technology to plan, implement and monitor the manufacture of a product. In the main, CAD and CAM systems presently tend to be used independently of each other but the advantages of linkage are evident since a CAD/CAM system blending mechanical and computer technology can facilitate the design and manufacture of a product. Design changes can automatically be reflected in altered production programmes. Ultimately, the integration of CAD/CAM with computer aided engineering (CAE) and computer aided testing (CAT), which allows prototypes to be modelled altering only computer software, may bring about the realisation of 'industrial boutiques producing parts on demand' (*Ayres,* 1991, p.98). Presently, CAD/CAM systems comprise a number of subsystems, including mathematical and mechanical models, computer graphics, design documentation, production planning, NC machines and group technology (*Bennett et al.,* 1987) which continue to evolve as integration possibilities come to light.

The decision to use CAD/CAM technology is difficult to analyse using conventional financial capital appraisal techniques because of the wide array of intangible benefits which are not easy to quantify (for instance, improved design drafts, better customer perception of products, increased productivity of draughtsmen and enhanced product quality). Cost control in CAD/CAM settings is also problematic because of the difficulty of setting labour standards for activities such as drafting and design. Moreover, with experience, these activities result in increased productivity and reduced operational time which generates the need to continuously update standards. Product costing is simplified when engineering and design costs can be ascribed to the production of a specific order. This is not always feasible however and it is easier simply to include costs in total departmental overheads with the attendant drawbacks of arbitrariness when costs are consequently assigned to individual products. Performance measures can be tied to improving setup times, material usage and manufacturing time, defect rates, product versatility and quality for which no simple measures exist but need to be custom-made for different production contexts.

Flexible manufacturing systems

A flexible manufacturing system (FMS) refers to a computer controlled production system to produce a family of parts. In an FMS, workpieces of different types travel between and are processed at various programmable, multi-purpose machine tools and other work stations. Parts flow through the system according to individual processing and production requirements by a materials-handling system (MHS) and possibly by DNC devices and robots. An advanced FMS can also include an automated storage and retrieval system (ASRS) for fixtures, raw material and parts featuring automated washing, assembly and inspection (*Bennett et al.*, 1987). Indeed, a number of companies utilise computer-controlled FMS running unattended on night-shift operations (*Merchant*, 1984).

Although robot manufacturers in the West have tended to retain secret proprietary operating systems which make it difficult to integrate robots with other machines in high-level computerised production environments, Japanese factories have benefited from developing CNC machine tools with compatible CNC robots. Consequently, the use of robots initially for stand-alone applications such as handling hot castings, spray painting and torch cutting mainly in the automotive industry, has progressed to spot welding and arc-welding with continually increasing reliability and timeliness (*Hegtler*, 1984).

The addition of vision and tactile sensors within robots over the past few years is expected to enable truly computerised fifth generation automation, encompassing adaptive controls for machine tools, pattern recognition devices, assembly robots with sensory feedback, and inspection machines (*Moxon*, 1987). Machine vision and sensors are the essential preconditions to introducing artificial intelligence (AI) into factory operations. For the time being, production technologies such as CAD, CAE, CAM, and robots are used to partially computerise factory environments such that FMS's contribute to 'islands of automation' (IA) buffered by intermediate storage of semi-finished/assembly products. IA's can be integrated to fully automate the production process under total computer integrated manufacturing (CIM). *Coulthurst* (1989a, p.33) suggests that in manufacturing:

> The ultimate goal is to link all facets of an enterprise, ie, design, purchasing, production planning and control, machining, assembly, inspection, marketing and accounting, through a common database to provide computer-integrated manufacturing.

In this respect, CIM represents a highly capital intensive approach to manufacturing, being the final step whereby the total factory is linked into one integrated system (*Romano*, 1987). Many manufacturing environments however can benefit from part-automation and indeed it is now possible to determine the appropriate level of technology for a specified industrial situation (*Leonard*, 1988).

The main advantages of an FMS over a traditional factory organisation structure include the ability to produce differing varieties and volume levels using the same technology, quick customer response, and reduced labour costs as materials-handling systems and automated storage and retrieval systems replace labour, in addition to savings from the actual automation of manufacturing processes which themselves cut down on human operators. Furthermore, product quality, setup times, machine utilisation, low inventory levels, space and enhanced information on production are all affected favourably by an FMS.

It is impossible to evaluate all these benefits in quantitative form, which makes it difficult to justify FMS expenditures in purely financial terms. Figure 2.1 shows an international comparison of FMS installed costs vs technical complexity of systems and Figure 2.2 indicates the reduced payback as a function both of installed cost and of technical complexity. Cost control, product costing and performance measurement problems arise principally from the reduction in direct labour utilisation and the high capital cost components of an FMS.

Figure 2.1 FMS installed costs vs technical complexity

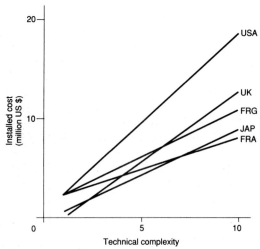

Adapted from Ayres, 1991, p.109

Figure 2.2 Payback time vs installed cost

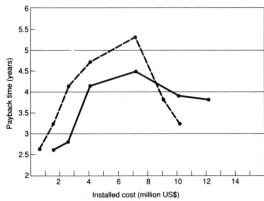

Adapted from Ayres, 1991, p.110

2.3 Management Innovations

Total quality management

The adoption of scientific management techniques advanced by Frederick Taylor from the late nineteenth century in the USA and in parts of Europe and the Soviet Union at the turn of the century (*Merkle*, 1980) was aimed at improving work methods in factory environments. 'Taylorism' essentially attempted to classify work into tasks and task elements which were individually timed and targeted. The underlying assumption was that individual task elements comprising a job are independent and separable and that efficiency and worker output could consequently be maximised on a piecemeal and progressive basis. A problem with the approach is that production processes are inherently interrelated especially in modern manufacturing environments. A factory process, for instance, may rely on the manufacture of parts which become inputs into sub-components later to be assembled. Manufacturing activities thus take place through complex sequential interactions; breaking up work into a myriad of very detailed independent tasks can potentially contribute to the build-up of aggregate slack. Moreover, the progression of materials and parts through the production process is accompanied by an increase in the value of input and concurrently the requirements increase for the enterprise to produce good parts and marketable products.

Total quality management (TQM) can be seen as a recognition that Tayloristic conceptions of the production environment are at odds with the integrated and interdependent nature of total factory processes. Errors and defects, if allowed to accumulate through to parts and assemblies, can become very costly to correct. The costs of error detection cascade exponentially as progress is made through each successive stage of fabrication into inspection. Rework and repair also escalate with increases in the complexity of assembled products. TQM is a direct attempt at addressing the problem. Having been first implemented in post-World War II Japanese enterprises as a comprehensive quality control philosophy, it emphasises the elimination of defects and rework. Although the application of TQM must be specific and unique to the needs and circumstances of enterprises, it can entail the training of groups of employees in techniques such as 'quality circles'.

A quality circle has been defined as

> . . . a group of four token volunteers working for the same
> supervisor or foreman who meet once a week, for an hour,
> under the leadership of the supervisor, to identify, analyse and
> solve their own work related problems (*Robson*, 1988, p.3.)

The economic benefits of quality circles have been viewed to be
high in most companies where they have been introduced, with a
worldwide average payback of between £5 and £8 for any £1
invested. The returns have been particularly high in Japanese
companies (*Lillrank and Kano*, 1989). But some companies have
been more concerned about the qualitative benefits (*Seddon and
Jackson*, 1990) including organisational culture change whereby
improvements become highly valued and sought after, decision-
making participation from line managers increases, and supervisory
skills become honed. Within the context of accounting techniques,
quality circles have been viewed as affecting communication in
terms both of quantity and quality. For instance, problems of over-
delivery of supplies, testing bottlenecks and stores organisation have
been identified, thereby suggesting potentially new accounting
measures and monitors (discussed in the following chapter).

Quality circles, however, only represent one form of quality
management approach. Different types of quality systems exist in
organisations which can be categorised into a progression of discrete
stages. The most basic level comprises the traditional quality
inspection whereby one or more characteristics of a product are
examined, measured and tested to assess conformity with pre-
specified requirements. It is a process applied to incoming goods, as
well as to manufactured components and assemblies at appropriate
points in the manufacturing process and is carried out by staff hired
for this purpose. Faulty goods may be scrapped, reworked or sold as
substandard. Progressing hierarchically from quality inspection is a
system of quality control (see Figure 2.3), whereby raw materials
and intermediate stage products are tested, with a certain level of
self-inspection by operators taking place. Elementary process
performance data and feedback of process information to operatives
and supervisors may be effected using an internal accounting system
or, more likely, some other part of the organisation's management
information system.

Figure 2.3   The four levels in the hierarchy of quality management

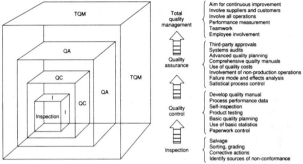

Adapted from Dale, Lascelles and Plunkett, 1990, p.4

Quality assurance is the penultimate hierarchical level in the progression of quality systems. Quality assurance contains all those planned and systematic actions required to provide adequate confidence that a product or service will satisfy given requirements for quality. This level thus entails the use of quality manuals, the determination of quality costs, use of statistical process control and quality audits. Quality assurance embodies a shift in emphasis from detection to prevention of non-conformance. The fourth and highest functional level entailing quality is total quality management (TQM), which is concerned with the overall implementation of quality policy under the direct responsibility of top management. TQM requires the principles of quality management to be applied in every branch and at all levels of the organisation including not just products and services provided but also sales, finance, personnel and other enterprise activities. The process may also extend beyond the organisation itself to include partnerships with suppliers and customers. As *Dale, Lascelles and Plunkett* (1990, p.5) note:

> Total quality management uses a variety of methods to involve, motivate and imbue people at all organisational levels with the philosophy that improvement is a way of life.

The quality circles approach represents one such method contributing to an organisation's TQM criteria. However, many quality management advocates have proposed their own approaches to TQM. For instance, *Deming* (1982) and *Tagushi* (1986) suggest a link between quality, productivity and competitive position and stress the use of statistical controls to reduce variances from predetermined quality targets (see also *Albright and Roth*, 1994). *Crosby* (1979) emphasises that enhanced quality reduces costs and raises profits whereas *Feigenbaum* (1983) sees quality management as being primarily customer driven. *Juran's* (1988) approach rests on implementing quality goals whereby the objective is to decrease the cost of quality, whereas *Hand* (1991) places particular importance on eliminating 'diversionary' activities to enhance the quality of business management. Although these TQM advocates offer different recipes for addressing quality issues, they place particular emphasis on pursuing quality targets as a 'state of mind' if not a 'religion'. No doubt, as *Price* (1990, p.37) notes TQM is 'simple but it is not easy'.

Quality control systems must become ingrained within the culture of organisations and may permanently establish new communication requirements. These can potentially become coupled with accounting mechanisms for identifying, processing and reporting quality information deemed relevant. Ultimately, TQM is about improving the usefulness of products and about reducing costs (*Woods*, 1989). Consequently, product quality is viewed as entailing costing issues. Accounting implications of quality management are addressed in the following chapter. The underlying rationale of TQM makes it applicable not just to the manufacture of goods but to the management, delivery and servicing of products whether tangible or not. Moreover, TQM can be readily applied to the management accounting function itself (see *Smith*, 1994). The guiding principle of TQM is commitment by all levels of management, the elimination of functional boundaries in organisations and the recognition that it is a continuous long-term process whose ultimate goal may be practically inachievable but which can serve as a guiding theoretical target.

Companies which have adopted TQM have reported significant improvements using a variety of measures. Motorola in the USA for instance began its TQM programme in early 1987 and has since reported a $250 million yearly saving in manufacturing costs. Also, Xerox has, since its implementation of TQM in 1984, noted a reduction in its product defect rate of 93 percent. It is to be noted, however, that TQM is concerned with mobilising action rather than quantifying its benefits at different stages. Placing quantitative cost-benefit criteria on TQM is not an essential exercise. To TQM enthusiasts, the ultimate test is a company's adoption and retention of TQM in the long run.

Materials requirements planning

Materials requirements planning (MRP) is concerned with maximising efficiency in the timing of raw material orders placed with vendors and with scheduling the machining and assembly of the final manufacturing product. It thus makes available purchased and company manufactured components and subassemblies just before they are needed by the next stage of production for dispatch. MRP can be implemented as a production and planning technique in traditional manufacturing contexts as it entails only a basic level of automation by way of computer software for back-scheduling the major events in a production process, given the required date for delivery of the final products to a customer.

MRP relies on information relating to expected demand and critical to its effective functioning are the structure, accuracy and timeliness of data input (*Archer*, 1991). Early MRP systems used in the 1970s depended on information based on weekly predictions, whereas the more recent manufacturing resources planning (MRP II) systems which link medium to long-term production plans with existing and planned capacities need daily updating. However, recent surveys of USA and UK companies implementing MRP II suggest that between 50 percent and 70 percent of such systems implementations can be categorised as 'unsuccessful' (*Barekat*, 1991). *Harrison* (1990) suggests that MRP II is in part based on a number of serious misconceptions such as the assumption of infinite capacity, fixed lead times and fixed batch sizes and that in focusing on the past, it fails to synchronise and thereby optimise manufacturing activities. However, the principal problem has not been a conceptual one but an applied one. The application of MRP has tended to take place in isolation from business strategy and manufacturing capability. Properly implemented, however, the objectives attainable with MRP include minimising inventory levels, production run disruptions, storage costs and the extra expenses incurred in accepting rush orders. One other important benefit of MRP is that it can provide forecasts of the production status of specific products and thus enable the preparation of pro-forma schedules of cost of goods sold, work in process and raw material inventory by aggregating individual product forecasts for each of these items.

MRP may not be incompatible with traditional cost accounting techniques in that it does not affect product cost mix, nor does it require a substantial capital outlay in its basic form. It can, in fact, be used to provide financial cost data not previously part of a traditional cost system. As *Campbell and Porcano* (1979, p.34) state:

> Without the MRP system, the cost accounting system will likely produce information that is not as useful as the information produced when the two systems are integrated.

Further, there are novel measures of performance relating to delivery timeliness, quality performance and routing accuracy among others (*Tatikonda and Tatikonda*, 1989) which MRP provides. What must be borne in mind is that simplicity and flexibility are key factors in the successful management of manufacturing enterprises. *Maskell* (1993, p.48) however notes that:

> MRP II contains a rigid, operations research approach to the solution of production and inventory problems that needs to be changed if the systems are to be useful in a world-class manufacturing environment.

Just-in-time systems

Whereas the MRP approach can be characterised as a 'push' system whereby production is initiated in anticipation of future demand, many organisations have sought to plan their manufacturing operations on a 'pull' basis. Just-in-time (JIT) systems operate on such a logic whereby production is initiated as a reaction to present demand. Just-in-time systems refer to the means by which the manufacturing process can be restructured to bring about more flexible, rapid and cost effective production. JIT systems effectively comprise two separate sets of activities: JIT purchasing, which attempts to match the acquisition and receipt of material sufficiently closely with usage such that raw material inventory is reduced to near-zero levels, and JIT production whereby production takes place only through a pull-system driven by the demand for finished products. JIT production's aim is to obtain low cost, high quality, on-time production to order by minimising stock levels between successive processes and therefore idle equipment, facilities and workers.

Whereas JIT purchasing involves the relationship between the firm and third parties (i.e. suppliers), JIT production is largely internal to the firm (see Figure 2.4).

Figure 2.4   JIT purchasing and JIT production

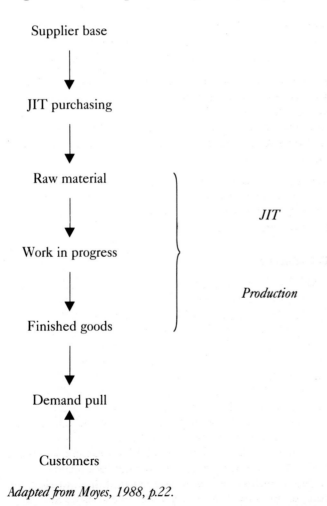

Adapted from Moyes, 1988, p.22.

Relevant claimed benefits of JIT purchasing include raw material stock reduction, control over delivery timing, close working relations with fewer suppliers, long-term contracts, quality assurance and raw material/subcomponent specifications (*Ansari and Modarress*, 1986; *Davis and Kramer*, 1991; *Manoocheri*, 1984; *O'Neal*, 1987; *Robinson and Timmerman*, 1987). But perhaps one of the most important features of JIT purchasing is the receipt of supplies in smaller lots more frequently (*Ramasech*, 1990). JIT production on the other hand stresses work in process and finished good inventory reductions, decreased lead and set-up times, zero-defects, flexible workforce, continuous improvement and quality control as part of the production process and producing to order. Like total quality management, JIT emphasises the detection of production problems as they occur rather than establishing procedures for dealing with problems after production has taken place and setting aside facilities for further processing. It has been suggested that JIT must address quality issues before considering quantity or throughput factors (*Crosby*, 1984). Indeed, under JIT production, the factory worker is encouraged to stop the machinery whenever a defect is discovered.

This combination of automation and autonomy is referred to as 'autonomation' (*Ohno*, 1988, p.48). Certain companies have implemented both TQM and JIT to reduce defect rates whilst bettering on-time delivery (*Ashton and Cook*, 1989).

The Kanban process can also support JIT production by acting as an information system through cards which relay information about type and quantity of inputs withdrawn from a container. Under Kanban, a card is sent from a subsequent process to the preceding process when an item is withdrawn. Kanban therefore connects all aspects in the flow of manufacturing within an organisation through the provision of information about the category and quantity of materials going through the system by linking one process to the prior process (*Harvey*, 1991). It can extend from vendors and subcontractors to the parent manufacturing firm (*Maskell*, 1986; *Moyes*, 1988; *Schonberger*, 1982b). Although MRP is a 'push' system, it is increasingly being seen as compatible with the 'pull' rationale upon which JIT systems rest. *Barratt* (1990, p.30) for instance reports on companies which use:

> . . . .'quick slice MRP', which adapts MRP in just-in-time situations

and on the 'marriage' of MRP II and JIT in companies such as Rolls-Royce Motors, Mitel Telecom and ICI Pharmaceuticals. Likewise, *Karmarkar* (1989, p.127) notes that MRP and JIT:

> . . . . are not mutually exclusive, and each has pros and cons. The best solution is often a hybrid that uses the strengths of both approaches.

It must be noted however, that companies successfully implementing JIT tend to define its scope and implementation sequence to suit their own unique competitive and internal conditions rather than to replicate procedures used by other companies (see *Schniederjans*, 1993; and *Vor, Saraph and Peterson*, 1990).

Some commentators have suggested that large firms using JIT tend to force their smaller suppliers to adopt the JIT philosophy (*Hutchins*, 1989; *Stokes*, 1989). As a consequence, the cost of working capital tied up in stock is externalised since small firms simply carry excess stocks to meet the needs of their large JIT clients (*Newmann and Jaouen*, 1986). Evidence, however, is emerging that small firms are increasingly embracing JIT successfully, reducing waste and improving quality in the process (*Stamm and Golbar*, 1991; *Inman and Mehra*, 1991).

A JIT system converts the structure of production into a process operation. Process costing methods may therefore be used to trace costs where production lines are treated as cost centres and unit costs are calculated by dividing costs of a period or an order over the units processed in that period. Direct labour may be treated as fixed and merged with overhead in the form of period costs. It has been suggested also that factory-wide pools for allocating overheads should be abandoned in favour of activity-linked bases (discussed in the following chapter). In this respect, JIT is particularly appealing as it enables the identification of cost drivers by highlighting non-value added activities (*McHilhattan*, 1987). Price variances should no longer be determined because of long-term contractual links with suppliers. Performance evaluation under a JIT system becomes altered as actual, rather than standard costs are stressed and variance analysis is likewise changed as attention is directed toward material quality, supplier service, zero defects and throughput performance.

The demand-pull emphasis on the physical flow of goods across the factory floor which underlies JIT production can be complemented by costs being determined retrospectively through an accounting record keeping technique called backflushing (see next chapter). This is in contrast to the traditional emphasis of pushing costs through the accounting system as production takes place (*Ferguson*, 1988; *Munro*, 1987).

2.4 Conclusions

This chapter has examined certain organisational and managerial innovations and automated manufacturing technologies increasingly influencing the way in which many enterprises operate. Some commentators have suggested that management accounting change must follow given the altering manufacturing cost mix, shifting cost behaviours and novel investment opportunities. Problems of allocating larger overhead pools, coping with a diminishing direct labour base and evaluating qualitative benefits pose new challenges for management accountants. It has been noted that the benefits obtained from our knowledge of integrating accounting and manufacturing data has so far only been 'the tip of the iceberg' (*Dilts and Grabski*, 1990, p.53). In this light the following chapter considers some of the issues raised here in more depth and explores the variety of ways in which normative accounting techniques are being transformed.

3
Emerging Cost Management Approaches

3.1 Introduction

Reasons for restructuring work processes and altering production technologies arise in part from decisions motivated by competitive pressures, strategic considerations, technical rationales and sometimes inspirational judgment (*Burchell et al.*, 1980). Management accounting information does not always enter the decision-making process in evaluating the potential of such change. However, once the decision is made to alter the operational structure of an enterprise, the accounting consequences are perceived to be significant. Thus, the increasingly widespread deployment of advanced manufacturing technologies alongside the growing application of altered work organisation techniques and management approaches have been viewed by some academics, practitioners, consultants and managers as having significant implications for cost management. The product cost mix comprising material, overhead and labour (if any) can undergo an important transformation. Likewise, changes in product diversity, variety and life-cycle can give rise to a range of costing repercussions. The adoption of flexible production technologies entails training, maintenance, service expertise and automation costs which, coupled with changes in organisational management practices, can induce an altered conception of the economics of production. This chapter seeks to describe and probe innovations in management accounting practices which are increasingly being pondered over by enterprise managers and accountants in many countries and which, in many instances, are applied by companies of differing sizes and industries. Accounting approaches, mechanisms and practices which remain more country-specific as well as further discussions on new directions in dealing with overhead issues appear in later chapters.

3.2 Total Quality Management and Accounting

Many companies in industrialised countries are adopting quality improvement as a primary corporate objective. Quality concerns affect management accounting practices in at least two ways. First the implementation of total quality management (TQM) ultimately must influence all aspects of a company's functional activities, including accounting processes, given the emphasis on 'totality'. It has been noted that:

> . . . there is no reason there cannot be quality control circles ... among accounting personnel just as there are among the production people. (*Wilson*, 1983, p.3.)

In this vein, *Morgan* (1990, p.49) has also suggested that the major areas covered by internal accounting systems including general ledger, accounts payable and receivable, the fixed asset register, etc.

> . . . might benefit from the operation of quality circles.

For instance, for an accounting department, excellence in performance may be measured on the basis of the number of times reports are generated and delivered on schedule. Such a monitor has quality implications for input data, computer system down time, and instructions from internal users among others. Sub-measures may include keeping track of incorrect accounting codes entered into the computer, and work planning to optimise the usage of computing time whilst also taking into account overtime incurred. An array of such measures can be developed in an organisation-specific manner depending on the nature of quality priorities identified by quality circles and other quality management approaches. There is emerging evidence that quality prioritisation within the management accounting function is taking place vis-a-vis defined enterprise pursuits (*Smith*, 1994). Ultimately, whatever the enterprise's goals, quality is deemed to impact on value-adding and non-value adding activities.

Subjecting accounting activities to quality controls represents but one side of the coin. The other perhaps more important way in which management accounting practices may be affected by quality concerns is in the situation where quality priorities are tied to enhancing the value of products and services which a company is in the business of providing to its customers. Quality control criteria are at times established through specific measures such as the proportion of deliveries made on time, the number of sub-standard products, the amount of reworks, the frequency and length of machine breakdowns, the launch time of new products and the number and gravity of customer complaints (*Coulthurst*, 1989b; *Thackray*, 1990). In spite of the use of such quantitative measures, worries continue to be expressed that accountants lack understanding of the relevance of quality to management accounting practices (*Allen*, 1991). To an extent, accounting based performance reports are employed by some companies in different countries which encompass quality measures (*Maskell*, 1989a) alongside data on delivery, production process times, flexibility and costs (*Maskell*, 1989b). But successful monitoring of quality depends on the availability and capture of the necessary data (*Garvin*, 1983) and more importantly on recognising and establishing relevant monitoring information. More innovative quality monitoring strategies that are organisationally defined are thought to be desirable. For instance, one measure of achieving quality improvement is the reduction of quality inspection by placing greater reliance on self-inspection (*Cole*, 1993). This underscores the need to achieve a subtle balance between information which can be quantitatively if not economically represented and that which must remain part of the process of production. Ultimately, an organisation must strike the 'right' mix between installing information systems for reporting on various dimensions of quality and relying on individual workers to monitor quality without requiring measures to be actually reported to other line managers. Such a balance must be organisationally specific (*Horovitz* and *Panak*, 1992).

In the UK, quality related costs have been reported to range from 5 to 25 percent of company turnover (*Plunkett, Dale and Tyrrell*, 1985) and of this total, 95 percent may comprise the cost of appraisal and failure. Eliminating causes of failure can not only reduce failure costs, but can also effect substantial reductions in appraisal costs. In this respect, TQM methodologies are often able to focus on the heart of the problem which is the identification and solving of operational problems. Quality costs may subsequently be categorised as relating to prevention, appraisal or failure. *Ponemon* (1990) suggests such a classification of quality costs so that prevention costs represent those expenditures which are incurred to ensure that unsatisfactory products are not produced by preventing the use or production of defective and non-conforming parts. In terms of assessing which prevention activities can reduce scrap,

Datar et al., (1993) report on the value of quality cost estimates. Appraisal costs help maintain quality levels by means of formal evaluations of product quality (such as testing, inspection, outside endorsements and quality audits). Finally, the cost of failure may be internal (scrap, spoilage and reworked material) or external (performance failures and customer complaints) whereby materials do not meet the company's requirements. Table 3.1 highlights these costs.

Table 3.1 Classification of quality costs

Failure costs. Costs required to evaluate, dispose of, and either correct or replace a defective or deficient product.

- Internal failure costs. Failure costs discovered before the product is delivered to customers. Examples:

— Rework costs
— Net cost of scrap
— Disposal of defective products
— Downtime due to quality problems

- External failure costs. Failure costs discovered after the product is delivered to customers. Examples:

— Complaint investigation and processing
— Warranty claims
— Cost of lost sales
— Product recalls

Appraisal costs. Costs of monitoring and inspecting products in terms of specified standards before the products are released to customers. Examples:

— Measurement equipment
— Inspection and tests
— Product quality audits
— Process control monitoring
— Test equipment expense

Prevention costs. Investments in machinery, technology, and education programs designed to reduce the number of defective products during production. Examples:

— Customer surveys
— Research of customer needs
— Field trials
— Quality education and training programs
— Supplier reviews
— Investment in improved production equipment
— Quality engineering
— Quality Circles

From Pasewark, 1991, p.47

Pasewark (1991) indicates that traditionally in the USA, products have been considered defective if they do not conform to standards that have been set internally. However, a consumer will not be interested in a product if his or her order performance expectation is greater than that of the manufacturer. The consumer of the future will expect a product to be guaranteed over its expected life. Thus expenditures will have to be geared toward making design standards conform to the expectations of consumers in the form of 'super prevention costs'. Indeed, *Pasewark* (1991, p.52) stresses that:

> Future superiority in global markets of manufactured goods will most likely depend on the speed of entrance into the super prevention area.

In this sense, the actual product will need to meet specifications set by external rather than internal expectations. The important thing is the consumer's perception of quality rather than that of the producer.

Differentation of quality costs into prevention, appraisal and failure has problems, however. It has been suggested that:

> . . . arrangement of data into these categories is usually done for reporting purposes, after the collection exercise. It adds nothing to the data's potential for provoking action (*Plunkett and Dale*, 1990, p.165.)

Further, *Heagy* (1991) suggests that this traditional classification ignores the cost of lost sales, which if included as a component of failure costs, will make total quality costs more accurate and meaningful. She suggests that:

> By focusing part of the measurement of quality cost on lost sales, this improved model requires management to bring the market place into the quality decision process (Ibid, p.71.)

Moreover, the quality activity elements represented by the traditional categorisation of quality costs do not match well with the cost information commonly reported by internal accounting systems. This is possibly a legacy of the traditional functional differentiation between organisational departments historically pervading many Western companies. However, as TQM approaches are put into place, which cut across arbitrarily defined functional boundaries, organisational information systems must cultivate elements of commonality and standardisation. Categorisation into prevention, appraisal and failure is a relic of quality department functioning which may be becoming increasingly anachronistic.

Knowledge about company practices can surface from benchmark programmes for quality management (*Russell*, 1991). Many companies are now moving toward alternative categorisations of quality costing such as highlighting the cost of conformance and the cost of non-conformance (*Crosby*, 1979). *Ostranga* (1991) suggests that it is possible to identify the cost of quality as long as it is tied to a specific plan of action to support the reduction in non-value-added costs. The focus should, according to him, be on investments in prevention which will allow a return on investment on quality expenditures to be identified and tracked. Such views, which differentiate between conformance and non-conformance or between value added and non-value added, are compatible with management accounting approaches to budgeting, variance analysis and performance evaluation.

The potential exists for TQM philosophies to blend into existing and emerging cost management practices and to thereby integrate quality costing within internal costing infrastructures. In this respect, CIMA's (1984) definition of quality costs as:

> The expenditure incurred in defect prevention and appraisal activities and the losses due to internal and external failure of a product or service through failure to meet agreed specification.

hints at the possibilities which exist for quality costing to complement management accounting approaches. Nevertheless, much ground remains to be covered and immutable accounting systems which maintain accountability bias toward traditional production cost concerns (even where use is made of novel approaches described later in the chapter) cannot provide courage to organisational decision-makers adopting and seeking to use wider managerial perspectives.

3.3 Accounting For Just-In-Time Systems

The choice of cost accounting techniques to be applied in particular situations is ordinarily seen as being dependent on organisational

needs. The installation of JIT systems is no exception. Indeed,
Foster and Horngren (1987, p.25) assert that:

> . . . JIT reminds us that any significant change in underlying
> operations is likely to justify a corresponding change in the
> cost accounting and management systems.

Accordingly, commentators in management accounting have
advanced what are deemed appropriate accounting responses to the
adoption of JIT systems. At one level, JIT is seen to demand novel
accounting measures (see below) and at another, it is argued to
make redundant certain traditional accounting techniques (*Harris*,
1990). In whatever way JIT has been interpreted by accountants,
normative accounting recommendations have been specific and have
been tied to the objectives of this work organisation philosophy.

The starting point of JIT implementation has been viewed as
important in considering accounting changes. *Miltenburg* (1990), for
instance, argues that when JIT is embedded in an MRP system,
then only those JIT benefits which MRP recognises as benefits will
be reported. Hence, a need exists to adjust costing procedures to
evaluate the benefits of JIT correctly. In evaluating the propriety of
a cost system for capturing JIT's consequences, there must be a
recognition of JIT's intended payoffs. These may encompass a
commitment to a high level of quality, continuous improvement of
the production process and final product, the simplification and
increased visibility of operational activities and the reduction of a
variety of costs including working capital, stock warehouse and stock
movement, and record keeping costs. An MRP system will not
record all of these. It may, for instance, report improvements in
quality which reduce the scrap rate since MRP typically tracks
allowed and actual scrap costs. But quality improvements that
reduce rework costs, lower warranty costs and increased customer
orders will not be captured by an MRP system. Nor will
improvements in delivery times, transportation costs, or stock-room
space reductions. It may be desirable to consider broadening the
information captured by the cost system to enable such factors to be
reported.

A JIT system enables more direct traceability of certain costs which
raises new possibilities for more comprehensive reporting. For
instance, materials handling facilities are often dedicated to a single
retail area or a single production line. Such operational costs can

therefore be classified as direct costs of individual retail areas or production lines. In effect, many activities which previously would have been classified as indirect costs would under JIT be considered direct costs (see Table 3.2).

Table 3.2 Direct vs Indirect Costs under JIT

	Manufacturing Environment	
	Traditional	*JIT*
Material handling	Indirect	Direct
Repair and maintenance	Largely direct	Direct
Energy	Indirect	Direct
Operating supplies	Indirect	Direct
Supervision	Indirect	Direct
Production support services	Indirect	Largely direct
Depreciation	Indirect	Direct

Adapted from McHilhattan, 1987, p.24

As already noted, a key aspect of the JIT philosophy is that it simplifies production activities. Likewise, JIT can allow accounting records to be simplified through backflush accounting whereby the level of detail with which product information is recorded is greatly reduced. A backflush costing system focuses first on the output of the organisation and then works backwards when applying costs to units sold and to stock. In contrast, conventional product costing systems track costs through work in progress beginning with the introduction of raw material into production (*Foster and Horngren*, 1988).

Backflushing focuses first on output and then works backwards when allocating costs between Cost of Goods Sold (CGS) and inventory with no separate accounting for Work in Process (WIP). Consider the example of ABC Company (adapted from *Bhimani and Bromwich*, 1991) which manufactures calculators and uses a backflush cost accounting system. The standard material cost per unit is £2.00 and the standard conversion cost (CC) is £3.00 per unit. Ten units are manufactured during its first month of operation and six units are sold. During the month, £24.00 of Raw Material (RM) are purchased on credit.

Under a backflush accounting system, the point at which a sale occurs is taken also to be the point at which accounting entries are made. The following journal entry depicts this for the six units sold:

CGS (6 units x £5)	..	..	..	..	..	30	
CC (6 units x £3)	..	..	..	..	..	18	
Creditors (6 units x £2)	..	..	..	..	..		12

Conversely, under a traditional cost accounting system, the following entries would be made:

(1)

Material Stock ..	..	..	..	..	..	24	
Creditors	..	..	..	..	..	..	24

To record purchase of raw material (RM) on credit.

(2)

WIP (10 x £2) ..	..	..	..	..	..	20	
Material	..	..	..	..	..	..	20

To record application of RM to WIP for 10 units.

(3)

WIP (10 x £3) ..	..	..	..	..	..	30	
CC	..	..	..	..	..	..	30

To record the application of conversion costs to WIP.

(4)

FG	..	..	..	..	..	50	
WIP ..	..	..	..	..	..		50

To record transfer of finished goods to warehouse.

(5)

CGS (6 units x (£2 + £3))	..	..	..	..	30	
FG	..	..	..	..	..	..	30

To record the sale of 6 units.

With the backflushing accounting system, accounts for stock are not kept separately and the purchase of raw material is recognised at the point of sale.

As an alternative, backflush accounting can be modified so as to record the purchase of raw material (where the RM account is integrated with WIP):

Inventory (RM and WIP)	..	..	..	..	24	
Creditors	..	..	..	..	..	..	24

and for the cost of the finished goods manufactured, the following entries are made:

Inventory-FG (10 units x (£2 + £3))   50
    Inventory-RM and WIP (10 units x £2)   20
    CC (10 units x £3)   30

and for sales:

CGS (6 units x (£2+ £3))   30
    Inventory (FG)   30

The inventory balance at the end of the month is as follows:

Inventory (RM and WIP)	£4.00
Inventory (4 units @ £5.00)	£20.00
	£24.00

The example above indicates the potential for cost reductions which can result from using a simplified and less extensive accounting record keeping system such as backflushing. A just-in-time system implies that physical material moves along the production line as sales are made rather than being pushed into production only to be stored in warehouses. Backflush accounting reflects the nature of this physical production flow by making accounting entries only as the demand-pulled production process takes place thereby reducing bookkeeping entries and their associated costs as shown above. As *Tatikonda* (1988, p.3) notes:

> Backflushing means looking at the product's bill of materials and reducing inventory records according to what parts went into the product.

Moreover, it has been argued that the lower investments in work in process inventories which emanate from the rationalisation of work processes according to the JIT philosophy and the reduced carrying charges associated with WIP (such as finance costs, obsolescence and scrap, material storage, material movement, insurance, stock flow accounting and production controls) can open innovative avenues for further cost cutting measures by manufacturing firms. In this sense, the implementation of the JIT philosophy which relies on a demand pull manufacturing process where production only occurs when orders are received can be more closely and narrowly aligned with data capture (as done by backflushing), rather than depend on a more general record keeping system which ignores the specific nature of production processes underlying accounting activities and which therefore offers little guidance for making further changes.

Just as JIT is seen to generate new accounting needs, it also alters the costing system, making certain traditional practices redundant. For instance, an organisation may ordinarily collect information on purchasing, warehouse and raw material inspection activities. These costs are subsequently placed into a cost pool along with others and a base such as warehouse space is used to allocate costs. Under JIT, long-term purchase contracts are used and the number of suppliers is typically reduced, thereby decreasing purchasing costs. Likewise, the goal of 'zero-stock' manufacturing eliminates warehouse storage requirements and quality and quantity inspection procedures are also greatly diminished. Such changes mean cost pools may alter considerably and allocation bases consequently have to be redefined.

Furthermore, under JIT purchasing factors such as quality of raw materials, availability of subcomponents and reliability of supplies often take precedence over short-term price advantages. Price reductions of raw material and bought-in parts are often achieved by deploying long-term agreements with suppliers. Consequently data on purchase price variances which may have constituted an important part of accounting based performance measures loses relevance in a JIT environment. What is of essence is not to judge the performance of the purchasing manager as an isolated activity but the evaluation of the production process as an integrated and complex set of interrelated functions. Likewise, recognising that JIT production entails a far-reaching form of decentralisation whereby each individual factory worker can halt the production process when a problem arises, renders the relevance of labour efficiency variances doubtful. The efficient use of labour cannot under a JIT system be captured by accounting monitors designed for use in Ford-type manufacturing environments. The use of variances for capturing performance information traditionally stresses incentives and responsibilities for workers in individual production cells. Conversely, JIT rests on continuous improvement of an aggregate type. It is therefore likely that where performance information of an accounting nature is desired, it will take the form of variance analysis at the plant level. Indeed, the underlying 'push' rationale of traditional manufacturing is replaced by a 'pull' philosophy under JIT. Here, the cost of idleness with the JIT system offsets the costs of overproduction in traditional manufacture and as such:

> . . . the new 'pull' production process under JIT renders the computation and use of traditional variances inappropriate. (*Green, Amenkhienan and Johnson*, 1991, p.51.)

It needs to be recognised however that an altered role for variance analysis does not extinguish the value of standard costs. Many companies after successfully adopting JIT techniques have altered their cost management practices, but have not shed their standard costing systems (*Ferguson*, 1988; *Phillips and Collins*, 1990). Other companies have shifted from the use of standard costs to actual costs since the former contain allowances for waste and defects which is counter to JIT notions of continuous improvement and zero-defects (*McNair, Mosconi and Norris*, 1988).

By the same token, the adoption of JIT as a work organisation technique forces a reconsideration of allocation mechanisms. Application of overhead costs may need to be revised in line with altered production strategies. JIT can, in instances, lead to apparent increases in product costs. As *Bicheno* (1991, p.135) explains:

> This is because the direct labour content may actually increase, due to activities such as self-inspection, setup, own maintenance, and so on. So even though leadtimes and inventories may be drastically cut, the products which have not yet been subject to JIT may actually appear to benefit.

Direct labour as an allocation base becomes inappropriate, not only because direct labour input becomes distorted by departmental work stoppages whenever a fault is discovered with the product being processed or even with the production process itself, but also because JIT implementation is often accompanied by a decline in direct labour usage and a consequent reclassification of all direct labour as indirect (*Dugdale*, 1990).

Performance evaluation indicators other than variances are affected by the application of JIT principles. Traditionally, the management accounting system reports an array of financial monitors on a periodic basis many of which are of little use given the growing importance of real-time information in many enterprises. In this context, *Cobb* (1991, p.38) has suggested that

> . . . a feed forward system which would predict a deviation thus allowing the process to be corrected before it occurred, would be preferable in a JIT company.

Although no company has been documented to have moved toward such a system of internal reporting, many firms report the enhanced use of non-financial monitors. In part, traditional accounting measures attempt to isolate the performance of individual organisational sub-units or departmental managers. The net consequence is often dysfunctional behaviour or excess emphasis on short-term profitability. Certain companies have therefore moved toward the use of monitors tied to quality objectives, reduction of stock, cooperation with vendors, on-time deliveries and process cost reduction (*Green, Amenkhienan and Johnson*, 1991). More specifically, measures including elapsed time, distance moved, space occupied and number of parts numbers (*Johnson*, 1988) have been proposed alongside the use of variances concerned with quality, cycle time and product complexity (*McNair and Mosconi*, 1987). What is evident to many is that technisource of ias JIT as one form of new manufacturing practice

> . . . necessitates changes in performance reporting and control systems (*Banker, Potter and Schroeder*, 1993).

McHilhattan (1987) delineates the differing emphasis of This process measures under a traditional system and JIT (see Table 3.3).

Table 3.3 Performance Measures: Traditional vs JIT

Traditional	JIT
Direct Labour (Efficiency, Utilisation, Productivity)	Total Head Count Productivity
	Days of Inventory
Machine Utilisation	Group Incentives
Stock Turnover	Customer Service
Cost Variances	Knowledge and Capability-based
Individual Incentives	Promotion
Promotion based on Seniority	Ideas Generated and Implemented
	Customer Complaints

Adapted from McHilhattan, 1987, p.25

Miltenburg (1990) has proposed that overhead be allocated on the basis of the amount of time that a part remains unused in the plant rather than on the extent of direct labour or machine time. This would induce the use of JIT principles since efforts would be made to reduce stock waiting times as well as lead times.

Although a wide array of accounting responses has been proposed in the literature in relation to JIT implementation, companies have in practice adopted a number of different approaches. They have effected changes reasoned on accounting premises as well as alterations not reflective of documented suggested accounting techniques (*Harris*, 1990). Ultimately some initial restructuring of the accounting system may be desirable when a JIT system is introduced but subsequently, as *Ferguson* (1988, p.48) notes:

> . . . a period of experimentation and gradual change is required.

3.4 The 'Tableau de Bord'

Cost management innovations might be expected to neglect national borders with the passage of time. There are many companies outside Japan which employ target costing practices and likewise, activity based costing is not an accounting approach confined to the USA (see below and later chapters). One important control mechanism used in French enterprises for more than forty years is the *tableau de bord* which has been seen as appropriate for use in enterprises outside France (*Lebas*, 1993). Effectively, the *tableau de bord* may be seen as an 'integrated communication device which permits management control of the enterprise' (*Ardoin, Michel and Schmidt*, 1986, p.143). It is a reporting system which focuses on key control parameters and which may trigger immediate managerial action. The *tableau de bord* provides, in part, a means of 'controlling the attainment of preplanned objectives' (Ibid) and therefore may be seen as a variance analysis report of sorts which underscores management by exception reporting. What is unique to the *tableau de bord*, however, is its stress on pyramidal analysis of different information facets of the enterprise's activities. These may include contributions to the balance sheet, future employment creation, return to shareholders, pollution abatement and customer satisfaction, aside from the operational activities of individual organisational segments such as sales, production and marketing. This tool, therefore, entails three-dimensional communication covering local, lateral and vertical information. Hierarchy may be reflected in the structure of the *tableau de bord* but so can the product-value chain from raw material to customer service and tactical manoeuvering to strategic management of local or global elements of the enterprise. There may thus be as many *tableaux de bord* as there are managers and each will be continually revised to implant corporate dynamism within this action-based control tool.

The *tableau de bord* is used in many French organisations and discussed in all French texts on management control within the context of general management practices. Effectively, it can be seen as a means of monitoring the pulse of the organisation and identifying any form of activity which requires action of one type or another. It is a highly customised tool according to the needs of different managers, reflecting the environment within which a company operates. The frequency of reporting may be daily, weekly, monthly or even annually, depending on the nature of the process being managed. Figure 3.1 below provides an example of a *tableau de bord* aimed at a responsibility centre management team.

Figure 3.1: Tableau de bord

	Realised in M	Realised in M-1	Realised in MN-1	Realised in M cumulated	Goal for M	Goal for M cumulated
Indicator 1						
Indicator 2						
Indicator 3						
—						

Adapted from Bescos et al., 1993, p. 321

Indicator rows in Figure 3.1 represent a variety of values, ratios and indices deemed relevant to the activities of the responsibility centre. Examples include turnover, market growth and efficiency. The first row provides information realised for the current month M. M-1 refers to the previous month and MN-1, the current month last year. The total to date is provided by the M cumulated column which can usefully be cross-compared to the Goal for the Month M and for M cumulated columns.

Accounting data may be integrated with graphical information, statistical tables and quantitative notes. Although financially orientated, the *tableau de bord* can provide an engineering or marketing or production-based focus. *Bescos et al.*, (1993) note that the *tableau de bord* cannot be:

> . . . a system of management information which is limited to reporting accounting data and running the risk of favouring only a particular type of thinking among operational managers.

The information systems designer must therefore conform to the preferences and priorities of the individual manager rather than simply establish a depersonalised financial tool for management control.

3.5 Automation and Activity Based Costing

The implementation of advanced manufacturing technologies and novel work organisation methods alongside the adoption of revised managerial philosophies has initiated a concern with the implications such changes have for accounting practices. Calls for management accounting reforms have been voiced particularly by those who see the changing nature of costs themselves as suggesting a need for reassessing traditional accounting approaches. Historically, manufacturing companies especially, though not solely, have changed considerably. From the 1940s production processes tended toward the repetitive manufacturing of homogeneous products. Although investments in heavy machinery to enable this was high, the emphasis on specialised production equipment for mass production coincided with an increased demand for focused labour. The net consequence of this approach was high labour costs comprising a significant portion of direct costs. It is argued however that more recently, direct labour costs have declined in relation to total manufacturing costs. As companies adopt advanced manufacturing techniques (AMT), such as numerical control machines, CAD/CAM systems and other forms of flexible production technologies, the need for direct labour input rapidly diminishes (*Brimson.*, 1991; *Jeans and Morrow*, 1989a; *Johnson and Kaplan*, 1987).

In contrast as investments are made into AMTs, overhead costs expand quickly. This arises not only from the attendant depreciation, insurance and maintenance costs, but also from a new category of costs associated with servicing the new technology. AMTs, for instance, may require computer expertise, software updates, personnel training, scheduling systems and integrating information systems to link and coordinate automated production activities. As a result, overhead costs can rise quickly whilst direct labour costs continue to decline rapidly. Trends experienced by manufacturing firms adopting advanced production methods, including AMTs, can be portrayed by delineating the cost behaviour patterns for inventory, direct labour and direct material (see Exhibit 3.1).

Exhibit 3.1 Cost behaviour patterns

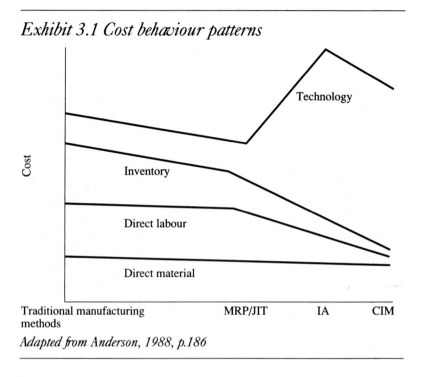

Cost

Technology

Inventory

Direct labour

Direct material

| Traditional manufacturing methods | MRP/JIT | IA | CIM |

Adapted from Anderson, 1988, p.186

From the perspective of traditional costing logic, such changes in the manufacturing cost mix can be particularly problematic. Conventionally, direct labour has served as a principal application base for indirect costs which tended to be low. But where the overhead numerator grows at a pace not dissimilar to the swiftly diminishing direct labour denominator base, an inappropriately leveraged burden (overhead) rate results (sometime of the order of 2,000 percent to 3,000 percent). To an extent, the growth in overhead costs has been conditioned by the application of innovative work approaches such as TQM and JIT which help contain certain costs.

Moreover, the managerial logic concerning the potential benefits which can be derived from economies of scale through bulk-buying and mass production is changing. There is now seen to be considerable merit in satisfying a greater diversity of customer needs by developing and producing a larger range of products and by providing a custom made product within a minimal time-frame. The availability of flexible advanced technology for this is not always the main motivating element. Rather, it is sometimes the only strategic option that a company can take in a dynamic and competitive market environment. Thus the fast pace of change in business pressurises companies to react if not to proact. The adoption of altered production technologies and work organisation approaches rests on transformed philosophies about 'best' business practices. Alongside the adoption of renewed managerial thinking comes product diversity, technological complexity and operational flexibility. One consequence of this is a reorientation of accounting practices. Below is a discussion of activity based costing (ABC), here taken to include activity based cost management (ABCM) and activity based budgeting (ABB) as one accounting approach advanced to tackle challenges posed by a changing business environment and the associated mode of thinking into which it has been moulded. It is to be noted that the term activity based management now covers a wide range of business tools and techniques which have developed out of activity based costing (see *Morrow and Ashworth*, 1994).

Activity based costing

The rationale

Businesses have conventionally attempted to achieve profitability by managing costs which in turn are indirect measures of resource consuming activities. Costs are reported on the basis of responsible organisational units and the objective has been to ensure that business decisions deliver value to the customer in excess of the costs required to produce that value. Consequently, costs are often regarded as generating value and measuring production activities rather than merely representing, in accounting terms, the utilisation of resources by organisational activities. Using cost as a substitute for activity does not pose any difficulty where the manufacturing process is relatively simple and produces homogeneous products. Here production costs may be readily traced and allocated to product units. In more sophisticated manufacturing environments however, product quality, diversity and complexity have been viewed as characterising the critical success factors for maintaining competitiveness. In these contexts, activity based information has been said to be more useful than traditional costing data as it attempts to capture cost causality factors more effectively. Some have even interpreted ABC as enabling the pursuit of reality in enterprises:

> The essential point about activity-based approaches is that they represent a return to reflecting reality in the way management information is compiled and reported (*Morrow*, 1992, p.1).

In addition, activity based management in complementing ABC attempts to provide

> . . . activity based information to focus employee efforts on continuously improving quality, time, service, cost, flexibility and profitability (*Cokins, Stratton and Helbling*, 1992).

Activity based information may be non-financial or of a strategic cost nature (*Johnson*, 1988) and may comprise any relevant data about activities across the entire chain of value-adding organisational processes including design, engineering, sourcing, production, distribution, marketing and after-sales service. This information focuses managers' attention on the underlying causes (drivers) of cost and profit on the premise that

> . . . people cannot manage costs, they can only manage activities that cause costs (*Johnson*, 1987, p. 51).

The manufacture of a product entails many processes which add cost to the product but not all such activities necessarily add value to the product. It is therefore possible, in principle, to differentiate between value-added and non-value added activities according to whether or not the elimination of an activity from the manufacturing process would result in a deterioration of product attributes such as performance, function, quality and perceived value and thus reduce value to the customer (see below).

Production approaches such as MRP, JIT and forms of AMTs place emphasis on eliminating waste, causes of delay, excess, and unevenness of product. It is potentially useful for managers to attempt to identify activities which waste organisational resources in these ways and to view these non-value adding activities as undesirable since they do not augment the customer's perception of a product's value. Such a perspective highlights a key aspect of what has been termed activity based management which is seen as offering a comprehensive guide to the theory and practice of new approaches which have been developed in the 1980s and early 1990s in response to business's growing need to understand cost behaviour and manage costs effectively (*Morrow*, 1992).

Non-value added activities can be classed as either production related activities such as inventory carrying, storage, expediting and production control, or as support activities such as strategic planning, product/process development, purchasing and financing. Non-value added activities are often erroneously perceived to be an essential part of the manufacturing process and become embedded as predefined requirements for the functioning of the organisation. For instance, it has been assumed in Western manufacturing operations that a trade-off exists between ordering/setup costs and handling/carrying costs giving rise to a theoretically optimal economic order quantity (EOQ). As the quantity of stock increases, the handling/carrying costs also increase because of enhanced working capital requirements, greater warehouse space utilised and possibly increased safekeeping costs until the stock is moved. Conversely, ordering/setup costs are decreased since invoicing and record keeping expenses are not affected by the size of the individual transactions they represent. On this premise, an optimal point exists for the quantity to be ordered at which both handling/carrying and order setup costs are minimised (see Exhibit 3.2).

Exhibit 3.2 Handling/carrying costs vs order/set-up costs

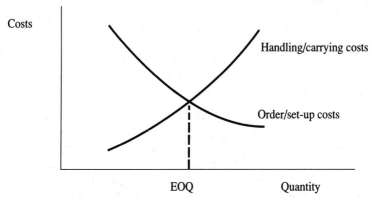

In contrast, the JIT philosophy would regard ordering/set-up costs as non-value adding activities which can be reduced. The economic order quantity can therefore likewise be lowered. This may be achieved by eliminating set-up time and costs and ultimately obviates the need to hold quantities of stock in volumes greater than one unit (the new EOQ). Reducing batch sizes and inventories also reduces the causes of defective output and thus improves quality. Quality, flexibility and costs can thus be managed in a mutually inclusive fashion by discarding notions of necessity in the case of activities which do not add value to the product being manufactured.

Problems may also arise where traditional cost accounting systems designed to value inventories for financial reporting purposes are assumed to provide a measure of the organisational resources used up in their production. This is because, in part, overhead reflects the cost of increased diversity (or scope) of output rather than the volume (or scale) of output. A traditional cost accounting system which allocates overhead on the basis of scale of output rather than scope of output will tend to 'overcost' high volume products and 'undercost' low volume products (see example below) relative to allowing for economies of scope (*Cooper and Kaplan*, 1987; *Cooper*, 1988). The resulting 'distorted' cost information claimed to be provided by conventional cost accounting systems can encourage managers to proliferate low volume product lines which may, indeed, be loss-makers. As *Cooper and Kaplan* (1987) explain:

> . . . low volume products create more transactions per unit manufactured than their high volume counterparts. The per unit share of these costs should therefore be higher for the low volume products. But when volume related bases are used to allocate support-department costs, high volume and low volume products are not treated differently because each individual unit produced represents the same volume of production. . . high volume products receive an excessively high fraction of support-department costs and, therefore, subsidize the low volume products (p. 218).

Most cost systems in manufacturing firms use a two-stage cost tracing procedure for non-direct cost, whereby the first stage assigns resources to specific segments of the production process. The second stage traces costs to products by using a measure of the quantity of resources consumed by each product. It is the choice of overhead application measure in this second stage which is seen as being able to distort costs if it is not chosen carefully (*Cooper*, 1987).

It is to be noted however that 'overcosting' of product, which ABC seeks to tackle, can in certain instances be desirable:

> . . . facing imperfect competition, it is sometimes optimal for firms to persist in using a single cost driver system (direct labor based) rather than switching to an activity based cost system (*Banker and Potter*, 1993).

Conventional accounting has differentiated between costs which remain constant per unit but vary in total with production volume (variable costs) and costs which remain constant irrespective of the total actual volume over a relevant range of production (fixed costs). Certain fixed costs are viewed by critics of conventional management accounting as being in effect long-term variable costs which vary with measures of activity (other than production volume), but not instantaneously. These have traditionally been thought of as fixed costs and have been apportioned on the basis of arbitrary allocation rules devoid of any defensible cause and effect link. Commonly used 'cost drivers' for allocating short-term variable costs include direct labour hours, machine hours and material £ (all of which are volume-based). The same bases are used also to allocate long-term variable costs by traditional cost accounting systems resulting in cost tracing which is regarded as inaccurate.

Cooper (1987) suggests that long-term costs which are variable with activity but not production volume are related to complexity and that increasing the volume of production does not increase the utilisation of support services such as set-ups, expediting, inventory movements and scheduling activities whereas augmenting the range of products will increase support costs rapidly. For instance, increased product diversity may increase the documentation and record keeping activities associated with set-ups since the number of set-ups increases when production lines utilising flexible technology switch from one product to another to increase the range of production. Under a conventional costing system, these increased record keeping costs become part of overhead and are allocated to products using an application base such as direct labour. Yet it is not direct labour utilisation or production volume which is responsible for the increased record keeping costs but some other measure of activity which represents increased product diversity. The cost drivers underlying increased record keeping costs mirror transactions which increase the scope of output rather than the scale of output. With this view, the choice of cost drivers for activity based costs should be based on factors which capture transactions, such as inspection hours, number of inspections undertaken, production lots manufactured, set-ups, shipments, orders and even the number of vendors. Some empirical evidence supports the idea of incorporating such operations-based cost drivers along with measures of volume in cost driver models (*Banker and Johnston*, 1993). However, *Cooper* (1987) warns:

> . . . there are no simple rules that pertain to the selection of cost drivers. The best approach is to identify the resources that constitute a significant proportion of the product costs and determine their cost behaviour. If several are long term variable costs, a transaction-based cost system should be considered (p.45).

ABC and the concept of activities

The underlying foundation of all ABC systems is the perception that the organisation is made up of activities. These activities transform resources driven by the requirements for the activity's operations into outputs demanded by the firm's other activities.

Thus, with an activity perspective, activities *consume* resources and cost objects *consume* activities. This is in contrast to traditional accounting where costs are *consumed* by cost objects (mainly products). The focus is not on the amount of each type of general ledger costs, such as wages, equipment, power and supervision incurred by a department but on the costs of the activities undertaken by the department. Thus, the conventional costs of a department would be assigned to the activities contributed to by the department. A department concerned with customer relations, widely defined, might undertake the following major activities:

Making quotations
Pricing orders
Checking creditworthiness
Issuing invoices
Customer liaison
Expediting orders

These are all very different activities which may make very different demands for resources. Ideally, an activity approach to accounting should be grounded on the management of the organisation by managing such activities rather than the traditional organisational functional unit. Activity based management has thus been defined as:

> A discipline focusing on the management of activities as the route to continuously improve both the value received by customers and the profit earned by providing this value (*CAM-I*, 1990).

This process includes cost-driver analysis, activity analysis and performance analysis and utilises activity based costing as a major source of information. There are probably few manufacturing organisations which manage purely on the basis of activities or processes. Generally, such a system runs in parallel with the existing management system.

The first step in determining an activity's cost is to ascertain the factors which determine the amount of resources required by the activity. The technology of the activity may be seen to determine the amount of resources used in the activity and therefore the demand for the activity's output and the size of the activity's cost pool. Thus, vetting an order for creditworthiness may involve a certain amount of staff time, data and paper processing and the use of a telephone or of a computer network. It is the technical operations required which determine the resource requirement of the activity. Ideally, the attribution of costs to activities should reflect this technology by tracing empirically costs based on the activity's resource driver; but in practice, judgement, interviews and diaries are often used in estimating the resource requirements of an activity.

It is the essence of the definition of an activity that it should be capable of being viewed as separate from other activities and that the output of the activity should be capable of being explained ideally by one and only one factor (the cost driver) which thus explains how costs change with variable demands for the activity output. Thus, for example, the amount of resources required for the activity of vetting creditworthiness may be felt to depend only on the monetary amount of the order from new customers. Cost objects, products or departments which want this service will bear a charge based on this cost driver: the larger the new order size, the greater the charge. This illustrates that activity costing is not only helpful for costing products but may also help to establish the cost of dealing with different types of customers. Cost drivers are one element in the charge for the activity's output and are used to determine the charge-out rate by dividing the cost of the activity by the total volume of its cost driver (the frequency of driver operations) in a period. Thus, for customer liaison the chosen driver may be the number of customers or orders, the type of customer or the location of the plants with which liaison is required. Ideally, the driver chosen should be deduced using empirical evidence and may be firm-specific. The usual types of drivers are:

- activity output volume, for example the number of set-ups, the number of quality inspections; and

- activity complexity, for example, creditworthiness checks may depend not only on order size but the type of credit arrangement required by the customer, conditioned by the total size of likely demands, such as the number of products, number of customers and suppliers and by the technology and the organisational structure.

A number of major points emerge from this description of the elements of ABC. Activity cost studies really give a snapshot of costs and technology at a specific time. Thus cost improvement is not automatically built into ABC. Rather, it is generated by activity based cost management processes. Activities may not heed organisational structure. Many different departments may contribute to an activity. Activity management may thus conflict with the usual management structure of the organisation. Ideally, ABC should be based on the empirical tracing of costs. Only in the last resort should ABC incorporate cost allocation.

The costs derived from ABC are of a different nature to traditional costs. They are argued to represent the costs of activities as seen at a time when the firm is able to rearrange its operating activities (*Cooper and Kaplan*, 1992). In a shorter time period, activity costs may not be able to be reduced because, for example, of labour contracts or because of indivisible capacity which technically cannot be reduced in the short run, and because managerial decisions about activities may reside with functional managers not responsible for the activities under consideration. Thus, ceasing to produce some product which is expensive in activity cost terms may not automatically lead to cost reductions. The departments responsible for these freed resources may not dispose or redeploy the resources. *Cooper and Kaplan* (1992) say that ABC systems need to highlight the usage of resources in a period rather than their accounting costs which may be fixed in the short run. Faced with unused capacity,

> Management, to obtain higher profits, must take conscious actions either to use available capacity to support a higher volume of business (ie, by increasing revenues) or to reduce spending on resources by eliminating the unused capacity (*Cooper and Kaplan* 1992, p.12).

However, this resource change process may be quite difficult to carry out. The type of unused capacity available in a period (often labour of a specific type) may not be of the sort that can be used to relieve the constraints which are restricting the otherwise profitable expansion of output. Moreover, additional increments of existing outputs may not be optimal because management should already be planning to produce the optimal volume of output. The following example shows how product costs may be distorted by conventional product costing exercises and how activity based costing can assist in assigning costs more equitably.

Activity based costing: an example

Consider the UK company which manufactures three products, A, B and C, in two production departments, 1 and 2. The production activities are supported by two service departments, purchasing and power. Product A is a simple product using only one raw material, X. Although Product A must be processed in both production departments, most of its time is spent in department 1, a labour intensive operation. Product B is more complex than Product A, requiring the use of raw materials X and Y. Material X is added in department 1 and material Y is added in department 2, a machine intensive operation. Whereas products A and B are high volume products, Product C is a low volume item entailing a relatively complex set of production operations in both departments 1 and 2 but using only raw material Z which is input in department 1. Thus, although department 1 is labour intensive and department 2 is machine intensive, all three products have some labour and machine operations in both departments. The same employees perform the labour and machine operations whilst also undertaking inspections of products. A different set of specialised workers is in charge of setting up the production line and effecting production changeovers.

Table 3.4 Cost requirements for each product

COST COMPONENT	PRODUCT A	PRODUCT B	PRODUCT C	COST
UNITS PRODUCED:	10,000	10,000	1,000	
RAW MATERIAL USED:				
(Kilograms) X	50,000	50,000	—	£800,000
Y	—	100,000	—	£1,200,000
Z	—	—	1,000	£5,000
DEPARTMENT 1:				
Direct Labour hrs	20,000	5,000	1,000	£390,000
Indirect Labour Hrs				
Inspection	2,500	2,500	5,000	£150,000
Machine operations	5,000	10,000	15,000	£450,000
Number of Set ups	200	200	500	£13,500
Machine Hours	5,000	10,000	750	£420,000
DEPARTMENT 2:				
Direct Labour hrs	5,000	5,000	1,000	£220,000
Indirect Labour hrs				
Inspection	2,500	5,000	7,500	£300,000
Machine operations	1,000	4,000	5,000	£200,000
Number of Set ups	200	400	600	£24,000
Machine hours	5,000	20,000	1,000	£832,000

OTHER DATA:
Power Costs   £400,070
Power Used (in kilowatt hours)

Department 1	1,500,000
Department 2	8,500,000

Purchasing Costs: £112,000
Number of Purchase Orders:

Material X	200
Material Y	300
Material Z	60

Building Occupancy Costs   £1,000,000
Square Metres Occupied:

Purchasing	10,000
Power	40,000
Department 1	200,000
Department 2	250,000

During the past period, 10,000 units of Product A, 10,000 units of Product B and 1,000 units of Product C, were produced. Table 3.4 shows the raw material, direct labour and indirect cost requirements for each product. The information is expressed in terms of kilograms, direct labour hours (DLH) and machine hours (MH), and indicates the number of set-ups, purchase orders, kilowatts hour power requirements, and square metres occupancy. Associated monetary costs appear in the last column. Part of this data relating to activities which drive costs such as the number of set-ups and the number of purchase orders may not be available in traditional cost systems. Conversely, volume-based measures are often provided by most accounting systems which attempt to charge overhead costs to specific products.

Under traditional costing, product valuation is ordinarily performed in one of two ways. The allocation of overheads to products may be effected by using either a plant-wide overhead rate or departmental overhead rates. Table 3.5 shows the stock valuation where a plant-wide rate based on direct labour hours is used. With this method, all production costs other than raw materials and direct labour are totalled and divided by the direct labour hours with a resulting overhead rate of £105.45 per direct labour hour (allowing for rounding errors). By charging each product with overhead at this rate, Product A has a unit cost of £343.62, Product B of £282.95 and Product C's unit cost is determined at £250.89.

Applying overhead costs using a plant-wide rate based on machine hours, as opposed to labour hours, for all costs other than labour and machines yields product unit costs for A, B and C of £173.45, £457.85 and £203.54 respectively. This approach to the calculation of product costs utilising a plant-wide overhead rate is quick and easy to perform although *Roth and Borthwick* (1989, p. 30) who developed some of the initial data used in this example suggest that:

> . . . the unit costs reported by this method are illogical.

The question may be raised as to why, using direct labour hours, the most complex product (Product C) should cost less than Product B to make, which in turn is less expensive to manufacture than the simplest Product A. Product B requires two raw materials and more machine hours in departments 1 and 2 than Product A. Likewise, the complexity of producing Product C far exceeds that of manufacturing Product B in terms of inspection, machine hours and set-ups. It is likely that a production manager overseeing the overall manufacturing process would place little faith in the costing calculations. The cost data would possibly be seen as misleading. The distortion arises because Product A requires more direct labour

Table 3.5 Product valuation under traditional costing

Production Costs	Product A	Product B	Product C
Raw materials			
X	£ 400,000[a]	£ 400,000	£ 0
Y	0	1,200,000	0
Z	0	0	5,000
	400,000	1,600,000	5,000
Direct Labour			
Department 1	300,000[b]	75,000	15,000
Department 2	100,000[c]	100,000	20,000
	400,000	175,000	35,000
Overhead	2,636,196[d]	1,054,478	210,895
Total Product Costs	£3,436,196	£2,829,478	£250,895
Cost per Unit	£ 343.62	£ 282.95	£ 250.89

[a] $\dfrac{50,000 \text{ kg}}{100,000 \text{ kg}}$ x £800,000 = £400,000

[b] $\dfrac{20,000 \text{ DLH}}{26,000 \text{ DLH}}$ x £390,000 = £300,000

[c] $\dfrac{5,000 \text{ DLH}}{11,000 \text{ DLH}}$ x £220,000 = £100,000

[d] 20,000 DLH (Dept.1) + 5,000 DLH (Dept.2) = 25,000 DLH x £105.45 overhead allocation rate (see calculation below).

Overhead Allocation Rate Calculation:

Indirect Labour			
Department 1		£600,000	
Department 2		£500,000	
			1,100,000
Set-ups			
Department 1		£ 13,500	
Department 2		£ 24,000	
			37,500
Machine Related			
Department 1		£420,000	
Department 2		£832,000	
			1,252,000
Power			400,070
Purchasing			112,000
Building Occupancy			1,000,000
Total Overhead Costs			3,901,570

Overhead Allocation rate:

$$\dfrac{\text{Total Overhead Costs}}{\text{Total Direct Labour Hours}} \quad \dfrac{3,901,570}{37,000} = £105.45 \text{ (rounded)}$$

hours than Product B. Product A has consequently been assigned a greater proportion of overhead costs even though Product B caused a greater level of machinery-related costs. Furthermore, the relatively higher production complexity associated with the manufacture of Product C is ignored by a volume-based overhead application rate such as direct labour. Consequently, the level of resources appropriated by Product C is not adequately reflected in its cost determination.

Traditional costing practices have overcome in part the problem of cost distortions by using departmental as opposed to factory-wide overhead rates. This entails determining departmental overhead figures by the allocation of costs associated with individual production departments. Thus building occupancy costs may be allocated on the basis of square metres occupied and power costs on kilowatt hours used. These bases may seem logical and economically plausible, but the allocation of purchasing costs is more problematic. Purchasing costs cannot as readily be assigned to production departments. It would seem logical to allocate them to the raw materials they relate to, but since all indirect product costs are allocated to production departments when departmental overhead rates are used, an allocation basis must be sought. One possibility is to use the kilogram weight of raw material used in each department. In this example, this basis allocates 50.2 percent of the weight to department 1 (50,000 kg of X and 1,000 kg of Z divided by 201,000 kg total raw material), and 49.8 percent to department 2. This basis illustrates the extent of arbitrariness assumed by traditional costing systems.

The use of departmental overhead rates is often seen as lending more credibility to the product costing exercise but does not resolve the cost distortion problem. In part, cost allocations are constrained by the simplicity of the costing approach but more importantly, the link between resource consumption and manufacturing processes for individual product lines is not satisfactorily addressed.

Activity based costing attempts to deal with some of these problems by attributing as many costs as possible directly to individual products based on the activities that cause the costs to be incurred. The example illustrates the differing levels of logic used in ascribing costs to products via activities. The starting point under ABC is normally to allocate support costs to departments and only then to products. Cost determination therefore entails two stages. For this example, Table 3.6 summarises the first stage allocations required for the sample data in Table 3.4. The first column lists the cost pools where costs are recorded. The second column provides the cost objects for the allocations, and the third column gives the activity used as the basis for the allocation. For example, purchasing costs are assigned to materials using the number of purchases ordered as the activity. The first stage allocations are for the service departments and building occupancy costs. Power and building occupancy costs are allocated to departments using kilowatt hours and square metres, respectively. Building occupancy costs are first assigned to service and production departments and purchasing and power costs including these costs are then assigned to their cost objectives.

Table 3.6 First stage allocation

Cost Pool	Cost Object	Activity Allocation Basis
Power	Departments	Kilowatt Hours
Purchasing	Materials	Number of Purchase Orders
Building Occupancy	Departments	Square Metres Occupied

Table 3.7 illustrates the first stage allocation calculations. Note that Table 3.7 does not account for the purchasing department's use of power costs although, if deemed more logical, this can effectively be adjusted for by using sequential allocation calculations or even reciprocal cost assignments (*Horngren, Foster and Datar,* 1994).

Table 3.7 ABC first stage allocation to departments

(a) Building Occupancy costs to Departments using square metres occupied as activity base:

Department	Square Mtrs Occupied	Percentage	Cost Allocation
Purchasing	10,000	2%	£ 20,000
Power	40,000	8%	£ 80,000
Department 1	200,000	40%	£ 400,000
Department 2	250,000	50%	£ 500,000
Total Building Occupancy Costs			£1,000,000

(b) Purchasing Costs to Raw Materials using the number of purchase orders as activity base:

Purchasing Costs	£	112,000
Building Occupancy Costs allocated (see above)	£	20,000
Total purchasing costs to be allocated	£	132,000

Material	Number of Purchase Orders	Percentage	Cost Allocation
X	200	35%	46,200
Y	300	54%	71,280
Z	60	11%	14,520
Total Purchasing Costs			132,000

(c) Power Costs to Departments using Kilowatt hours as activity base:

Power Costs	400,070
Building Occupancy Costs allocated (see above)	80,000
Total Power Costs to be allocated	£ 480,070

For purchasing costs, the relevant cost driver is the number of purchase orders which enable these costs to be assigned to raw materials. Raw materials thus serve as the cost objects in the first stage allocation. Likewise, kilowatt hours and square metres occupied serve as cost drivers of power and building occupancy costs respectively.

The second stage allocations in Table 3.8 summarise how the indirect costs are assigned to products. The cost object for assigning all costs in this stage is the product. The hours spent on machine operations and inspections are the basis for assigning labour costs for the activities. Power, machinery-related and building occupancy costs are allocated based on machine hours which may be seen as an appropriate cost driver in this instance.

Table 3.8 Second stage allocation

Cost Pool	Cost Object	Activity Allocation Basis
Indirect Labour	Product unit	Hours worked
Power	Product unit	Machine Hours
Machinery-Related	Product unit	Machine Hours
Building Occupancy	Product unit	Machine Hours
Set-ups	Product unit	Number of Set-ups
Purchasing	Product unit	Materials Used

Under ABC, separate cost pools may exist for significant work stations or departments where the cost in each cost pool is strictly proportional to the level of activity in that cost pool. *Noreen* (1991, p.9) notes in this respect that:

> In such systems, occupancy costs (i.e. building depreciation, property taxes, utilities) are often allocated to the work station cost pools on the basis of square feet. The work station costs in turn are allocated to products based on an activity measure such as machine time. This allocation process implicitly assumes that occupancy costs are strictly proportional to machine hours. But are they? Is it necessarily the case that a cost is strictly proportional to its activity measure?

Not only does ABC normally require the use of many cost drivers in the second cost allocation stage (*Drury*, 1990), but the choice of cost drivers in the second stage is in certain instances difficult to identify where the primary objective is to tie resource consumption to activities. Certain cost drivers will find more ready acceptance than others. As such, the use of materials used and the number of set-ups act as effective cost drivers for purchasing and set-up costs, respectively.

Table 3.9 illustrates the second stage cost allocations to products and Table 3.10 shows the calculated product unit costs under activity-based costing. Tracing costs from activities to products gives unit costs of £163.04 for product A, £415.27 for product B and £733.42 for product C.

Table 3.9 ABC second stage allocation to products

Cost (cost driver in bracket)	Product A	Product B	Product C
Indirect Labour:			
(Hours worked)			
Dept. 1 Inspection	£ 37,500[a]	£ 37,500	£ 75,000
Dept. 1 Machine Operations	£ 75,000[b]	£ 150,000	£225,000
Dept. 2 Inspection	£ 50,000[c]	£ 100,000	£150,000
Dept. 2 Machine Operations	£ 20,000[d]	£ 80,000	£100,000
Set-ups: (Number of Set-ups)			
Dept. 1	£ 3,000[e]	£ 3,000	£ 7,500
Dept. 2	£ 4,000	£ 8,000	£ 12,000
Machine Related: (Machine Hours)			
Dept.1	£133,333[f]	£ 266,667	£ 20,000
Dept.2	£160,000	£ 640,000	£ 32,000
Power: (Machine Hours)			
Dept. 1	£ 22,860[g]	£ 45,720	£ 3,430
Dept. 2	£ 78,473	£ 313,892	£ 15,695
Building Occupancy: (Machine Hours)			
Dept. 1	£126,984[h]	£ 253,968	£ 19,048
Dept. 2	£ 96,154	£ 384,615	£ 19,231
Purchasing Costs: (Number of Purchase Orders)			
Material X	£ 23,100[i]	£ 23,100	£ 0
Material Y	£ 0	£ 71,280	£ 0
Material Z	£ 0	£ 0	£ 14,520
Overhead cost	**£830,404**	**£2,377,742**	**£693,424**

a. $\dfrac{2,500 \text{ DLH}}{10,000 \text{ DLH}} \times £150,000 = £37,500$

b. $\dfrac{5,000 \text{ DLH}}{30,000 \text{ DLH}} \times £450,000 = £75,000$

c. $\dfrac{2,500 \text{ DLH}}{15,000} \times £300,000 = £50,000$

d. $\dfrac{1,000 \text{ DLH}}{10,000 \text{ DLH}} \times £200,000 = £20,000$

e. $\dfrac{200 \text{ set-ups}}{900 \text{ set-ups}}$ x £13,500 = £3,000

f. $\dfrac{5,000 \text{ MH}}{15,750 \text{ MH}}$ x £420,000 = £133,333

g. $\dfrac{5,000 \text{ MH}}{15,750 \text{ MH}}$ x £72,010* = £22,860

h. $\dfrac{5,000 \text{ MH}}{15,750}$ x £400,000** = £126,984

i. $\dfrac{50,000 \text{ Kg}}{100,00 \text{ Kg}}$ x £46,200*** = £23,100

* see ABC first stage power costs allocations.

** see ABC first stage building occupancy costs allocations.

*** see ABC first stage purchasing cost allocations.

Table 3.10 Product valuation under activity based costing

Production Costs	Product A	Product B	Product C
Raw Materials			
X	£ 400,000	£ 400,000	£ 0
Y	0	1,200,000	0
Z	0	0	5,000
	400,000	1,600,000	5,000
Direct Labour			
Dept. 1	300,000	75,000	15,000
Dept. 2	100,000	100,000	20,000
	400,000	175,000	35,000
Overhead*	830,404	2,377,742	693,424
	£1,630,404	£4,152,742	£733,424
Cost per unit	£ 163.04	£ 415.27	£ 733.42

* see first and second stage ABC calculations.

Costs determined under ABC better reflect a particular conception of the extent of manufacturing complexity which in this example is the highest for product C and lowest for product A. In effect, if traditional cost determinations are used to make pricing decisions, then it may be argued that the price of A would be set too high and that of B, and especially C, too low under direct labour based costing (though under machine hours in this example, product C only would be underpriced).

What is also evident from this example is that the magnitude of the price reversal between products A and B captures the impact of product complexity in cost terms. But in addition, that between product C and products A and B points to the effect of output volume on costs. In general, high volume products may be seen to subsidise low volume ones following ABC recalculation given that certain costs relate to batches rather than batch size. Where costs are falsely assumed to be volume related and are allocated on that basis, the potential for cost distortion is greater than where cost drivers are used to represent resource consuming activities not related to volume. The activity based system

> . . . recognises the differences in relative input consumption and traces the appropriate amount of input to each product (*Cooper*, 1988, p. 48).

Conventional cost accounting systems which presuppose that volume-unrelated resources consumed by a product vary in direct proportion to the quantity of volume-related input consumed lead to distorted product costs being reported relative to ABC. Factors which affect input and which may not be volume-related include the diversity of production run, size, complexity, material and set-ups. *Cooper* thus holds that it is because of the diversity and complexity of products and their use of advanced manufacturing processes that product costs are determined more by transactions than by volume.

The merits of activity based costing

One major purpose of a cost accounting system has generally been seen to be the provision of product cost information. Market prices and competitive forces often determine price structures but many companies continue to rely to some degree on product cost determinations for setting prices, especially in the case of customised products which do not have readily available market prices (*Cooper and Kaplan*, 1987). Moreover, a knowledge of product costs may enable an enterprise to concentrate on attaining what is considered a more profitable product mix as well as allowing managers to avoid loss-making activities (*Drury*, 1989). Where managers use costs for decision-making, costing can become a strategic tool. However, ABC advocates hold that distorted product costs which emanate from traditional costing practices can lead firms to choose inappropriate strategies. For instance, under conventional costing, *Shank and Govindarajan* (1988, p.31) suggest that

> . . . low-volume, speciality products appear to be more profitable than they actually are, tempting firms to concentrate on low-volume business.

Conversely, if managers understand and have confidence in the mechanism through which costs are determined, then a strategic use of costs becomes a more readily attainable organisational reality. It is to be borne in mind, however, that not all companies which have access to ABC derived data actually 'make the transition from analysis to action' (*Cooper et al.*, 1992, p. 307).

As illustrated in the above example, ABC provides an alternative mode of cost determination to that used traditionally. ABC offers a viable alternative to full costing which, it has been argued, has primarily served external financial reporting purposes (see Chapter 7). In effect, ABC extends the variable costing rationale in an attempt to render cost determinations more useful for managerial purposes. Whereas variable costing focuses on short-term volume related costs, an ABC cost determination includes long-term variable costs which traditionally are grounded in overhead cost pools. As *Collins and Werner* (1990, p.134) suggest:

> The cost-driver approach, with its focus on cost causes and behaviour, leads one to examine not only short-term variable production costs but also long- term costs that were considered committed or fixed.

Thus, ABC recognises that some conventional overhead items although not variable with periodic output are variable with enterprise activities which are usually assumed to be unaffected by the volume of output in the period (see *Brimson*, 1991, and *Morrow*, 1992). ABC does this by seeking to trace the cost variations which are caused by alterations in activity volume. Thus, for example, the use of electricity can be metered and labour hours can be coded to activities in the same ways as direct costs, variable with output volume in conventional accounting, are traced to output. Thus, where this is possible, some activity based costs can be traced empirically to activities in the same way as material and components are able to be traced to product units in conventional accounting. Here, ABC renders a clear contribution to understanding costs which are obscured by conventional accounting using allocation bases which have little to do with cost causality. ABC goes beyond a contribution margin analysis in that it quantitatively addresses cost behaviour in terms of short-run volume changes as well as longer term cost trends independent of volume changes. This approach offers an element of rationality and compelling logic which thinking managers often readily identify with.

As discussed earlier, the identification of value added and non-value added activities is often an important benefit of installing an activity-based costing system which:

> . . . helps reinforce the mind-set of opportunity in minimising or eliminating non-value added and optimising value added costs. (*Ostranga*, 1990, p.45.)

In this sense, ABC is not unlike JIT in its effects (*MacArthur*, 1992). The search for appropriate cost drivers forces managers and accountants to reconsider operational processes in a comprehensive manner and within an economic frame of reference (just as with the application of zero-based budgeting). *Kingcott* (1991, p.36) suggests that it is the process of ABC and not the end result that brings benefits to the company since:

> . . . it forces management and supervisors to consider the drivers which affect costs.

Costing implications of manufacturing operations come to light and, in this sense, accounting information can point to more desirable production strategies such as the design of products with common parts, the discontinuance of low-volume products necessitating complex manufacturing processes and the identification of cost drivers which can lead to the adoption of altered production technologies (*Stec*, 1989). Indeed, it has been suggested that for internal purposes, non-value added costs which appear not to add future value to a product ought to be characterised as period costs and immediately expensed in the income statement. Accordingly, the notion of product cost would undergo a revised definition encompassing only materials and conversion costs of value-added activities (*Mecimore*, 1988). This stance also complements the view that a cost driver represents:

> . . . the cost of an activity from which the company derives its competitive advantage. (*Ayers*, 1988, p.6.)

Such an accounting representation of operational concepts enables managerial attention to be focused on enhancing the internal functioning of the organisation. Thus, ABC can offer an organisation information about not only the profitability of its output but also about the gains that may emanate from altering organisational processes.

Activity based management has been considered to complement business process re-engineering (BPR) which effectively seeks to

> . . . change business processes by envisioning new ways of working, getting the organisation to accept that vision, adopting appropriate technology, empowering employees, and then changing the organisation (*Brinker*, 1993, p.3).

Essentially, if BPR is about doing 'the right things right' then so is activity based analysis. This is because activity based analysis is perceived to offer possibilities of benefiting from radical change of business practices rather than of simply addressing the cost implications of doing something without regard to overall efficacy.

One important factor relating to the implementation of ABC is that it is not seen as necessitating a total departure from traditional cost control techniques. For instance, the view that there is some natural or random variation in repetitive processes even when performed efficiently is a traditionally accepted view by management accountants.

Statistical process control (SPC) as a means of measuring the parameters of a process and of assessing when variability exceeds the random variation inherent in the process is well established. In keeping with such managerial thinking, SPC has been seen as being able to supplement the ABC approach (*Hollander and Roth*, 1991). Likewise, in the context of using costs for strategic reasons, *Dugdale* (1990, p.40) notes that:

The product costs generated by an activity-costing exercise are appropriate for strategic decisions and need only be calculated infrequently or when such decisions have to be made.

In this sense, ABC need not necessarily be seen as a replacement for traditional product costing approaches.

An additional benefit of ABC has been said to be that it provides data more useful to non-financial managers than traditional product costing information. By linking overheads to activities rather than products or periods, ABC provides the benefit of making them 'much more visible' (*Harvey*, 1991a, p.43). As such, inter-unit cost comparisons where improvements between plants can be made, and subsequent inter-temporal comparisons for effective cost control over time, can more readily be performed by non-financial managers.

In sum, activity based costing is viewed as having many advantages over traditional cost systems. *Cooper* (1990a, p.42) summarises these as follows:

> ABC systems have attracted attention in recent years because they provide three major benefits:
>
> - More accurate product costs.
>
> - An improved understanding of the economics of production; and
>
> - A picture of the economics of activities performed by a company.

Ultimately advocates of ABC claim that the 'goal is to increase profits, not to obtain more accurate costs' (*Cooper and Kaplan*, 1992). Nevertheless, activity based costing is not a general panacea to costing challenges or to the pursuit of profits, and poses certain problems. Proponents of ABC recognise fully that there are organisational environments for which an ABC system would not be useful.

But broader factors must also be assessed within which ABC as a general costing approach can be considered. ABC's appropriateness cannot be taken as given and it is to such issues that the chapter now turns.

ABC: caveat emptor

The manager making use of costs on a regular basis will appreciate the management accountant's maxim 'different costs for different purposes'. No one accounting approach can provide costs devoid of judgemental input. A certain degree of discretion is always exercised in determining costs and consequently any costing exercise is value-laden depending on the decision context. In this sense, it must be recognised that a 'true' cost does not exist – only one that is tailored to the purpose and even this may be an imperfect measure. Research from different quarters supports this view. It is widely acknowledged that: 'superiority of one costing system over another cannot be established unambigously in the absence of knowledge of the true product cost' (*Gupta*, 1993, p. 210) which of course is not available. Consequently, an activity based costing system (or any other costing approach) cannot generate true costs but only costs that are more accurate within an alternative managerial logic. The value of an ABC system stems from its contribution to better understanding of costing relationships within such a distinct logic. Advocates of ABC are careful to define activity costs within the limits of the technique. Thus, *Cooper* (1988, p.48) has noted that:

> In an activity based system, the cost of a product is the sum of the costs of all activities required to manufacture and deliver the product.

Such a definition focuses on one facet of the organisational process. Conversely, *Brimson* (1991, p.109) states that:

> An activity cost is the total expense of all traceable factors of production assigned to perform an activity.

Adopting a broad conception of 'factors of production', he qualifies this:

> A product cost becomes a summation of the cost of all traceable activities to design, procure material, manufacture, and distribute a product. (Ibid, p.202.)

The traceability of ABC costs

The definition stresses traceability of costs. What needs to be made explicit is that the ABC approach helps determine costs which within the context of the total functioning of an enterprise, may reflect only a portion of the financial implications of producing a product or of providing a service. Costs incurred at a level that is functionally or temporarily removed from the production process cannot always be captured by an accounting system. It may be argued, for instance, that any process relating to a product ought to be accounted for within the overall cost determined for that product including the cost of managerial decision-making. If such decision-making relies on product cost determinations which in turn rest on the use of sophisticated costing techniques, such as ABC, then ultimately, even the cost of implementing ABC could be expected to be linked to products. Yet, an ABC system does not seek to account for itself at the level of product costing. More importantly perhaps, cost causing activities cannot always be identified because of commonality or the jointness of costs. Should, for instance, set-up costs in switching from one product to another and back be allocated to both products equally? How are costs associated with switching on a flexible manufacturing system to be spread over a range of products which have to be processed over the course of one day's operations? Such general problems of overhead allocation cannot easily be resolved through a change of cost system. Joint costs cannot be dealt with by ABC, nor can the fixed costs associated with activities (this is further discussed below).

Thus, certain costs will not be amenable to ABC analysis and will, for a variety of reasons specific to an enterprise, remain unattributable to the production of given goods and services. ABC as an accounting technique cannot overcome this problem fully.

The cost function for an activity entertained by ABC advocates is asserted ideally to vary proportionally with activity output and to allow any cost variations for changes in the volume of an activity to be explained by the use of a single cost driver. This cost function also allows the costs of sub-activities within an activity to be added together to yield the cost of the overall activity. Similarly, the total activity costs of an organisation can be found by simply adding together activity costs (see *Cooper*, 1990b).

Thus, ABC produces a linear cost function of the same type as is familiar in practice in treating direct materials and direct labour. The conditions required to allow this approach to be used legitimately are stringent; the number of costs conventionally treated as fixed overheads which are likely to be found to be amenable to ABC treatment will therefore be limited. Among these conditions are that the level of operations of one activity should not affect the costs of other activities, and that there exist neither economies of scope between activities nor fixed or indivisible costs attached to activities (*Bromwich and Wang*, 1993). However, when these conditions apply, it is possible to use ABC with overheads. This allows the identification of those activities, the cost of which can be separated from those of other activities, and the identification of the 'cost drivers' which explain how costs vary with activities (*Christensen and Demski*, 1991). There are however a number of problems with this approach.

Generally, treating costs as activity costs requires that each activity can be treated as being entirely unaffected by the level of other activities (i.e., that there are no economies or diseconomies of scope). This allows us to build up activity costs, and the proportional relationship between cost drivers and activity outputs yields a linear cost curve for activity costs.

Of course in practice, some activity based costs are either unable to be traced to activities using strict empirical evidence or their use generates an uneconomic number of 'cost drivers'. Therefore, additional allocation bases are added to those used conventionally which are believed to capture the perceptions (however obtained) as to how alterations in activity volumes impact on costs while keeping the number of separate activities manageable. Such exercises are often said to 'attribute' costs to activities. These exercises involve some arbitrary allocation and cannot be defended on the basis that they fully trace activity costs. They may, however, give some signal as to activity costs in so far as the allocation bases are correlated with the functions which cause individual activity costs to change.

Similarly, it is intuitively clear that the degree of distortion introduced by using only a few 'cost drivers' will reflect the heterogeneity between activities in the same cost pool, the technologies used, the size of the unit costs not reflected in the chosen cost drivers and the relative amount of different products utilising different resource requirements using the cost pool (*Cooper*, 1989b; *Noreen*, 1991). The importance of any such distortions may also depend on the market conditions for the products involved. This is because the unfavourable impact of using an erroneous cost curve in decision making may depend on the market conditions facing the enterprise.

How far analysis of the distortions introduced by using allocations in ABC helps managers is not clear. It is difficult to see how managers can estimate these distortions and allow for them in their decision-making and performance measurement activities without knowledge of the costs given by being able to fully measure the cost of activities.

ABC: a conceptual framework

It is for this reason that activity based costs are increasingly interpreted within a more focused perspective. In this context, *Cooper* (1990b) has reported on a five year study to develop a conceptual framework for the design of cost systems. He suggests a four-category hierarchy of activities which differentiate between cost drivers. At one level, cost-drivers may represent 'unit-level' activities also used in traditional cost systems which relate to resource consumption every time a unit is produced. At the next level appear 'batch-level' bases which assume that certain inputs are consumed in direct proportion to the number of batches of each type of product produced. 'Product-level' cost drivers assume that certain inputs are consumed to develop or permit production of different products. Finally, at the highest point, 'facility-level' activities take place to sustain a facility's general manufacturing process. This relationship means that the fixed costs of activities in a short time period are not encompassed by ABC. More generally, the assumptions underlying activity based cost functions are the same as those which apply to variable direct costs in traditional accounting. This restricts substantially the scope for ABC.

Cooper (1990b, p.6) stresses that facility-level activities make up a category that:

> . . . contains costs that are common to a variety of products and can only be allocated to products arbitrarily.

Accordingly, *Cooper and Kaplan* (1991a, p.133) warn that:

> Only unit, batch, and product-sustaining expenses should be assigned to products. Therefore, in ABC, facility-level expenses are kept at the plant level and not allocated to products.

ABC can consequently be seen as going beyond the allocation of short-term variable costs in linking 'batch' and 'product' level costs to products but still leaving the problem of the 'overhead glob' (*Vangermeersch*, 1986) which it sets out to address unresolved in part. Certainly, attempts are being made to develop algorithms which managers can use as practical guides in choosing the best allocation base for each cost pool (*Hwang, Evans and Hegde*, 1993). This does not suffice however. Joint facility costs are essential to the manufacture of individual products but are not allocated by ABC because they cannot be. ABC is limited in its ability to reveal links between activities and resource consumption and, therefore, the notion of full or comprehensive 'product costs' within an ABC context must be severely restricted. What also must be borne in mind is that there is a balance which must be sought between accuracy benefits and costs of data collection, storage and processing (*Babad and Balachandran*, 1993). Thus, implementing ABC entails further managerial considerations of this trade off.

The cost of changing accounting systems

Of significant concern to companies considering the implementation of activity based costing is the fact that 'redesigning a cost system is expensive and time consuming' (*Cooper*, 1989a, p.77). The above discussion of the refinement of activity based costing indicates the degree of difficulty in producing ABC data. Large enterprises can readily use expertise to design and implement an appropriate ABC cost system, but this is not the case for all companies. *Parker and Lettes* (1991, p.37) stress that:

> . . . while major corporations can use complex accounting systems such as activity-based costing to help determine product costs, a scale factor limits the complexity that small companies can handle and may prevent them from using similar systems.

Although ABC software packages are sold over a range of prices tied to degrees of complexity and functions (*Walkin*, 1991), a wide array of other costs are implicated, including training of staff, design and data gathering (*Cooper*, 1990a) and ensuring acceptability of a systems change. This extends to cognitive and emotional costs as well as:

> . . . dislike of the results because the model yields higher and more variable costs than conventional costing. (*Staubus*, 1990, p.249).

Although managers may fail to use traditional costing data because of disbelief in the credibility of the information, costing that is deemed more accurate by accountants, such as an ABC system, but unintelligible to managers, may meet with equal resistance. ABC implementation may within a comprehensive cost perspective be prohibitive in itself, if the expense of training managers to understand its complexities until they find its logic compelling is accounted for. Even where such logic becomes evident to a manager, resistance may have other sources (*Argyris and Kaplan*, 1993). Sales managers for example may prefer to ignore signals generated by an ABC system if their incentive remuneration is greater under traditional cost systems (see for example *Bhimani and Pigott*, 1992b).

Although ABC systems have been viewed as providing information of strategic value (*Cooper*, 1988; *Shank and Govindarajan*, 1989), it actually enhances managers' focus on internal activities of the organisation (*Gietzmann*, 1991). Rather than direct their attention externally to the market environment within which their firm must compete, ABC attempts to highlight the economics of its production processes. Investing in a sophisticated costing system which shifts managers' concerns away from outward changes and external factors toward internal processes must be an option which needs to be viewed in the light of what more outwardly oriented and strategic management accounting techniques have to offer (see Chapter 5).

What has been viewed as another 'major limitation' (*Roth and Borthick*, 1989, p.32) of using activity based costing is that not only are some costs subject to arbitrary allocation (facility-level costs), but arbitrary time periods still must be used in calculating costs. Measuring the profitability of a product over its entire life may be preferable to interim measures, but unless a product has a short life, it is not likely that companies would wait until the end of it before evaluating product cost behaviour (see Chapter 7 on product life cycle costing). Thus, interim measures require allocation and, in this respect, ABC does not overcome this form of arbitariness. ABC systems tend to encompass a limited set of organisational functions and time-frames. This and the effects on managerial outlook can be viewed as costs of altering accounting systems.

ABC's view of cost hierarchies

As indicated, the essence of ABC is the categorisation of activities into a number of separate classes depending upon the overall cost driver for each class of activity with each category being assumed to be independent of activity in other classes. Most crucial to ABC is the distinction between volume driven activity and batch driven activity (unit and batch level in *Cooper's* terminology (1990)) and the treatment of these activities as independent of each other. This suggests that volume is a more important determinant of activity costs than the above argument suggests as does the empirical evidence (see Chapters 7 and 8). It is doubtful whether this distinction can always be maintained, at least where volume is substantially variable. A very large change in product volume is likely to require substantial alterations in the management of batches. A large increase in volume can be expected to be scheduled in a different way from that required to cope with a smaller volume. Similarly, a large increase in volume may change the process of ordering material and components. Maintenance schedules and product planning resources may similarly be radically affected by the envisaged level of product volume. Thus, the level of resources and their planned usage may be a function of, at least, large discontinuities in planned or actual product volume.

Schoenfeld (1974; 1990) and other writers on German cost theory have indicated the importance attached to the intimate relation they perceive between volume and other elements of the production programme (activities in ABC terminology). One strength of German cost theory is its concern to select, prior to decision making, the optimal set of ways to adjust production operations to planned volume changes from the possibly very large number of different methods of adjusting to such changes, varying from adjusting one factor leaving all others constant to altering all or some factors simultaneously (see *Schoenfeld*, 1974, pp. 105-110 and pp. 162-166). Exploration of such methods of adjustment convinced these writers that to talk about production volume in a period independently of other variables was difficult. This led to the substitution of the whole production programme in all its ramifications as the overall cost determinant instead of production volume and other supposedly independent volume related variables. Production volume emerges as a purely independent determinant of resource usage only when many other decisions, such as those associated with scheduling and capacity concerning how production should be adjusted to planned volume have been made. Reasoning of this sort allows *Schoenfeld* (1974) to write that one of the leading authorities on

German cost theory, Heinen, said that volume cannot be regarded as a separate independent cost determinant (p.158). Similarly, it implies that production related activities cannot easily be regarded as independent of each other or of production volume in a period.

For instance, greater production in a period may reduce set-up and switching costs but increase supply and logistic costs. Thus, the division of activities into product level, batch level and unit level is only possible on the assumption that all the superior decisions in the product hierarchy have been made and are likely to remain stable in the future. Otherwise, accounting needs to reflect the possible interrelationship between activities of these types depending on the degree of adjustment available to the decision maker.

In the end, the acceptability of theories about the relationship between the production variables relative to the assumptions of ABC is a matter of obtaining relevant empirical evidence. Some studies in this area are now beginning to be undertaken but little evidence is yet available (*Young and Selto* 1991, pp. 16-20).

The above re-emergence of the importance of production volume in ABC should come as no surprise. Indirect inputs and capital investments are ultimately purchased because of the net cash flows which will be generated by the output which they help to produce.

ABC's critical assumptions

ABC rests on certain underlying assumptions which are not made explicit and which provide a simplistic if not a distorted view of the realities that organisations must confront. One such assumption is, according to *Azzone and Bertele* (1990), that product demand behaves deterministically. Their starting point is to view product demand as being random and to then consider the implications of introducing a new product to an existing line. First the effect of introducing the new product must be evaluated in terms of the quantity and timing impact over other products produced by a company. Such effects may represent an opportunity cost which must be compared to the contribution of ABC determined profitability of the new product. Effectively, the suggestion is that idle capacity cannot always be viewed as a period cost reflective of the inefficient use of resources. Rather, a given degree of idle capacity can represent a value adding activity. Indeed, idle capacity enables 'timeliness' criteria to be met and related cost implications need to be accounted for:

> . . . idle capacity must not be considered, as in the works of
> Kaplan and Cooper, just as a period cost, but is needed to
> satisfy demand peaks and provide the timeliness regained from
> the market. (*Azzone and Bertele*, 1990, p.274.)

More importantly, it is well accepted that many other costs are best
described as discretionary. That is they are not driven by production
volume, scheduling or non-production related activities. Rather, they
are determined by managerial decisions which are not constrained
by production and other technologies. Associated costs are often
committed at the time of what have to be fairly arbitrary decisions,
and the agreed programme of activities continues until these
decisions are revised. In modern enterprise environments such
decisions impact on many costs. For example, quality decisions
affect variable costs (such as via the use of superior material), set-up
costs and engineering costs. Most of these costs are not captured by
existing quality accounting systems and are generally treated as
overheads. More generally, many decision driven costs are treated as
fixed overheads. Tracing costs of this type and linking them to
conventional and variable costs makes their contribution to the firm
visible and aids decision making (see Chapter 4).

One approach is to seek to describe the characteristics which
determine the different nature of the resources used in the firm. It
has been found that a very rich set of descriptors are required for
this purpose, each of which has implications for costing. It is
important to emphasise that all costs are direct relative to some
factor at the level in the organisation at which the decision to
acquire the resources is made. Conventional accounting control
techniques can be used at this level but allocations below this level
may merely cause confusion. Concentrating on the characteristics of
resources suggests that many are better monitored in terms of non-
financial measures.

This perspective suggests that there are at least three classes of
resource: those which are traceable to specific final goods outputs or
to process outputs; those which are not traceable in this manner
because resource outputs are generally available throughout the
organisation, such as information systems and general procedures;
and those which produce outputs which are common to more than
one cost object and which may fall into either of the other two
classes. The contribution of ABC has been to strip overheads of
those resources in the first class and treat them as traceable. The

second class of resources which simultaneously provide the same service throughout the organisation need a very different accounting treatment.

This approach to viewing resource consumption suggests that more attention should be paid in accounting to those resources which constrain the enterprise and that therefore some attempt should be made to measure their opportunity costs. Similarly, it can be shown that measures of idle capacity are more informative than perhaps they seem with conventional treatments. Properly formulated and reported at the correct level of aggregation, they provide very important inputs into decision making (*Bromwich and Wang*, 1993).

Another promising approach is to ask for each resource what drivers affect its use. There is clearly a large number of drivers but the effects of a given driver may not be generally independent of the chosen levels of other drivers. Generally, drivers cannot be treated as independent as they may be in ABC in the absence of clear evidence that such an assumption does apply to the former operations. Thus, volume of output in a period cannot be treated as independent of production scheduling unless all scheduling decisions are frozen. The conditions that have to be placed on the interaction of resources in order to yield independent resource pools are very restrictive and more constraining when cost pools are considered. This view suggests that volume related factors are far more important than some ABC advocates suggest.

One further problem is that activities and their outputs are not obviously directly related to enterprise cash inflows, that is, the costs of activities may not be obviously linked to sales revenues in any clear way. Each activity which is not volume related is free standing from any relationship with any other enterprise operations including those which yield present or future net cash flows. One method used by the advocates of ABC, who tend to be concerned with manufacturing operations, to seek to overcome this problem is to first link activities to higher level cost drivers, such as the number of batches and the number of products maintained; and secondly to allocate these costs to cost objects such as product or organisational units. With this view, many ABC resources and costs represent one element of the incremental resource demands and costs of cost objects. They thus represent general set-up resources and their costs (for example, so much per batch of a product) and the resources and costs required to maintain the existence of these cost objects (the cost of maintaining a product in the firm's product portfolio). Both resource demands and costs will alter with changes in the character of these cost objects. The concern of ABC with incremental resources makes the economies of scale resulting from combining these resources with variable resources more visible than under conventional accounting.

The incremental character of these costs also means that they cannot be legitimately treated as part of the unit costs of products obtained by dividing these costs by product volume, for example, by dividing the costs associated with producing a given batch of a product by the number of units in the batch and by allocating the costs of ordering a batch of components to the individual components in the batch.

Many, if not all, ABC studies do this. (See, for example, *Cooper and Kaplan*, 1987 and *Yoshikawa et al.*, 1993, pp.114-119). This is an allocation which yields a constant average cost per unit, which would differ depending among other things on the volume basis used (for example budgeted volume or actual volume) and the chosen level of the selected volume base. The problem with this approach can be seen even more clearly to be an allocation where the product in mind consists of two or more variants.

This method of attributing costs to product units implies that what commenced as a non-volume based activity ends up being treated as a cost variable with production volume and therefore suggests in decision making that varying the volume will change activity costs, for example, batch costs. However, such numbers do not measure the opportunity cost of changing batch size or of altering the volume of products within a batch. This approach has been defended by *Cooper* (1990a) because it does not change the total costs charged to the product as a whole.

The correct approach to such resources from an economic perspective and one which reflects their technological characteristics is to consider them in decision making in the aggregate at the level of the cost object at which they become incremental, – that is, at the level of the product or organisational hierarchy, the existence of which causes these costs to be incurred. Variations in these costs are explained by alterations in operations at these levels of the hierarchies. One reform that can therefore be suggested is that if problems are experienced in costing at a given level of disaggregation of operations, accounting should be willing to move up to the level of aggregation at which the costs become incremental. Thus, decisions should be made at the product level if product unit costs make no economic sense. For some costs, this process may have to be taken further and costs evaluated at the product group level (see *Bromwich*, 1993). This is the standard economic approach to these problems and has also been the standard approach urged for use in accounting for decision making.

This is another way of saying that decision making concerning resources should occur at that level of the organisation which allows the technology of the resources to be correctly reflected in decision making. Thus the reforms suggested here are consistent with economic theory and some of the accounting literature (but not generally in practice). This view of some activity-based costs as incremental costs of production means that at planning time their amount is affected by planned volume. Such ABC costs are thus a function of aggregate product volume and can be treated in this way if so required.

In sum, with this view, ABC costs are generally incremental costs of production activity. They should be reported at that level of the product hierarchy or of the organisation at which they become incremental with this view. Such costs should not be allocated to product units.

In broad terms, the notion that ABC activities cause costs and that products consume activities to justify the adoption of activity based costing may be questioned. The suggestion is that cost causality is not uniquely explained by activities. Some costs are dependent on the passage of time or may be decision-driven. ABC in this sense cannot claim a monopoly over cost causality visibility. The underlying basis of cost changes cannot be explained within the narrow confines of activity analysis. ABC advocates are aware of this problem and have distinguished between resource consumption patterns over a period of time and the accounting for them (*Cooper and Kaplan*, 1992). Monitoring resource usage in a period indicates the need for additional decisions which are not rendered visible by accounting. This argument does not negate the value of adopting an ABC system but places it within the context of the type of information sought by managers. If accuracy of costs is determined and explained within the perspective of expenses tied to activity level changes, then activity based costing will provide relevant information.

ABC's bottom line

It has been suggested that the use of ABC may help us understand some costs which are presently treated as fixed overheads but this use of ABC is limited because ideally it requires an empirically based exercise to ascertain how costs vary with activities. The use of ABC also requires certain very stringent conditions to be met. Strictly, the use of ABC allows costs to be traced only to the point of the product or organisational hierarchy at which these costs become incremental. Such costs are likely to differ depending on production volume. No theoretical justification for assigning activity based costs to individual product units or for using a richer set of allocation bases than is usual in conventional accounting in the expectation that they will capture activity costs has yet been found.

To confront some of the criticisms discussed here, the ultimate test is whether, in the long term, companies which adopt ABC become more profitable. Such evidence is not available on an aggregate basis and is unlikely to ever produce definite results because of the difficulty in assigning profitability to changes of a single factor such as a costing system. At the case-study level, enhanced profitability has been reported anecdotally but even here increased profits may accrue for a variety of reasons including the possibility that ABC's unintended effects impinge on the bottom line (*Bhimani and Pigott*, 1992b).

Some have suggested that theoretical models are presently unable to test the logic of ABC, and ultimately one must rely on the practicality of ABC attributed by the market place to decide on the usefulness of this system (*Fox*, 1991). Subsequent chapters, therefore, consider the uptake, utilisation and retention of not just ABC but other accounting approaches as well in different countries. For management accounting, the ultimate objective must be the applicability and deemed usefulness of practices rather than theoretical propriety or abstract logic. This is what subsequent chapters explore.

4
Fixed Overheads: New Directions

4.1 Introduction

The earlier report *Management Accounting: Evolution Not Revolution* (*Bromwich and Bhimani*, 1989, p.100) identified some of the challenges facing accountants in the late 1980s in the field of the planning and control of overheads and in seeking meaningful ways of accounting for overheads. One challenge identified was 'the accounting and control of overhead costs which do not vary with activity, diversity of output or production complexity'. Similarly, it was stated that 'overhead allocation and control has always been seen to present major challenges for cost accountants' (p.100). It was also hoped that an increased emphasis on market factors in product costing rather than on seeking 'accurate' full product costs would yield solutions to many of these problems.

Many surveys and comments by practitioners suggest that accounting for overheads is one of the major areas of dissatisfaction with management accounting methods in practice (see Chapters 7 and 8).

This part of the report discusses a number of new methods which have been suggested for accounting for fixed overheads. Fixed overheads are those costs which do not vary with output volume in a period. The aim of these suggested innovations is to improve on conventional accounting in reflecting the technological, economic and managerial characteristics of overhead resources and hence in explaining cost behaviour for decision- making and control. The need to reflect these characteristics in accounting is clear because current technology is often very different from the large scale mass production technology implicit in conventional accounting (*Howell and Soucy* 1987a, 1987b; *Kaplan* 1983). *Howell and Soucy* (1987b) make the point that:

> Automation and increasing reliance on 'information workers' in
> the factory are removing labour and increasing overheads in
> product costs, pushing labour based overhead rates to
> extraordinary heights (p.27).

The promise of ABC and its variants for planning and control of
some costs which are conventionally treated as fixed overheads has
been discussed in Chapter 3. The first part of this chapter suggests
new treatments for discretionary or decision driven costs and for
costs imposed by regulators. Both types of costs are often treated as
fixed in accounting practice. Methods of dealing with the most
difficult problems in overhead accounting, the treatment of joint and
common costs are then considered in some detail. New methods for
dealing with both types of costs are discussed. Finally, a new type of
accounting report is presented, which seeks to reflect in a more
transparent way the characteristics of overheads which are required
to be understood in planning and control. This type of report also
allows the adverse effects of overhead allocations to be avoided.

There is general agreement that modern manufacturing systems
reduce very substantially those costs which are variable with product
volume in a specific time period and increase very substantially
other costs, especially those which have been treated as fixed costs
in traditional accounting:

> Automation is increasing the spread between variable and full
> costs (*Howell and Soucy*, 1987b, p.27).

One of the better known attempts to help deal with this problem is
the recommended usage of ABC (and its variants) which recognises
that many of the costs included in fixed costs are variable with a
variety of causes. As *Cooper and Kaplan* (1987) say:

> A large and growing proportion of total manufacturing costs is
> considered 'fixed'. This paradox - that what we call 'fixed'
> costs are in fact the most variable and most rapidly increasing
> costs - has seemingly eluded most accounting practitioners and
> scholars (p.225).

As indicated in Chapter 3, one contribution of ABC where
appropriate is to strip out of traditional fixed overheads those for
which a cost driver can be found.

All the suggestions discussed here are attempts to deal with the technological and economic characteristics of resources of a fixed nature in a given time period, the cost of which will therefore also be fixed. These characteristics seem often to be neglected by accountants. Few textbooks spend any time on the detailed relationship between technology and accounting and on how these factors mutually interact. Similarly, until recently this relationship was also neglected in the research literature.

Many studies indicate that the usual method of allocating, at least, manufacturing overheads to products is to use labour hours and, sometimes, machine hours. Thus, in practice, little attempt is made to reflect the economic or technological characteristics of fixed overheads. For example, capacity costs are generally fully allocated without any distinction being made between used and unused capacity and no special treatment is accorded in accounting to capacity constraints.

Conservatism in accounting

It would seem there is a great deal of conservatism in accounting and great doubt as to the worthwhileness of changes suggested in, at least, accounting for overheads. The very enthusiastic early reception given to ABC by senior managers and practising management accountants has not yet resulted in a revolution in management accounting. Surveys suggest that even now many large firms are still considering the installation of ABC, and with some outstanding exceptions, installations tend to be limited to parts of the firm or involve pilot studies of one kind or another.

Recent surveys of UK and USA enterprises might suggest that only some ten percent of large firms are practising ABC in anything like a comprehensive way. Most questionnaires to firms concerning all types of changes in accounting systems over, say, the previous two to five years suggest that a substantial number of alterations have been made. However, many of these changes are not really innovative in that they do not alter the basic structure of the accounting system being used (see, for example, *Bright et al.*, 1992). With regard to changes to accounting systems, *Drury et al.*, (1993) found, in their survey, that:

> Most of the replies focused on improvements relating to information processing . . .

and

An examination of all the replies gave a general impression that there was no evidence of new innovative techniques being implemented during the past five years (p.71).

Not surprisingly, when firms are asked what alterations they envisage over a similar future period, responses are much more innovative. It would seem that major accounting innovations are very difficult to implement because of a large number of barriers to change such as the costs, the lack of requisite skills and technology, management inertia, organisational factors and the financial and intellectual investments in existing systems (see, for example, *Bruns*, 1987, and *Scapens and Roberts*, 1993).

It can be argued that the possible reasons for encountering conservatism toward accounting goes far beyond the rather pragmatic barriers to change listed above. Managers learn to live with accounting systems which poorly reflect the current environment. They develop informal methods of adjusting for the major distortions introduced by current accounting systems, by using informal information and non-financial data and by recognising these distortions in extensive managerial discussions. The use of these informal systems and different perceptions of costs by managers, allow managers freedom in negotiations in the firm. Accounting systems are an integral part of the management system of the organisation and manifest a complex and mutual interrelationship with this system.

Management accounting systems may also reflect and render visible the formal and informal organisational structure and managerial power distribution in the organisation. Similarly, the firm's existing accounting system impacts on enterprise culture and reflects that culture. Finally, accounting may be used differently depending on the organisation's strategy and performance measurement processes. Changes do not come easily to such firmly embedded systems (see, for example, *Brunsson*, 1990).

In a more practical vein, it can reasonably be said that these and other factors result in a wish for accounting innovations to be kept simple. Experience and the literature suggests that practising accountants and senior managers shy away from seemingly complex accounting innovations. The solutions to overhead problems suggested below are therefore kept as simple as possible. The discussion commences by considering possible treatments of discretionary or decision driven costs which in practice are treated as fixed overheads in the absence of better conventional methods.

Thus, the next two sections look at possible accounting treatments for two categories of costs which include substantial overhead elements and which cause accountants many problems. These two cost categories are discretionary costs (also called here decision driven costs) and the less familiar set of costs which reflect the activities of regulators. These are both types of costs which accountants find difficult to manage.

4.2 Discretionary Costs and Overheads

Decision driven costs

The costs of decision driven resources may fall into any of the cost categories utilised in the accounting literature. These costs feature in management accounting textbooks but generally have been accorded only a brief treatment, often with an implicit admission that accounting can be of little help with these costs in decision making and that they are capable of accounting control only in the aggregate and often in rudimentary ways (see *Horngren and Foster* 1991, pp 432-443 and *Kaplan and Atkinson*, 1989, pp.29, 193 and 531).

In the accounting literature, these resources and their costs are generally held to have at least three important features. The first is that they arise from periodic decisions; usually as part of the annual budgeting exercise where programmes of expenditure are committed until decisions are revised or agreed commitments cease. The second is that their link with corporate objectives is often not clear and no obvious relationship exists between outputs and inputs (normally mainly labour) because the underlying technology is not well understood making it difficult to predict the effects of managerial intervention. Finally, many discretionary costs are seen as the result of a portfolio of one-off and ill-defined activities. These assumptions concerning discretionary costs make them difficult to manage. Examples of decision driven costs often include advertising, public relations, training, research and development, health care and some activities of general and administrative departments such as accounting, industrial relations and human resources.

Few attempts have been made to define decision driven costs. A definition which can be applied to these resources and which can be expanded and stated in more technical terms is as follows:

> Decision driven resources are those which are not technologically determined in that they are not essential to the production of either product or process outputs, where an essential input is one of which a positive amount must be provided if the production of output is to proceed at any level of volume (*Bromwich and Wang*, 1993, Chapter 5).

The essence of decision driven resources is that their amount is not determined by the technology used by the organisation nor by production needs but rather by managerial decisions. This suggests that their planning and control may take a different form from that for production driven resources. It also suggests that the usual treatment of their costs as fixed and their allocation as part of these costs confuses them with other types of costs and renders invisible any special characteristics they possess.

The above definition suggests that many resources and their associated costs that are conventionally treated as discretionary are not really decision driven. This is especially important because it is often said that conventionally defined discretionary costs represent an increasing proportion of overall costs.

The familiar descriptions of discretionary costs are very wide and may include resources and costs which possess, at least, some characteristics of non-fixed resources and their associated costs. While it may be generally the case that discretionary resources are not product volume related, many clearly contribute to activities. Other conventional discretionary resources represent, in part, set-up and infrastructure costs, that is, they are similar to many other fixed resources employed by the enterprise.

The above discussion of costs which are correctly described as decision driven suggests that it is difficult to understand why such resources would be employed by a profit maximising firm. However, it can be suggested that at least some discretionary costs should be appraised in terms of the benefits they provide to consumers for which the consumers are willing to pay (*Bromwich*, 1990): that is, their role is to sustain or expand demand. This consumer value approach provides the missing link between inputs and outputs for many processes which are generally treated as discretionary and provides a way of understanding the contribution of decision driven resources to the organisation. At least, some types of discretionary resources are employed either to maintain demand in the face of competition or to increase demand. With this approach, the benefits provided by products to customers by decision driven costs which provide enterprise revenues are seen as the ultimate cost drivers. From a strategic perspective, this category of cost drivers dominates those cost drivers used in traditional accounting and in activity costing when, as seems to be often the case, this approach is used in a routine way to attribute costs to products and not to the benefits which the activities represented by these costs provide to the consumer.

With the customer value perspective, each resource possessed by the enterprise is seen as being able to be linked to providing benefits which help meet the needs of customers, except for some resources which are incurred to meet regulations imposed by authorities external to the firm (see below). This approach is described in Chapter 6 as being used by many Japanese firms. What is called strategic cost analysis allows the cost of these resources to be integrated with operational plans because it makes visible the links between costs and the customer benefits to management at the operational level. It is not being suggested necessarily that detailed calculations are required. For many purposes, the assurance that decision driven costs will be covered by increased revenues may be sufficient.

With this approach, the utility of training costs, for example, becomes much more transparent. Training should be carried out only if it generates specific benefits to customers for which they are willing to pay more than the cost to the firm of providing these benefits. This test can be applied to training decisions at all levels in the organisation, thereby allowing the integration of the strategic benefits of training into operational plans. It has always been impossible to provide this type of integration within conventional management accounting where strategic planning activities, more generally, have had to be decoupled from current operations because accounting systems report only the costs of current enterprise operations.

Relating the output of decision driven processes to the market benefits they provide also allows strategy to be driven down the organisation. The output of each process in terms of market benefits provided can be related to the resources employed to achieve these benefits and the costs of these resources. This approach may be especially helpful for understanding decision driven decisions seemingly far removed from attracting the consumer. Additional administrative or central resources can be appraised in this way by linking these resources with the increase in customer benefits believed to be provided.

In practice, once the relevant decision concerning decision driven activities is made, the costs of decision driven resources are treated by placing them into the cost categories which are seen as appropriate to their cost behaviour. Thus, the costs of quality related decisions which affect direct product costs may be treated as if they were variable costs. Similarly, the cost of capital resources required to obtain a desired level of quality would be treated in the same way as other capital costs. However, this method of cost categorisation ignores the special characteristics of, at least, some of these resources which is that their usage and costs depend on decisions made in order to affect the level of market demand. Here, the responsible decision makers should regularly receive reports that indicate how the fruits of their decisions compare with expectations at the time of the decision. This suggested approach represents an important reform to accounting which tends to ignore decision driven resources and where it does consider them tends to focus on their costs and not upon their impact on the market. The conventional accounting categorisation of discretionary resources as fixed and their costs as overhead costs, also ignores the property that the amount of these resources may be changed more easily than other inputs which are technologically determined (see *Bromwich and Wang*, 1993, Chapter 5).

Not all discretionary costs can be dealt with in the way suggested above. Indeed, *Horngren and Foster* (1991, pp. 432-445) generally discuss discretionary costs as if they always have the characteristics of 'difficult to manage' costs and emphasise their indirect link with corporate objectives and the ill-defined nature of discretionary activities. However, many discretionary processes can be treated using activity based costing and activity based management (see Chapter 3). Similarly, the control of decision driven costs may lend itself to using non-financial indicators, where the nature of the processes can be defined in these terms, if not in financial terms. These approaches do not solve any problem arising from any possible ill-defined link between decision driven activities and corporate objectives. This is because both of these approaches treat the activities involved as separate processes and use measures not clearly linked to the enterprise's cashflows and objectives.

The next classification is one which does not generally figure in accounting. It encompasses all those resources which are devoted to satisfying regulatory requirements, demands which have increased substantially.

4.3 Regulatory Resources

The resources required to satisfy regulatory requirements may fall into any of the usual cost categories. Thus, some health and safety regulations may affect direct or indirect labour, by requiring additional production operations, but most of these regulations probably affect equipment and capital resources. Regulatory requirements are wide ranging and may affect many corporate activities. For example, the accounting department has to respond to a very wide range of regulatory requirements, including the collection of taxes, preparing statutory accounting reports and following accounting standards.

Regulatory requirements which impose variable costs

Few management accounting reports set out the costs of such activities separately. This may be because the characteristics of the costs associated with these resources make them indistinguishable from other similar costs. Thus, those variable product costs required by health regulations are in many ways indistinguishable from other variable product costs. Similarly, activities or process related costs imposed by regulation generally can be treated in the same way as other process costs and be charged to the cost object requiring the process activity. Such variable costs may be able to be designed out of the cost object in the same way as other variable product or process costs.

However, it is important to understand that the usage of such resources is not technologically determined but rather represents costs imposed at the discretion of others. Such requirements may be thought of as of two types. First, those which the company can only avoid by ceasing the production or process with which the regulation is associated, such as specifically defined items as safety requirements on vehicles. Secondly, there are those costs to which the firm can respond in some way, by planning out the use of a regulated material, component or operation. For planning purposes, it may be useful to report separately these two types of costs, especially as the definition of inescapable regulatory requirements indicates that they have a characteristic which is normally associated with fixed costs: they cannot be avoided if production is positive. For planning and control purposes they should therefore be treated in the same way as will be recommended here for other fixed costs with the same characteristics. Including them in conventional overhead recovery processes is unlikely to reflect their character correctly in that this would amount to treating regulatory requirements as if they were variable with production.

The second set of problems connected with treating fixed overheads to be discussed in this report arise from the problems of jointness between resources and therefore costs. This is the subject of the following main section of this chapter. The final section of the chapter suggests a revised form of report to management which incorporates many of the reforms suggested in this report and respects the technological character of resources and the economic characteristics of costs. The suggestions in these sections are discussed in more detail than is usual in this report because of their novelty and because of a lack of detailed literature in some of these areas. Again unusually, the discussion in these sections focuses especially on the work of one of the authors of this report because little other recent work has been undertaken in the areas to be covered.

4.4 Joint Costs and Common Costs

Much of the economics literature and some of the accounting literature does not distinguish between common and joint resources and costs. Used in this way, the term 'common' may encompass an element of jointness between cost objects, such as organisational units or products. Jointness arises where two or more cost objects necessarily use the same resources or are the joint outputs of the same resources (*Manes and Cheng*, 1988, pp.1-3). In accounting, specific definitions of the terms common and joint are often used with reference to costs and implicitly also apply to resources. With this approach, *common costs* are defined as applying

> to a setting in which production costs are defined on a single intermediate product or service which is used by two or more users *(Biddle and Steinberg*, 1984, p.5).

In contrast, *joint costs* apply to a setting in which production costs are a non-separable function of the outputs of two or more products (*Biddle and Steinberg*, 1984, p.4). The term 'non-separable function' means that the output of one product necessarily involves production also of, at least, a second output (though proportions may vary). Thus, an *unavoidable* jointness between the outputs for cost objects is a crucial part of the definition of joint costs. This jointness in costs is generated by a dependence arising from the technology used to produce the joint outputs.[1] That is, the process used automatically and unavoidably produces more than one output.

One of the major problems facing management accounting generally is thus that resources and therefore their costs may be joint between outputs. Such costs have to be treated as fixed overheads. This is because they cannot be logically traced to individual cost objects using only empirical evidence.

Indivisible factors where an input must be purchased in discrete units larger than required for current operations may possess these characteristics, as may many costs necessary to set up production or to allow it to proceed at all. Excess capacity with regard to plant and equipment also provides examples. Many of the resources used in modern manufacturing which are often very information system orientated have these characteristics. Once made available for one use, such resources can be used simultaneously for a number of other uses because the quantity of resource is not reduced by use (at

---

[1]Much of the academic literature covering these matters attempts to deal with common and joint resources and costs by converting them into items that can be treated as constrained in supply with variable product outputs and therefore any jointness disappears. This approach applies mathematical programming methods to these types of inputs and their costs. With suitable assumptions, these exercises yield opportunity costs or shadow prices which may be used to charge common and joint costs to their outputs (see *Manes and Cheng*, 1988). It would seem unlikely that this approach is likely to be taken up strongly in practice.

least, up to a capacity constraint). Production of computer programmes and software provides examples, as do many information and planning systems and their associated data banks. Such problems arise, perhaps, in their most extreme form with regard to utilities like telecommunications and electricity generation and distribution where capacity depends on peak demands and off peak demands can be met at a very low cost. Thus, capacity is a public input which once made available for peak demands is also automatically available for off-peak demands. The conventional approach to treating overheads in these industries by allocating them on some supposedly equitable basis across all demands does not reflect the economic reality of these industries. This may give rise to complaints from those enterprises which buy from capacity suppliers, such as local electricity companies and other telephone companies (which generally require use of the British Telecommunications network to complete their customers' calls) in order to supply their customers.

Such factors can be called public inputs reflecting that once made available, they are simultaneously usable by the whole firm or parts of the firm.

From a technological and economic perspective, the jointness of fixed resources and their costs often reflects their general nature as 'set-up' costs required before production can proceed either for the whole firm or for parts of the organisation. Such resources thus provide service capacities to the organisation (*Baumol et al.*, 1988, p.280; *Kaplan and Atkinson*, 1989, pp.28-29). With this view, these fixed costs are related to resources like buildings, machinery and information systems without which production cannot commence and which provide capacity used jointly by parts of the organisation. This suggests that accounting for them is intrinsically similar to acounting for capacity; an area where traditional accounting is not strong. The amounts of such resources required are explained by, among other factors, the expected level of planned production, the type of manufacturing operations and the attributes of the product to be produced.

The problems raised for the accountant by these characteristics include the fact that their economic character means these costs can be treated only as incremental (avoidable) to all the cost objects which use the underlying resources. Reflecting their technology, these costs should not be allocated to individual units of the cost objects or to the different cost objects utilising their services because there is no rational ground for making such allocations. These costs are incurred because the level of the resources provided is necessary for the planned level of production and their costs are unaffected by usage by cost objects.

It is important to attempt to alter accounting practice in this area which generally allocates both common and joint costs between organisational elements on some seemingly arbitrary basis. Much of the remainder of this section looks at some suggestions for accounting for joint costs. The next section first discusses accounting for common costs which do not also have the characteristic of jointness or of being public inputs.

Common costs

Just because inputs are used in common, either within the firm or by suppliers, does not necessarily mean that the resources and costs involved cannot be traced to outputs. Thus, current practice has no difficulty in tracing, to outputs, the costs of units of identical components or parts used by more than one output. Similarly, labour used for more than one task in a period can with an appropriate measuring system be traced to the outputs that require these tasks. Thus, many items which are treated as 'common' or 'joint' in conventional accounting may be able to be traced to output or other cost objects with suitable measurement devices. For example, there is nothing intrinsic in the character of the utility services used by the firm, such as electric power and telecommunications, which means that they cannot be traced to cost objects within firms. For example, they can be metered to users if appropriate. Recognising this, the essence of activity costing is to strip out of conventionally defined fixed overheads just those resources and costs which are variable with activities. Thus, it might be suspected that many resources which are treated as joint or common in accounting and therefore included in overheads are in fact traceable.

Joint costs

The cost of the resources which manifest jointness between products or organisational units cannot be traced to the consumption of their outputs by any organisational constituent except where they are provided for a given organisational unit, such as a cost centre, plant or division *and* are excluded from use by other parts of the organisation. Thus, the costs of joint outputs and resources may be difficult to trace other than to the set of *all* organisational units which require their use and which cannot be excluded from their use. Thus capacity inputs, such as storage space used by only one plant can be traced to that plant. Similarly, resource usage in maintaining a database required by only one division can be traced to that division. Many resources of this type are sited at the division, group and corporate level and cannot therefore be further traced down the organisation.

The characteristics of resources generating joint costs

This class of inputs generates many of the most difficult problems accountants have to solve. This type of input pervades the modern organisation and represents a major category of resources which is, perhaps, not yet well handled in accounting.

The cost structure of a joint resource will generally resemble that associated with fixed costs where the initial supply requires a large outlay and the supply of the resource or service has a zero or very low variable cost. Thus, because of the low cost of their supply once established they can be supplied simultaneously and jointly to more than one user and employment by one part of the firm does not reduce the supply to other users. This attribute does not apply in the case of a conventional factor, such as a unit of raw material, where usage for one purpose denies use for any other purpose. A second characteristic of public joint resources is that of non-exclusion. This means in the context of the firm that organisational units cannot be excluded from the enjoyment of the resource or service. Once available a corporate-wide credit ranking provides a good example. It is impossible to exclude any part of the organisation generally identified with the corporation from enjoying any benefits flowing from this credit ranking. Similarly, it may be impossible to avoid the firm's reputation being exploited by individual organisational units. (For a general review see *Atkinson and Stiglitz*, 1980, pp. 482-518).

That joint resources involve providing capacity rather than inputs which are used up directly in production leads to a major suggestion in this report which is substantially at variance with conventional management accounting. This is that capacity resources and their associated costs should be accounted for in a way that reflects both capacity provision and the public or joint characteristics of such resources. In the accounting literature, very few articles have considered resources with public good characteristics (see, however, *Cohen and Loeb*, 1982).

'Opting out'

The above non-exclusion assumption may well not apply in all organisations where potential users may often be able to be excluded by management decree or sufficiently ingenious administrative arrangements. It may however be difficult for organisational units to exclude themselves without corporate agreement. Many firms require that their organisational units use services provided by the firm rather than opting out of any provision or purchasing supplies on the market. This often seems to be the case for services provided at group or corporate level (see, for example, *Drury et al.*, 1993, where 68 percent of their sample permitted divisions to buy outside the firm but this right was limited where interdivisional transfers represented a large amount of the activities of the firm).

Where either the exclusion of parts of the organisation or opting out by organisational units is possible, the costs of any resources giving rise to joint costs can be traced to the overall set of organisational units or products using the joint resources in mind (see *Baumol and Ordover*, 1986, pp. 91-98 and *Sharkey*, 1989, pp. 35-42).This is because all resources are used for something and should be able to be linked with at least their immediate output. This linking of resources and their direct outputs may not be possible using accounting numbers and may require the use of non-financial output measures in planning, relating expected resource use to expected outputs over a planned time schedule including milestones and critical events. Similarly, control may be exercised using non-financial performance measures. Thus, one way to approach the problems raised in this section is to use a variety of non-financial performance measures. Such measures are as yet little used by accountants and clearly are not necessarily owned by them. However, with the use of such measures, there is a need to ensure that the accounting system and any information system using non-financial signals either provide consistent signals or the outputs of both information systems are available to decision makers. The use of non-financial indicators may not ensure optimality where they cannot be linked to ultimate organisational objects and where therefore the trade-offs between performance measures cannot be quantified.

Ascending the cost hierarchy

Another way to gain an understanding of the input/output relationships of joint resources is to move up the organisational hierarchy. Often any ambiguity as to the output of a unit when considered at one organisational level is resolved when it is considered at a higher level. For example, at the level of the cost centre, outputs cannot be measured in money terms but they can be so measured as part of the resources employed by the profit centres to which they contribute. Physical outputs and inputs can be related at this organisational level. For many expense centres, such as the legal and public relations departments, the outputs to which they contribute is made clearer by ascending the organisational hierarchy until that organisational level is reached where the resources are deemed avoidable on its closure. The full cost of the process can therefore be charged to that organisational unit. For many processes of this type, the use of their resources will only become avoidable at the level of the organisation as a whole. Moreover, that an economically rational cost object can be found does not mean that the efficiency of the level of services can be judged because the relation between the services and the output(s) of cost objects may still be ambiguous.

Using market prices

Many of the above problems disappear if the output of the resources used for these types of activities are available on the market. Such market prices measure the opportunity cost of the internal provision of the activity and give an external valuation of these activities (*Faulhaber*, 1975). The existence of such a market price provides an external cost for the activities which may be more useful in decision making than treating these costs as a fixed cost to be allocated in some way. Any cost charged to organisational units should not be greater than the cost of free standing provision by the market, ignoring any other intra-organisational effects. If, indeed, the services are available on the market, consideration should be given to allowing organisational units to use this market to fulfil their needs. This would at least ensure that the amount purchased had to be considered by the buying unit in a rational economic way where such units are profit centres. Major problems here are that the technology used by market suppliers may not reflect that of the organisation seeking to deal with joint costs and that the purchasing units may not take into account any firm-wide effects of their decisions.

Thus, in principle, an economically sensible transfer price can be ascertained for the use of joint resources where exclusion is possible or where opting out is permitted, especially where equivalent services are available on the market. As suggested earlier, firms may have a larger number of tools to enforce exclusion than the market. Thus, accountants should seek to distinguish between those joint resources which are excludable and those which are not. The former should be more amenable to charging for use than the latter.

Problems with transfer prices

However, there are still many problems with the use of internal (transfer) prices especially where market prices are not available. Negotiations between supplying and purchasing organisational units will generally involve small numbers of participants (*Musgrave and Musgrave*, 1980, pp. 81-82). Any transfer price that emerges from such negotiations is therefore not equivalent to a market price generated by the matching of demand and supply in the market in a way that is neutral relative to all characteristics of the participants except their demand and supply prices. Intra-organisational bargaining may give less weight to economic attributes and may rather reflect many other characteristics, such as the organisational status and power of the negotiators. Recourse to arbitrary overhead allocations may therefore reflect a desire to avoid the difficulties that may attend such negotiations.

Charging what organisational units say they would be willing to pay encounters the difficulty that these units may understate their willingness to pay at the time of the decision to acquire joint resources, especially where the provision will be made anyway, the method of charging may not reflect such declarations and the units cannot opt out of the agreed supply as is often the case in practice (*Mueller*, 1989, pp. 124-134). However, the centre of the firm has a very large number of ongoing relationships with other organisational units and the information systems associated with these relationships give the centre a large amount of information about subordinate units and their optimal conduct.

The above suggestions of the possibility of using market prices or internal transfer prices to charge for overheads is conditioned very strongly by the organisation structure. This suggests, more generally, that accounting systems and the organisational structure of the firm mutually interact with each other. Accounting systems if they are to work well therefore have to be designed to fit with the rest of the organisation and its culture.

Overhead costs as 'taxes'

As was indicated above, it may also be possible for an organisation to exclude an organisational segment from enjoying joint resources. Such an excluded part of the organisation may be willing to pay for using the resource. This yields some evidence of the value of that input to the organisational unit. This declared value amounts to a contribution or *tax* which the unit would be willing to bear to help to ensure the recovery of the cost of the joint resources which it needs to utilise. In this section, it will be suggested that overhead allocations make more sense if seen as taxes meant to recover the costs of joint resources. Strictly, such charges should not be used in decision-making because they do not measure economic costs. However, the taxes discussed here and below are designed so that any distortion to profits caused by their use in decisions is minimised.

This approach suggests two economically meaningful methods of dealing with joint costs. Both involve charging a tax on the users of joint resources in order to attempt to recoup the cost of the underlying resources. One method is to charge any overhead cost relating to joint costs as a fixed charge to the aggregate of the profits from all products or organisational units using the joint service. This is an application of the approach suggested earlier in this chapter. This charge should be levied at the point in the product or organisational hierarchy at which the resource's use and therefore costs become incremental. This approach is used extensively in the service sector especially in the hotel and catering industry (*Fitzgerald et al.*, 1992) where an annual capacity charge is often made for departmental space.

It also accords with German management accounting practice where contributions (revenues less incremental costs) are often calculated for orders, for products, for product groups and for each of a hierarchy of organisational units (for treatments in English, see

Strange, 1991, and *Kilger*, 1990). Thus, in Germany and a number of other countries, contribution analysis is used much more extensively than in Anglo Saxon countries to provide a hierarchy of contributions both for products and for organisational units. Thus, considering products as an example, the approach suggested here is that the cost of joint resources should be charged as a lump sum tax to the aggregate contribution of all the products which use the services of a joint resource. As the charge represents a lump sum, it will not distort long-run or short-run decisions if used in decision making. Ideally, this tax would measure the incremental opportunity cost of rendering the service providing that this tax measures the fall in the economic value from using the service during the period — the user cost. Estimates of user costs measure the consumption of the service and are only equal to accounting costs by chance, at least in the short run where capacity is not adjusted optimally to demand. Otherwise, in the short run, any tax or charge for joint resources has to be treated as fixed as this cost does not measure the economic cost of the resources.

Allocations and joint resources

In principle, the ideal economic approach to *funding* or *charging* for joint resources is to levy a charge on each user which reflects the benefits they perceive from the resource, assuming that such preferences are known to those setting the charge. This levy is really a 'tax' which aims to recover the cost of the joint resource (*Cohen and Loeb*, 1982). This approach is in many ways similar to that used by a full price discriminating monopolist selling conventional goods who is able to tailor prices to the individual demand of each user thereby extracting the maximum amount each individual is willing to pay for all units of the conventional good desired.

In decision-making, the provision of a joint resource by the firm should be extended until the total incremental benefits to all users for which users would be willing to pay is equal to the marginal cost of obtaining that level of provision. These benefits will reflect how provision of the resource will affect the revenues obtained from the final outputs produced by users. Levying a charge or tax to each individual unit equal to the benefits obtained from that level of provision would thus just cover costs, if everything goes according to plan. The incremental benefits obtained by a unit for any level of provision of the public resource is the change in its profit with respect to an alteration in the provision of the public good; that is, these benefits measure the marginal profitability of provision.

One problem with this approach is obtaining truthful statements of willingness to pay from resource users (*Mueller*, 1989). A second is that the use of these prices to charge organisational elements may require the use of lump sum taxes and transfers between organisational units. Organisational units dissatisfied with the charging arrangements may seek to withdraw from enjoying the resource.

This approach also requires a great deal of information from organisational units which may not be easy to obtain. Where the required large quantity of information can be obtained, it may be wondered whether using this in decision-making at the centre may be inimical to decentralised management.

There is another method of taxing or charging for public resources which is less likely to run into these two problems. The aim here is to calculate a charge to the users of joint resources which recoups the cost of these resources over time from the users but minimises the distorting effect of these charges on profits (*Baumol et al.*, 1988, Chapter 8). This approach is used to determine overhead charges which ensure that the costs of joint resources are met over time assuming that plans, at the time of acquiring these resources, turn out to be correct. This approach has an advantage over traditional allocations. If these charges were used in decision-making, this would cause the least distortion to profits whilst still recouping the cost of overhead resources.

Basically, the recommendation here is that the charge for joint resources to organisational units should be levied as a mark up on the marginal (variable) costs of products. This mark up is not based in any sense on usage. Rather, it is based on 'what the product will bear' where the ability to 'bear' is defined in a specific way. This ability to bear additional costs is measured by the relative constancy of the quantity demanded by the market of the product of an organisational unit in the face of a price increase. Commodities showing a smaller negative response in quantity to price changes thus can bear more of the cost of the joint resources. If such charges were incorporated into cost plus prices, they would affect least the profits of price inelastic products, the demands for which are relatively insensitive to price increases.

For example, the approach suggested here would levy a charge for capacity normally in the form of a total 'rental' charge on the users of that capacity distinguishing between unused capacity and utilised capacity. This type of charging is sometimes advocated by those buying in bulk from utilities. This type of fixed charge for the capacity provided in a period reflects the pattern of resource usage of capacity resources. Separating this charge into that part relating to used capacity and that relating to unused capacity should help decision-making. This charge is not an allocated cost but rather is the contribution required to fund the resource in accordance with plans made to finance the resource at the time of its acquisition based on the market environment faced by users. Ideally, the charge for utilised capacity should be based on the price of obtaining this service on the market as is frequently done for floor space in hotels and departmental stores where organisational units are charged the market price of the square footage of the space allocated to them. If not, the charge should be based not on allocated costs but on seeking a contribution to joint costs based on what products or organisational units can bear.

German management accounting theory comes to somewhat similar conclusions. This theory suggests that manufacturing capacity should be accounted for entirely separately from costs directly variable with output volume. Rather a charge should be levied for the provision of the capacity to provide services. However, in Germany, in practice, the charge for manufacturing capacity is based on accounting depreciation (often calculated using replacement costs).

Summary

With the above view, if it is wished to distribute the cost of joint resources, the charges to organisational elements and products within the firm should be recouped by levying a 'tax' on products reflecting their demand sensitivity. This approach is also recommended for charging for other fixed costs where it is felt necessary to charge users in some way. This requirement to charge users is a seemingly dominant wish according to empirical studies on overhead allocation (*Atkinson*, 1987b; *Fremgen and Liao*, 1981; *Drury et al.*, 1993).

On a more practical basis, and in conventional accounting language, this approach suggests that overheads should not be allocated using a base which reflects usage poorly or not at all. Rather, the financing of overheads should be based on sales. Such an approach provides an imperfect but practical guide to the ability to bear overhead charges. This suggestion is not so far removed from practice as might be expected. Several studies indicate that many firms do allocate fixed costs, especially corporate and divisional fixed costs, using measures based on sales (see, for example, *Fremgen and Liao*, 1981 where over 25 percent of firms surveyed allocated indirect corporate expenses on the basis of sales, p.50). In support of the approach suggested here, they say that:

> Few respondents mentioned ability to bear as the criterion that was used to select bases, but it appeared to be the dominant factor underlying the actual bases employed (*Fremgen and Liao*, 1981, p.55).

The various suggestions in this chapter, and some of those in other chapters of this report, can be illustrated by a revised form of accounting report. This report incorporates the suggestion that many of the problems with overheads can be overcome by adopting a report which uses a contribution approach for each element of the organisation and the product hierarchy as suggested above. Such a statement shows an ascending set of contributions either for organisational elements or for parts of the product hierarchy (see *Bromwich and Wang*, 1993, Chapter 9). Variants of such statements are used in Germany (see *Strange*, 1991; *Schoenfeld*, 1974, pp.5-39 and *Boons et al.*, 1992). Indeed, *Seicht* (1990) states that:

> At least a third of all German and Austrian industrial companies have transferred their cost accounting to a system of marginal cost and contribution income accounting (p. 619).

4.5 An Accounting Report Based on Cost Characteristics

Earlier parts of this study indicated that the costs for resources can be linked to a wide variety of cost objects in either product or organisational hierarchies in a very flexible way reflecting the technology and structure of the enterprise. The exact linkage selected will be specific to the firm, to the structure of its product portfolio and to its chosen organisational structure. The approach used here is to categorise costs according to the causes of their variability and the character of the resources underlying each type of cost, to report all costs in the same category together and to link these cost categories with managerial responsibilities. The aim is to trace costs initially to the lowest possible relevant component in the organisational or product hierarchy.

The statement presented here reflects the organisational hierarchy. A similar statement for the product hierarchy would focus more on product costs and present contributions at each level of the product hierarchy.

For simplicity, the report displayed assumes that the lowest level of organisational unit reported upon is a division which manufactures and sells two different products; therefore, costs can be deducted from revenue to yield a series of contributions. Statements can also be produced for manufacturing divisions, departments, cost and expense centres where transfer pricing is practised as it is in Germany where somewhat similar statements are used (see *Kilger*, 1990, on contribution costing in Germany).

The report starts in Part I at the divisional level then reports in Part II on divisions in the same organisational group and then for the firm as a whole. The detail of the statement given here focuses upon the division. The actual format of the statement depends on the technology of the firm, the organisational hierarchy and the responsibility of the various managers. The actual arrangement used will be firm-specific. Where relevant, each major product and organisational category also contains costs which are charged to that category as a whole, where it is not possible or desired to distribute these costs to subsidiary units within the category. Such an approach has been recommended in this study where resources are not traceable to lower levels in the product or organisational hierarchy. The cost categories are only illustrative and are not meant to represent an exhaustive list. These categories and the costs within them will differ between firms and industries.

In order to make sense of the contribution of each product or organizational category, it is necessary to deduct from the unit's revenue all the incremental costs of the unit. A greater use of contribution analysis than is normal in Anglo-Saxon accounting is thus being suggested.

The suggested general format for an accounting report is presented overleaf. A report of the type shown in Part I of the statement is required for all organisational units. Thus there would be one of these statements for each organisational unit. Part II of the statement applies to combinations of units and therefore commences by aggregating the individual unit statements. Thus the contributions obtained from organisational units are combined at the beginning of Part II of the statement.

Part I of the statement shows the contribution yielded by a division which manufactures and sells products. It does this by presenting an ascending set of contributions. The lowest level contribution is equal to revenue net of only the cost of product volume based activities. In control terms, this contribution may be useful for monitoring the performance of the operating manager(s) charged with producing the planned volumes of the products at a specific variable cost. The next contribution deducts from this first contribution the activity related costs of the products and may be useful for monitoring operating managers; it serves to remind managers of the cost of activities and indicates the contribution from the production programme. These two contributions together may be useful for short-term decision making, such as whether to take an additional special order. These costs are those of the operations essential to allow production.

Deducting capacity related costs from the contribution after deduction of costs variable with volume and with production activities yields the contribution generated by divisional production. This may help in monitoring the divisional manager's operating performance relative to variables within the divisional control. More general activities which often are decision driven are reported in the fourth set of costs shown in the statement. Here, the following are deducted from the contribution from divisional production: costs for decision driven services, especially those relating to services provided by superior organisational units; costs for the activities sustaining the model programme; and product related decision driven costs. This yields the contribution obtained from the division's product group.

The next step is to deduct the costs which can only be traced to the division as a whole. This yields the divisional contribution. Finally, deducting general administration attributable to the division yields divisional profit.

Figure 4.1 Suggested revised accounting statement

PART I

	Products		
	1	2	Total
1. Revenue (or transfers to other divisions at transfer prices)	●	●	●
less Costs variable with output	●	●	●
Contribution From Output Volume	●	●	●
2. *less* Production costs variable with production related activities	●	●	●
Contribution From Production Programme	●	●	●
3. *less* Capacity Costs (excluding unused capacity; charged as 'tax' or opportunity cost)	●	●	●
Contribution From Divisional Production	●	●	●
4. *less* Activity costs of sustaining model programme	●	●	●
Non-divisional product related costs	●	●	●
Product related decision driven costs	●	●	●
Contribution from Product Group	●	●	●
5. *less* Unused capacity			●
Non-distributed divisional costs			●
Divisional Contribution			●
6. *less* General administration attributable to division			●
Divisional Profit			●

PART II

7. Aggregated Divisional Profits			●
less Non-distributed Group costs			●
Group Profit			●
8. Aggregated group profits			●
less Non-distributed Corporate costs			●
Corporate Profits			●

Part II of the statement also provides a set of ascending contributions. Here, however, they are aggregated for the organisational units coming under the umbrella of the highest superior organisational unit being considered. This means that units of the product organisational hierarchy are nested in the hierarchy of organisational units.

The first contribution in Part II of the statement shows the contribution of a given organisational group. Deducting those costs associated with the organisational group and any regulatory costs yields the divisional contribution. Aggregating the contribution of all such organisation groups and deducting non-distributed corporate costs yields the firm's profit. This would be subject to a variety of accounting adjustments if it were wished to reconcile this profit figure with that in the financial accounts.

The classifications used in this statement may be thought to be much clearer than those in conventional accounting statements. The suggested statement uses mutually exclusive cost categories and exhaustively assigns costs to one and only one category. These cost classifications respect the underlying technology of the resources being costed. Similarly, a clear logic runs through the statement in that the various contributions have clear meanings for control and decision making purposes. Reflecting this, the format looks cleaner than many conventional accounting reports. The above report is really an ideal. In practice the logic of contributions may be difficult to trace and some costs may not fit into simple cost classifications.

Discussion of the suggested accounting statement

The arguments in favour of the individual components of this statement are contained in the body of this chapter and other chapters. One aim of the statement is to ensure that each accounting cost shown is consistent both with the technology of the resources underlying it and with the relevant managerial responsibility. The need for this consistency between accounting and technology of an increasingly dynamic character is a major challenge to accounting. Without this, accounting signals may become increasingly dysfunctional.

A second aim of this statement illustrates a suggested objective of this report generally and of modern management accounting which is to reduce the number of resources and related costs which are treated as fixed overheads in conventional accounting where they would be allocated to products and cost objects. The statement treats as attributable to a cost object only those resources and costs which are traceable to that cost object and collects together all those costs traceable to the same cost object. Thus for each organisational unit, all costs variable with production volume are collected together and reported separately from costs variable with those activities which are chargeable to the product. This assumes that such a separation is feasible given the possible interdependence of product volume and activities (see Chapter 3). For control and for decision making purposes all these categories have to be considered together where production programme activities are interdependent. Budgets have to be flexed for all the variables in the production programme, not just volume.

The section of the statement that deals with activities (Part I, sections 2 and 4) assumes that these are traced to products (not to product units) or product groups except for those activities which are themselves a function of volume (if these are not included in the first cost category).

As was argued earlier in the study, many activities defined in the conventional way are not traceable to products but may be traceable to other cost objects and thus may be included in other categories in the statement. Such a format is consistent with *Cooper's* fourfold characterisation of activities (1990). Such activities are not shown explicitly in the statement as activity analysis is viewed as a tool for understanding cost categories and cost behaviour.

Another major aim of the statement is to structure the reporting of costs in a way which collects them together in separate groups depending on the causes of their variation and on their sharing the same underlying technology in terms of the factors which cause their underlying resources to vary. Thus, for example, in the statement, costs variable with output volume are reported separately from those which depend on capacity provision. The final aim of the statement is to obtain contribution figures which are meaningful for each element of the organisation hierarchy and which also reflect managerial responsibilities. Thus Part I of the accounting statement divides the contribution from a product into meaningful segments. The first segment of Part I shows for each product costs variable with volume and in conventional accounting terms shows the contribution yielded prior to support costs (activity costs) obtained from other direct production departments within the division. Support costs are dealt with in the second section.

The third cost segment shows the costs incurred because of the decisions to provide a certain level of capacity to the division producing the product. This part of the statement also yields signals as to whether this capacity represents a constraint on production or is provided in excess amounts. Constrained capacity could be signalled by using opportunity cost based charges in the statement. Thus, the approach suggested in Part I of the statement yields useful figures for planning and control for separable cost components relating to the product and organisational hierarchy. The same approach is used on the second page of the statement which encompasses multiple products.

This type of statement is very flexible. Thus, it could be compiled using standard costs and budget figures rather than actual figures. The results obtained from the statements can be transformed to reconcile with actual profits by consolidated adjustments at the end of the statement.

The format of the statement, the categorisation used therein and the focus on contributions may seem somewhat different from conventional management accounting statements. However, this approach is used in Germany successfully and a much simpler variant is recommended by *Horngren and Foster* (1991, p.503). There is some evidence that contributions are being resorted to in practice where the traditional approach to overheads seems not to produce useful information, especially in the service sector.

4.6 Conclusions

The first substantive section of this chapter addresses discretionary or decision driven costs. It was suggested that these tend often to be treated as fixed overheads in practice and may be neglected. Adopting a customer value perspective was suggested as a way of better understanding these costs. In decision making the question to be asked was suggested to be: how much is the customer willing to pay for the benefits provided for decision driven expenditure? This provides the key to understanding and controlling many of these costs.

Separate accounting for regulatory resources was suggested in the next section to be of importance because of their special characteristics and because it was important to understand whether such costs were escapable by managerial action. It was recommended that where the costs imposed by regulators were not escapable they should be treated as joint costs but reported separately.

A major part of the chapter was addressed to discussing a variety of ways of dealing with common costs and joint costs. It was suggested that many common costs could be traced to cost objects with appropriate measuring devices.

It was suggested that one possible treatment of joint costs was to report them at the point in the product or organisational hierarchy where these costs become incremental. The worthwhileness of providing a joint resource can be ascertained by determining the contribution yielded to meet the cost of the resource. This approach avoids cost distortions which flow from seeking to allocate costs to lower level cost objects in these hierarchies.

The next suggested reform can be applied where the services provided by a joint resource within the firm are also available in the market. The suggestion here is that the price of such services on the market should be used within the firm to guide charges for such resources provided that users within the firm are free to use the market for their requirements. Market prices can be used to provide guidelines for transfer prices where the firm does not wish the use of the market by its divisions.

Finally, a scheme was suggested that allowed the costs of joint resources to be recouped if this is required. This scheme, by levying charges for joint resources on the basis of 'what the product will bear', avoids the arbitrary allocations generated by conventional overhead allocations.

The scheme suggested ideally bases charges on the sensitivity of demand of products, with those less sensitive to price increases bearing more of the costs of joint resources. This ensures that costs generated in this way may be used in decision making as they will minimise deviations from optimal decisions. More practically, this suggestion comes down to suggesting that allocations should be based on sales rather than using cost based recovery methods. This approach is often used in practice for divisional and corporate expenses.

The final part of this chapter suggested a form of accounting report which by reporting for each level of organisational hierarchy attempts to reflect the technology of resources and the economic characteristics of costs.

Basically, the report first presents an ascending set of divisional contributions commencing with the contribution due to the volume of output of a product in the period and then indicating the contribution after meeting product programme costs (the non-volume costs of production). Finally, the contribution from the division after meeting all incremental costs is calculated. The remainder of the statement calculates the contribution from all divisions in the same organisational group. The contribution for each organisational group is shown which when aggregated yields the firm's total contribution.

5
The Strategic Dimension

5.1 Introduction

Casual observation indicates that Western management accounting practice still focuses almost exclusively on costing and helping to control activities within the enterprise by concentrating on the understanding of internal costs. Most textbook expositions also adopt this perspective, providing detailed analysis of a variety of conventional cost categories and regimes. The concern seems to be to spotlight the costs of products and of departments within the firm and to monitor these internal costs relative to plans. With regard to information external to the firm, few management accounting systems seem to go beyond reporting sales revenues and even the presentation of historical market share information in management accounting reports is fairly rare (*Howell and Soucy*, 1987 (a & b)). More generally, a *Harris Research Centre* report (1990), commissioned by KPMG Peat Marwick, found that in strategy formulation

> the use of external information is generally rare . . . . Company annual reports are the most popular published sources [of strategic information]. p.10

Advocates of activity or transaction costing, such as *Cooper and Kaplan* (1987) and *Johnson and Kaplan* (1987), reinforce this emphasis on internal costs by seeking to attribute these costs to the enterprise's products in a way that better reflects the activities incurred in their production. More recent attempts to reduce non-valued added activities still tend to concentrate on costs rather than seeking to assess the views of consumers on the value added characteristics of products (*Brimson*, 1991).

This approach can be contrasted with the role that accounting is said in Chapter 6 to play in many Japanese companies, where its aims are to help achieve target prices set to reflect the enterprise's strategic aims and to help provide product characteristics which yield greater value added to the consumer than rival products (*Hasegawa*, 1986, pp. 59-60). Chapter 6 also indicates that in product planning and development in Japan, a great deal of time is spent in seeking to estimate how consumer demand will respond to possible variants of a product and how the life time revenue accruing from such variants compares with their costs (see *Tanaka*, 1989). Management accounting when used as a control or evaluation device in Japan is utilised to encourage the continual search for cost reductions and generally serves to reinforce long-term manufacturing strategies which represent one of the special characteristics of Japanese management usually emphasised by commentators.

Porter (1985), chapter 1, says that satisfying consumer needs is a necessary but not sufficient objective for sustained competitive advantage. The firm also needs to have a competitive advantage over actual and potential competitors. He says:

> Value is what buyers are willing to pay for, and superior value stems from offering lower prices than competitors for equivalent benefits or providing unique benefits that more than offset a higher price. (1985, p.3)

This advantage may be achieved either by providing a superior way of meeting consumer needs (by offering a clearly differentiated product or set of services related to the product) or by marketing a relatively low cost product. Competitive strategies may span the whole product range of an industry or may be focused on only a target segment. Accounting has a clear role in helping to formulate strategies of this type. Differentiation is only worthwhile if the revenues obtained exceed the costs of satisfying consumer needs. Accounting obviously plays a major role in achieving a cost leadership strategy and in maintaining this strategy by continuing cost engineering.

Given the importance accorded to accounting systems in Western decision-making, the costs of offering strategically excellent products need to be fully integrated into enterprise cost systems and reported on by these systems. This is one of the objectives of what has come to be called *strategic management accounting* (SMA). This new approach to management accounting helps to focus managerial efforts more on their markets, where customers have to be won and retained and competitors repulsed, and on the costs of these market activities. The second aim of strategic management accounting is to ascertain the enterprise's cost positioning relative to its rivals (see *Bromwich*, 1990, pp.37-46 and *Shank*, 1989). This positioning is crucial in determining the sustainability of the firm's product characteristics and price/output strategies against competitors. For such sustainability to be achieved the enterprise needs to have cost advantages over its rivals.

The next section briefly introduces strategic management accounting and outlines its necessary characteristics. The following section reviews the relationship between some variants of strategy theory and strategic management accounting. It also outlines how strategic management accounting relies on the strategy literature. The next two sections review the two major approaches to strategic management accounting briefly outlined above.

The final section of the chapter gives some conclusions and reviews some difficulties with the approach.

5.2 *Strategic Management Accounting Defined*

The aim of this approach is to allow management accounting, in addition to its conventional fields, to concentrate upon the consumer value generated relative to competitors. It also aids in monitoring the firm's performance in the market place using a whole range of strategic variables over a decision horizon sufficiently long for strategic plans to come to fruition. These concepts form the core of the new concept of strategic management accounting. The aim is to provide, in cooperation with other enterprise functions, information concerning the firm's markets and its competitors, with the emphasis being placed on the long term.

A working definition of strategic management accounting is:

> The provision and analysis of financial information on the firm's product markets and competitors' costs and cost structures and the monitoring of the enterprise's strategies and those of its competitors in these markets over a number of periods. (*Bromwich*, 1990, p.28)

Providing a strategic perspective in management accounting requires the role of accounting to be extended in two directions. It first requires that costs are integrated into strategy using a variety of strategic cost analyses. The aim is to align costs with strategy. The second element of strategic management accounting is to discover in a fairly general way the cost structure of competitors and to monitor

changes in these over time. There seem to be two dominant
approaches to strategic management accounting. One seeks to cost
the product attributes provided by a company's products. It is these
attributes which are seen as attracting consumers. The other
approach is to seek to cost the functions in the value chain which
provide value to the consumer.

The importance of strategic management accounting

Although the term strategic management accounting is new, firms
have practised elements of this approach for a long time. Many firms
when faced with competitive challenges hastily undertake
competitive investigations of product benefits offered by themselves
and their competitors. Often, however, the costs of providing such
benefits are not considered in this process. These costs are subject
to the same swingeing overall cuts introduced to beat off the
competitive threat as all other costs even though these costs may
need to be increased to meet this challenge. Such information is also
often gathered in connection with takeover bids and is sometimes
crucial to either a successful takeover or a successful defence.
Similarly, in automotive firms, for example, product planners when
developing a new model are often provided with figures based on
product characteristics. Many consultants offer services in this area.
Indeed, *Shank and Govindarajan* (1988) assert with regard to the
USA that

> There is a billion dollar-a-year market in strategy cost analysis
> consulting services dominated by firms such as Bain &
> Company, Boston Consulting Group, Booz Allen & Hamilton,
> McKinsey & Company and Monitor.

Similarly, for example, variants of this approach have recently been
successfully introduced in large European firms in the computer,
pharmaceutical and steel industries.

Strategic management accounting gives additional strength and a
stronger role to the surprisingly large number of the Fortune 500
controllers who participate in strategic planning activities but only
by giving informal advice or providing data or analyses. Perhaps the
adoption of strategic management accounting will increase the figure
of 25 to 33 percent of controllers who presently claim to get involved
in choosing options or to be involved in all the phases of the two

crucial steps of developing the mission and establishing objectives (*Fern and Tipgos*, 1988).

Harnessing the finance department to corporate strategy may give additional impetus to the need to match the strong strategic thrust of many global competitors. There is ample evidence that Western firms lag behind in this area. A recent study of product development in Japan, Korea and Denmark indicated that Danish firms tended to allow the problems experienced by existing customers to drive product development whereas the Japanese relied much more on innovative product research and competitor analysis and employed a substantial number of market scanning devices. Similarly, the *Harris Research Centre* study (1990) of information for strategic management in large UK companies found that the use of external information is generally rare. Only about half the companies used competitor information and market research results with any frequency. Annual financial reports seemed to be the major item of public information used.

Strategic management accounting is still in its infancy and its successful application yields results which are commercially sensitive. This makes it difficult to give many examples of how actual enterprises use the approaches advocated here. *Allen* (1986) gives an example of strategic financial management in a UK company which emphasises the appraisal of future plans by determining their present value.

Similarly, many firms have attempted to isolate their key strategic success factors which they must sustain if the firm is to survive and succeed and to determine the strategic dimensions of the goods and services they provide. It is well known, for example, that the McDonald's Corporation uses as major items of strategic importance detailed measures of quality, cleanliness and value. Similarly, a large supplier to the aircraft industry has identified a number of customer orientated strategic objectives including reduced delivery times resulting from shortening lead times, reliability and high quality, incorporating the need to obtain zero defects and to provide flexible responses to customer demands whilst matching industry innovation levels at a low buyer cost.

Without the adoption of strategic management accounting, the control and monitoring of strategic objectives may have to take place outside the financial management system using disaggregated measures. It is then difficult to consider the overall impact of the enterprise's achievements in these areas.

The excitement generated in the profession and in industry generally concerning strategic management accounting does not yet match that which now surrounds activity costing. There may be a number of reasons for this. The required revisions to current management accounting for SMA are much more radical than those needed to implement activity costing and are not as well founded on existing management accounting expertise. Strategic management accounting requires that accountants embrace new skills extending beyond their usual areas and cooperate much more with general management, corporate strategists, marketing and product development, who may not have a good image of accountants.

Strategic management accounting does, however, help resolve major concerns that management have about the inability of conventional management accounting to deal well with strategic matters. *Porter* expresses the existing role of accounting in strategy formulation as follows:

> While accounting systems do contain useful data for cost analysis, they often get in the way of strategic cost analysis, (1985, p.63).

It also raises many problems which at first glance seem insoluble to those inexperienced in this area. For example, the usual reaction to being told to consider competitors' cost structures is that it can not be done even in the face of evidence that many global competitors devote considerable resources to this endeavour. A firm involved with its competitor in a joint venture learnt about its competitor's costs but did not use them in competitive analysis because the competitor used a different system of overhead allocation. It is difficult to see how a business can be managed without a broad understanding of the enterprise's competitive cost structure.

5.3 *Strategic Management Accounting and Strategy*

Both of the approaches to be briefly reviewed in this chapter build substantially on the work of *Porter* (1985). Porter has produced a very clear and relatively simple approach. (For an alternative presentation see, for example, *Grant,* 1991.) His concern is to establish what causes the differential profitabilities of different industries and to consider how firms (strategic business units) with different strategies manage to survive in some industries. He sees each industry being affected to different degrees by five competitive forces:

(1) the threat of new entrants

(2) the threat of substitute products and services

(3) the degree and character of competition within the industry

(4) the bargaining power of suppliers

(5) the bargaining power of customers.

The interplay of these forces determines whether an industry is capable of earning sustainable profits in the longer run. The balance of these forces can change over time suggesting that the firm in the industry, or the relevant strategic business unit, should monitor its environment to identify changes in industry structure and in competitor strategies. The firm needs to be pro-active in its strategy in the face of actual and expected changes both in the competitive forces faced by the industry and in the strategies of competitors who may be external to the industry narrowly defined. *Porter* (1985) sees the aim of firms or strategic business units as being to select strategies which yield them sustainable competitive advantages over their rivals by choosing their optimal strategy having considered these forces and the firm's comparative advantage, if any, over its competitors.

The firm in choosing its strategy needs to understand its strategic cost drivers and work on them to reduce the cost of the firm's strategy relative to its competitors. The cost drivers influencing a firm's cost structure are much wider than those used in ABC. They are the factors which determine the form of the cost structure of the firm and of its rivals. Some of these drivers result from the economic structure of the industry and some are beyond the control of the firms within the industry. Others can be altered by enterprise action. Some of the key cost drivers identified by *Porter* (1985, pp. 70-83) are familiar, others are less so. The identified key drivers are economies (diseconomies) of scale, linkages between the firm and its customers, suppliers and other units within the firm, learning potentialities, patterns of capacity utilisation which affect unit costs, integration between units in the organisation, interrelationships within the business, timing, discretionary policies, location of the unit and institutional factors impinging on the firm. All these elements determine the value chain which can be defined as

> the linked set of value-creating activities all the way from basic raw material sources through to the ultimate end-use products delivered into the final consumer's hands. The focus is external to the firm seeing each firm in the context of the overall chain of value creating activities of which it is probably only a part (*Shank and Govindarajan*, 1989, p. 179).

The value chain emphasises the total value of all operations, not just those which the firm carries out itself. Thus, the value chain covers more than the conventional concept of value added which ignores important linkages with both suppliers and customers by focusing only on value added within the firm. *Porter* (1985, p.37) sees this wider value chain as comprising five primary activities and a number of support activities. The primary activities are defined sequentially as inbound logistics, operations, outbound logistics, marketing and sales and services. Secondary or support activities encompass activities relating to the following: firm infrastructure, human resource management, technology and procurement. Porter seeks to assign costs and resources to each important part of the value chain and to use these in guiding the firm towards reconfiguring the value chain, that is, deciding on those areas of the value chain in which the firm has comparative advantage and those which it should source to suppliers, or in other words, how vertically integrated the firm should be and what are its core competencies.

Because of different cost structures and other advantages, firms in the same industry may have very different value chains. Thus, the oil industry consists of almost fully integrated firms, those which concentrate on retail, specialists in exploration, often only in specific parts of the world, and dealers on the oil markets. Porter emphasises that

> The value chain displays total value, and consists of *value activities* and *margin* . . . . Margin is the difference between total value and the collective cost of performing the value activities (1985, p. 38).

Thus, Porter does not seek to attribute the profit or margin generated by the value chain to individual activities or processes making up that chain.

The costs and resources assigned to elements of the value chain will depend on how the industry and firm's cost structure impact on each part of the value chain and the ability of the firm to control the cost elements affecting its activities.

Porter seems to see no difficulty in this exercise of attributing costs and resources to individual parts of the value chain but it may produce major problems for the accountant as allocation will often be necessary (see *Porter*, 1985, pp. 64-73). For example, many of the support activities are likely to contribute to many products and are therefore likely to represent joint costs. For a review of the promise and problems of costing the value chain, see *Shank and Govindarajan* (1989). In order for the firm to seek competitive advantages, exercises of this sort should also be undertaken for rival firms or business units.

Porter suggests that the firm, which fully understands the value chain and competitor value chains, has a choice of three strategies in order to obtain competitive advantage:

(1) Diversification

(2) Cost leadership and

(3) The use of either of these on a focused segment of the industry.

Porter's approach emphasises the need for the firm to consider the whole stream of its activities, their linkages and the impact in a competitive market of its fight to obtain a competitive advantage. Traditional management accounting in contrast tends to focus on manufacturing activities, ignore support activities, departmentalise activities (thereby ignoring linkages between them) and look inwards towards the factory rather than looking outwards to customers and to competitors.

Porter's work can be criticised from a number of other stances (see *Mintzberg*, 1987, and *Miles and Snow*, 1978). First, it treats as very structured decisions those which many regard as very fuzzy, involving subjective views and much debate and bargaining within the organisation. A very different perspective on the strategy process can be found in *Mintzberg* (1987). Second, the evidence is that many firms follow more than one of Porter's three strategies and seem to avoid the danger he sees of getting 'stuck in the middle' with two unsuccessful strategies and thereby being unable to sustain a competitive advantage. It can also be argued that Porter tends to avoid the dynamics of the strategy process and to offer little guidance on how firms should generate the strategies with which they hope to gain comparative advantage.

Accounting researchers have played a strong role in making Porter's work practical in an accounting context. *Bromwich* (1990) has sought to compare the relative cost of product attributes to what the consumer is willing to pay for them, thereby seeking to assign revenues to elements of the value chain which provide clear customer benefits. *Shank and Govindarajan* using what they call strategic cost analysis have sought to cost the value chain and more generally have sought to integrate Porter's work into accounting. The next two sections look briefly at these two approaches.

5.4 Approaches to Strategic Management Accounting

There presently exists only a very small body of literature describing these approaches, explaining models which can be used in applying a strategic approach to management accounting and providing a theoretical foundation.

The credit for coining the term and for being the first advocate of the approach goes to Kenneth Simmonds, a CIMA member, in a paper presented to an Institute technical symposium in 1981 (see *Simmonds*, 1981a). At this time, he also set much of the later agenda for strategic management accounting especially in the area of determining competitive cost position. His wish was to incorporate the findings of the relatively new subject of business strategy into management accounting. He argued that accounting should be much more outward looking and should help the firm evaluate its competitive position. He first outlined the importance of the learning curve and the strategic importance of the long-term behaviour of costs yielded by this approach in terms of providing competitive advantages. He emphasised the importance of costing competitors in order to determine relative competitive positions and their likely responses to changes in the enterprise's business strategies and investments. Simmonds also joined a number of other commentators who were urging the use of market related data in management accounts and arguing that variance analysis only made sense if it was interpreted in the light of market changes (see *Simmonds*, 1981a and 1981b).

Strategic cost management

The leading proponents of strategic costing in the USA are *Shank and Govindarajan* who call their approach strategic cost analysis. A good indication and selection of their work is given in their recent book (1989) and a more general view is given in *Shank* (1989). Their approach relies heavily on the work of *Porter* and other competitive strategists. They commence their studies of a firm by determining the firm's or the strategic business unit's value chain which isolates each activity that creates consumer value and spans all the functions of the organisation from supply to customer after sales service and the honouring of warranties. The next step is to assign costs and assets to each value activity comprising the chain and to identify the cost drivers for each activity to ascertain the total costs of the value chain and the resources it uses. The final step is to build sustainable competitive advantage either by operating on the cost drivers to reduce costs or by rearranging the value chain, focusing on those activities in which the firm has competitive advantage. Here, the cost drivers in mind are really the cost characteristics of the value activities and of their linkages which may give competitive advantage.

Mainly using the case study method, *Shank and Govindarajan* seek to change accounting systems so that they better fit with the organisation's strategy and can contribute to the formulation of strategy, the communication of strategies throughout the organisation, and the development of methods to implement, monitor and change strategies. Their work suggests that existing accounting methods which were designed for different purposes cannot be expected to aid greatly in the strategic area. This is, perhaps, most startlingly illustrated in their Kinstead Equipment Company case where they look at profit variance analysis from a strategic focus (1989, Chapter 6). (For a similar UK criticism see *Goold*, 1986).

Because of their case study approach, it is difficult to review their work briefly. Here a couple of illustrative examples will be presented. These illustrations cannot capture the full richness of their approach.

Probably their most famous work is the 'Baldwin Bicycle Case' (*Shank and Govindarajan*, 1988). Here, a relatively small cycle firm in the USA in the early 1980s has spare capacity and is offered a relatively low price to supply 'store name' bicycles to a departmental store. A traditional contribution analysis suggests that this offer should be accepted as it yields a very attractive short-run contribution over all incremental costs.

Shank and Govindarajan's approach goes beyond this analysis and considers what accepting the order would do to the strategic positioning and cost structure of the Baldwin Bicycle company. The major concern was that the offer would erode the quality image of Baldwin's existing products and the supplying of the departmental store with lower cost products would provide direct competition to Baldwin's existing customers, retail specialist bicycle shops who may well transfer their demands to other suppliers. Accepting the offer was seen by Shank and Govindarajan as likely to force the firm to reposition itself into the very competitive low cost bicycle market. More generally, by looking at the company from a strategic rather than a traditional accounting short-run perspective, they found that the firm had to adopt a new strategy if it was to survive in the long run.

Shank and Govindarajan (1989a, 1989b) seek to explain the importance of analysing the value chains for the entire industry and not just that part of it accounted for by the firm or strategic business unit being analysed. They also argue there is a need to analyse the value chains of competitors. In each of these analyses, the accountant plays a strong role because

> Each value activity has a set of cost drivers that explain variations in costs . . . Thus, each value activity has its unique sources of competitive advantage (1992, p.182).

They give an example of a firm manufacturing two similar products in the paper board industry in the USA. One product is used for high quality and one for non-differentiated, low quality packaging. The firm is presently focusing on low level packaging, a declining market. They seek to determine the cost structure of the firm and where its profits come from by looking at the entire value chain not just of the firm but also including firms filling the packages and ultimate retailers. It proved not too difficult to determine the costs of each of the value activities in the two value chains for the two packaging products. It was found that those who used differentiated packaging had a very different cost structure from those using undifferentiated packaging. They are able to cost all parts of the value chain, both that part in which the packaging firm is located and those elements outside the firm. They show not only the cost of manufacturing the packaging but also the proportion of packaging costs in each part of the selling process outside the firm. They also estimate the profit in each stage of the process. The profit from undifferentiated packaging represented only about one third of the profit over the whole value chain relative to the total value chain of differentiated packaging. Sales of the non-differentiated product had been declining at about three percent per year whereas the market for differentiated packaging had been growing at ten percent per year and was expected to grow faster still.

This costing of the value chain was used to consider whether the firm should strategically reposition itself in the differentiated packaging market. This would require major investments amounting to some $60 million in a sector where the firm had a weak market position, being regarded mainly as a 'back up' supplier. Moreover, the great majority of the total profit in the differentiated packaging value chain accrued to the buyers of the packaging which gave them great buying power. They would therefore dominate packaging suppliers. Shank and Govindarajan argue that only a value chain analysis could give these insights and any one of the usual methods of decision making would suggest focusing on the undifferentiated packaging market segment. Their hope is that this analysis

> Will encourage more widespread attention to the empirical estimation of value chains as a useful extension of modern strategic cost analysis (1992, p.197).

There is no doubt that their work is innovative and has major practical significance. The approach strongly links accountants to strategy.

Costing product attributes[1]

The crucial point here is to recognise that from a strategic perspective, each of the activities undertaken by the enterprise and

---

[1]This section builds on *Bromwich* 1990 and especially *Bromwich* 1991 with permission.

each of the resources employed should yield an identifiable benefit or set of benefits to consumers for which consumers are willing to pay. The firm should therefore seek to trace the costs of enterprise activities and resources to these benefits, so as to be able to compare the revenues generated by these benefits with their costs. This exercise should be subject to the benefits of this information exceeding the cost of its collection in each case. Each enterprise cost should ultimately be driven by the benefit or benefits it provides to customers. It is these which ultimately drive costs. This category of cost drivers therefore dominate those used in traditional accounting and in activity costing which are utilised to attribute costs only to products and not to the benefits which the activities represented by these costs provide to the consumer.

Focusing on the costs of customer benefits allows the firm's strategic plans to be integrated with its routine operations. It has always been impossible to provide this link within conventional management accounting where strategic planning has generally had to be decoupled from current operations because accounting systems report only the costs of the enterprise's current operations.

Adopting a strategic perspective emphasises that each of the firm's strategies for products and markets should yield the customer some benefit. Figure 5.1 illustrates the link between product benefits and strategies.

Figure 5.1   Market strategies

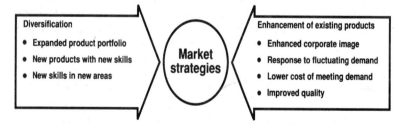

The left and right hand boxes illustrate respectively component elements of two usual strategies: diversification and product enhancement. Each component element of these strategies yields customers possible benefits. For example, an expanded product portfolio provides the consumer with more choice (the left hand box) and the enhancement of an existing product to improve its quality (right hand box) yields the customer clear benefit if this improvement of product quality is relative to competing firms.

Customer benefits need to be sufficient either to retain existing customers or to win new ones in a market where rivals compete in terms of lower product cost, higher quality, and delivery times and, as corporate strategists recognise, where competition is to be expected across a wide range of strategic product variables, not simply price. Indeed, the price of the given package of benefits contained in a product may not be a decision variable for many firms in strongly competitive markets. Concern with consumer benefits suggests that a wide range of techniques are required to produce a detailed analysis of the firm's products and the offerings of its competitors.

Product attributes

The key perspective that allows strategic management accounting to be introduced is to see each product not as a whole or as a unity but as comprised of a number of separate characteristics offered to the consumer each of which the customer is willing to pay for. On this view, products comprise a package of attributes or characteristics which they offer to consumers (*Lancaster*, 1979). It is these attributes that actually constitute commodities, and which appeal to consumers so that they buy the product. Demands for goods are derived demands stemming from the demands for their underlying characteristics. These attributes might include a variety of quality elements, such as operating performance variables; reliability and warranty arrangements; physical items, including the degree of finish and trim; and service factors, like the assurance of supply and of after sales service. It is these elements which differentiate products and appeal to consumers. A firm's market share depends on the match between the attributes provided by its products and consumers' tastes and on the supply of these attributes by competitors.

Only products which yield the *maximum* amount of a *specific* bundle of characteristics for the amount of money the consumer wishes to spend will survive in a well organised market with well informed consumers. Whether a product represents an efficient way for the consumer of buying the bundle of characteristics offered by the product depends on product prices as well as the quantities of characteristics offered by the products. If the price of a product decreases, for example, the quantity of the characteristics per monetary unit it offers increases and more would be spent on it to the detriment of other products. Changes in the prices of products and in the amount of characteristics obtainable for a given price would change which products were regarded as efficient ways of obtaining the bundle of characteristics they offer (see *Bromwich*, 1990).

With this perspective, product characteristics and product cost (and therefore price) can be seen to be deeply intertwined. None of these matters can be considered in isolation.

The market share accruing to each product will depend on consumer tastes and on product prices. Each product will attract that clientele of consumers who like the bundle of characteristics it offers, conditional on its relative price. The firm's strategic decision is therefore to determine the amount of characteristics which will be offered and the product price. A change in market share can be won by offering a different bundle of characteristics, that is by differentiating products, by offering a greater bundle of characteristics at the same price by, for example, introducing cost saving technology and by supplying an existing set of characteristics at a lower price. Introducing a cheaper way of obtaining characteristics should attract demand from the other products depending on competitors' technology and cost structures (and, more generally, on their strategic behaviour in the face of a challenge). The amount of any increase in market share will also depend on consumers' preferences. The introduction of a cheaper way of obtaining characteristics may mean that existing products are no longer worthwhile.

New technologies that allow additional combinations of characteristics will yield new products. Products which mimic the characteristics of existing products have to sell for no more than the price of these existing products. Similarly, new products which offer combinations of characteristics which combine or span the characteristics offered by existing products must be priced so that the characteristics they offer are no more expensive than with the competing existing products.

In real world markets, firms supplying outputs which otherwise would be inefficient in terms of the mixture of characteristics they provide may well survive in the market. Such products may survive in market settings where products are not divisible and cannot easily be used together, as with some consumer durables, provided that they yield a combination of characteristics desired by some consumers. However, such firms are unlikely to be able to resist entry because they are charging a higher price for units of characteristics offered by other firms which are either charging less using the same technology or using a lower cost technology.

This approach may allow Western firms to approach their product strategy in a similar way to that used in Japanese firms. These companies are said to choose a bundle of characteristics which is larger and richer than those offered by many competitors and then determine a price based on a target cost aimed to give them the desired market share. Cost savings are then targeted over time in order to ensure the sustainability of their characteristics and price strategies and to increase their market share over time.

Consumer benefits in strategic cost analysis

The emphasis used in strategic cost analysis will depend on the strategic approach adopted by the enterprise. Those which aim to succeed by producing at a high volume similar products at a relatively low cost to those offered by competitors will generally concentrate on competitors' costs, looking at product attributes only when it is expected that a change in product specification will be made either by the firm or by its competitors. Enterprises which benefit from barriers to entry may concentrate on the costs of maintaining these barriers in strategic cost analysis rather than being concerned with competitors' costs or the costs of providing product characteristics. These latter factors would be considered at times of strategic challenge. Strategic cost analysis of the type suggested here which is concerned to cost product attributes will be used by enterprises which compete in terms of product characteristics they offer and their costs.

The aim of this type of strategic cost analysis is to attribute some of those costs which are normally treated as product costs to the benefits they provide to the consumer for each of those benefits which are believed to be of strategic importance. Not all costs can necessarily be attributed to consumer benefits and for some costs and benefits such an attribution may not be worthwhile.

The first step in a strategic cost analysis of this type is to list separately the product benefits offered to consumers. These benefits will differ fundamentally depending on whether the customer in mind is in the final goods market or is an intermediatory firm in the chain leading to the final customer. With the latter type of customer, the strategic cost approach facilitates analysis by customer rather than product. This is an exercise that many firms are finding difficult in the confines of conventional management accounting.

Table 5.1 provides extracts from an exercise which attempts to model a fast food supplier which provides prepared and partly processed products to its network of selling outlets. An illustrative set of consumer benefits is shown on the vertical axis of the table. To simplify the presentation, it is assumed that all the firm's products provide similar consumer benefits. These benefits can be categorised in a number of ways. In the table, those items directly related to a unit of product (items 1–7) are shown separately from those relating to sales outlets (items 8–11). Product advertising (item 12) provides an example of other benefits not related directly to the other two categories but which can be attributed to the product. The total of costs which can be treated in this way are shown in the row labelled Total Costs Attributable to Consumer Benefits. The penultimate row in the table is for those product costs that can not be attributed to consumer benefits. It is included so that the analysis can be reconciled with product costs prepared in the conventional way where this is appropriate and thought desirable.

Table 5.1 Strategic cost analysis

Illustrative Costs:	Product-Volume Related Costs	Activity Related Costs	Capacity Related Costs	Decision Related Costs	Total Costs
PRODUCT BENEFITS	●	●	●	●	●
1) Texture	●	●	●	●	●
2) Nutritional value	●	●	●	●	●
3) Appearance	●	●	●	●	●
4) Taste	●	●	●	●	●
5 Consistency of above, over outlets & time	●	●	●	●	●
6) Quality	●	●	●	●	●
7) Low cost relative to competitors	●	●	●	●	●
OUTLET BENEFITS					
8) Service	●	●	●	●	●
9) Cleanliness	●	●	●	●	●
10) Outlet facilities	●	●	●	●	●
11) Location & geographical coverage	●	●	●	●	●
OTHER BENEFITS					
12) Product advertising	●	●	●	●	●
Total costs attributable to Consumer benefits	●	●	●	●	●
Product costs *not* attributable to consumer benefits	●	●	●	●	●
Total product cost	●	●	●	●	●

Product volume related costs include material, labour and variable overheads, each of which may be reported separately. Activity related costs include material handling and transport, quality control, monitoring quality and service and site and facilities maintenance, each of which may be reported separately. Capacity related costs include land and building occupancy costs and depreciation and leasing charges, each of which may be separately reported. Decision related costs include product and site design, product and site engineering, quality improvement, marketing, including product advertising and personnel and administration, again each of these costs may be reported separately.

The number of consumer benefits or packages of consumer benefits to which it is sought to assign a cost will depend on the strategy adopted by the enterprise. Thus a firm which concentrates on giving high benefits for only a few characteristics will report only the costs associated with these characteristics. The list of benefits shown in the table is deliberately rather detailed to illustrate the richness of the possible benefits offered even by a seemingly simple product.

An alternative method of proceeding would be to identify the 'core' characteristics offered by competitors and to report only upon the costs of the additional benefits offered by the firm's products.

Costs in strategic cost analysis

The second step in strategic cost analysis is to decide on a set of cost categories for the product. Often a variant of the firm's usual cost classification will be best because this will encompass the matters seen as of concern to that firm and thus reflect its economic environment. In Table 5.1 the overall cost categories chosen are variable product costs, capacity related costs and decision related costs. These cost categories can be further sub-divided into other categories.[2]

Generally, an analysis of the type suggested here will be undertaken separately for each group of similar products. There will also be a need to provide additional statements at the level of the strategic business unit or the enterprise to encompass any customer benefits flowing from diversification of the enterprise product portfolio and other benefits generated at this level in the firm, such as non-product related advertising and providing a 'high-tech' image for all the firm's products.

A UK company selling a number of home cleansing products mainly through large stores practised some of the approaches suggested here (*Rickwood et al.*, 1990). It sought to evaluate the attributes yielded by its products and those of its rivals by market research, by

---

2 Surprisingly, the technical but important problem of joint costs may also arise in strategic cost analysis with respect to costs which are variable with output or with activity, whereas this problem is generally encountered with respect to overheads in conventional management accounting. These cost problems arise in strategic cost analysis because with costs such as materials, labour and variable overheads, each cost component may contribute simultaneously to a number of product characteristics and it may be impossible to attribute part of these costs to each of the product attributes to which they contribute. For example, in a confectionery business, an operation which blends two or more raw materials together may contribute to a number of consumer attributes, such as appearance, taste and texture. Any assignment of the costs of the operation to these attributes would be arbitrary.

One approach to this problem is to bundle these benefits together for this cost category. For example, a fast food supplier which sought to be seen as a lower cost provider of its products using minimally sized and equipped outlets might well only cost the relative value of its products and the costs of providing a good geographical coverage in convenient locations. A more up-market supplier would report on more product and outlet benefits.

contacts with wholesalers and by analyzing marketing literature. A clear thrust towards strategic management accounting was illustrated by the involvement of accountants in these tasks. The benefits of one product were established to be twofold. One benefit was the ease of use of the product relative to competing products. However, the second benefit and the product's overwhelming advantage to the firm was its container which was distinctive but smaller than those offered by rival firms. This meant that the cost of buying a unit of the firm's product was less than the cost of a unit of rival liquids.

This distinctive packaging and smaller container size, by making it difficult for consumers to see whether the product represented the cheapest way of buying the commodity, allowed the firm to disguise a price premium per unit of liquid substantially greater than that of competitors. This analysis helped the firm when a rival firm was found to be aiming to bring out a similarly packaged product.

The firm did analyze in a general way the performance of its rivals but did not seek to collect competitors' costs nor attempt to attach a cost to the major attributes of its own products, although it tried to minimise the use of arbitrary allocations. The threat to its product required it to undertake these exercises which represent important elements of strategic management accounting.

The firm's revised strategy of reducing the price of the product under threat and undertaking a modest advertising campaign (this amounts to adding to the product's attributes in the context of this section) was successful despite a direct cost advantage accruing to the rival firm which was discovered in the study leading up to the new strategy. The continuing need for strategic management accounting is illustrated by this firm's experience. Their rival returned to the attack using its cost advantage and attempted to outperform in terms of product ease of use.

An alternative approach to the above which has been used by Coopers & Lybrand among others is to seek to cost the achievement of key performance indicators providing that these are linked with strategy. With this approach the relative differences in performance on key performance indicators (say, quality and transport) between the firm and its rivals as perceived by customers could be ascertained. The cost of improving a poor performance could be thus compared with the predicted benefits of such an improvement. A growing number of firms practise this approach albeit in a broad brush way.

Strategic investment appraisal

An example of using a strategic cost analysis approach in the appraisal of 'high tech' investments is *Bromwich and Bhimani* (1991). They advocated, with examples, the use of strategic investment appraisal to allow for less easily quantified benefits. This has since been used by a number of consultants. With this approach, a matrix such as Figure 5.2 is used.

Along the top of the figure are shown the potential benefits of a 'high tech' investment. Along the left hand side are the strategy objectives of the organisation. The various benefits of the project are then appraised in terms of the contribution to the firm's strategies. Benefits are of three types. The first is those benefits which can be directly stated in monetary terms; the second is those non- financial benefits which can with ingenuity be translated into monetary terms; and the third is those which cannot be expressed in monetary terms. These, such as the risk reduction and the enhanced firm image believed to be generated by product acceptance, therefore have to be scored subjectively by management. The final score is obtained by weighting each of the scores. The importance of incorporating each type of score will depend on the strategic importance ascribed to the various corporate objectives to which the project contributes. The importance of all benefits in appraising 'high tech' investments is indicated by a firm that accepted such an investment costing $1.86 million even though the project monetary benefits were only about half of this cost. The above approach helps quantify such a difference and aids in indicating the strategic significance of such a project.

Figure 5.2   A strategic planning matrix

Strategies/Benefits	Improved revenues	Lower costs	Higher reliability	Better supply response	Meeting customer require-ments	Fit with other products	Enhanced image	New skills	Better information	Risks of not investing	Cost of investment	Costs of operation	Organiza-tional plans	Total
Product enhancement	X*			X*			X**							
New Products	X*			X**			X**	X**						
Risk reduction				X**										
Cost advantages		X		X										
Improved organizational structure														
Company wide impact														
Monetary items														
Items which can be expressed in monetary terms*														
Scored items**														
TOTALS														

*Items which can be converted into monetary terms
**Items which cannot be expressed in monetary terms scored on a 'points' scale (1 to 10)

From Management Accounting (USA) March 1991

5.5 *Conclusions*

It is not difficult to think of many problems with the approaches suggested in this chapter. It should not be forgotten that some competitor nations do seek in a variety of different ways, reflecting the differing business environment they face, to do much of what is suggested here. The Japanese use of target costing provides an example (see Chapter 6).

In many senses, the consequences of these approaches for accounting are of less importance than the fact that some group of people in the firm are considering strategy in some of the ways suggested in this chapter.

One obvious problem is that, until recently, accountants were not educated in strategy (it now, for example, figures strongly in CIMA's examinations) and may not have played a strong role in strategy formulation. Even today, they may not be asked to input information to this process because accounting information may not be structured in a way that helps strategy formulation. This may mean that the financial consequences of strategies are not sufficiently investigated in decision making.

It is not being suggested here that the accountant should take over the role of strategy formulation or expect to provide all the information required in this activity. Rather, it is being urged that accountants should cooperate with others who 'own' other information relevant to strategy.

Other managers may not wish to share this information and may doubt whether conventional management accounting approaches can portray it correctly. The need for the accountant to cooperate with managers in the organisation is a theme which runs through this book. The evidence is that this is not easy and requires great efforts by all within the organisation (see *Armstrong*, 1985 and 1990). A major problem seen by many critics with this approach are the very considerable information requirements. Formulating a value chain needs information about the market and about competitors. Similarly, costing product attributes requires knowledge of the market, the use of an innovative accounting approach and knowledge of competitor cost structures. This is not really a problem generated by strategic management accounting. Without this information, how can firms make competitive decisions? Many competitor firms in other countries devote a substantial amount of resources to providing this information.

Often, the information does not need to be very accurate. For SMA, we are interested in fairly broad brush estimates: are the costs of competitors ten percent higher or 200 percent higher than those within the firm? Estimates of cost structures can be obtained by studying the technologies used by competing firms. Benchmarking also helps here.

The sources of information are much wider than is often thought and can be obtained from unlikely sources. *Ellis and Williams* (1993) in a book on corporate strategy and financial analysis, devote three chapters to information sources. As an example, investment analysts are often well positioned to provide a great deal of information about an industry in which they specialise. Most industries now have consultants who have great expertise concerning firms in that industry. Quite often firms in the same industry may be willing to share information because their major competitors are overseas.

The implementation of strategic management accounting may be regarded as a principal problem facing accountants. Concerns about strategies and the costs of those strategies are very great. If accountants cannot provide the relevant information others will.

The need to consider the firm's comparative advantages relative to competitors and the benefits for which customers are willing to pay and their costs is the main theme of strategic management accounting. Providing the relevant accounting information configured in a way in which it can be used for strategy is thought by many commentators to be a major contemporary challenge to accountants.

6

Japanese Management and Japanese Management Accounting

6.1 Introduction

This chapter examines the management systems and management accounting practices of Japanese manufacturing firms in the light of research studies of Japan, personal interviews with Japanese managers, discussions with networks of Japanese academics and businessmen, an evaluation of published empirical surveys and articles written in English or translated into English.

The first part of this chapter looks at the social and economic environments of Japanese companies. It also introduces some of the management practices used in large first division Japanese firms and considers their ease of transferability. The impact of both of these sets of factors on accounting is also discussed. The second part of the chapter looks in more detail at Japanese management accounting.

6.2 Japanese 'Magic'

The success of the Japanese economy is legendary. During the 1960s an unprecedented rate of economic growth exceeding 10 percent per year was attained. The major economic shocks of the 1970s, including two major oil crises, were weathered and the average annual economic growth in the 1970s and 1980s was 5 percent and 4 percent respectively. In comparison, generally economic growth in the USA has not exceeded, at most, 3 percent over any significant period.

The Japanese share of world exports has grown from about 2 percent to well over 6 percent per annum in a 30 year period to the mid-eighties while the world share of USA exports has declined by 6 percent to 11 percent over the same period (*McMillan*, 1985). From 1985 to 1991, the Japanese gross national product rose on average by approximately 4.6 percent per annum and exports similarly increased by 6.7 percent per annum (*Financial Times*, 14 August 1993, p. 4). Only Germany came near to matching this record of economic growth and only the USA could match the increase in exports. Even in the last two years Japan has coped relatively well though the impact of recession in 1992/93 is now substantial with zero growth likely to be declared for 1993, with industrial output falling by 4 percent and possibly negative growth figures for 1994. Moreover, it is not yet clear how the problem of the recession, which some see as structural, will be overcome. Substantial voluntary redundancies and early retirements have been declared and bonuses which constitute an important part of some salaries have begun to be cut substantially.

Japanese industrial success is relatively narrowly focused on a number of industries which require a great deal of pre-production planning, can be conducted mainly as assembly operations, embody modern technology, and reward the philosophy of high quality and low costs. Japan has been especially successful in motor vehicle manufacture, electronics of all kinds, the computer industry, office machinery and optics. This portfolio of successful products changes with time. Sunrise industries are strongly encouraged by the government and industry, while sunset industries are ruthlessly rationalised.

The literature in English explaining Japanese management accounting practices, still generally referred to as cost accounting in Japan, has increased considerably over the past few years, often concentrating on what has come to be called 'target costing' and related techniques (see, for example, *Inoue*, 1992; *Morgan and Weerakoon*, 1989; *Sakurai*, 1989; *Worthy*, 1991; and *Yoshikawa et al.*, 1989). Often the available literature explicitly or implicitly urges the use of Japanese practices in Western firms. For example, many authors have taken Hiromoto's suggestions that Japanese management accounting predominantly plays a behaviour influencing role to indicate that Western accounting should be re-orientated towards this perspective (*Hiromoto*, 1988). This tendency may have been aided and abetted by the title of the article: 'Another Hidden Edge – Japanese Management Accounting'. Japan's high levels of manufacturing productivity and quality have also been attributed to its superior system of education, large-scale corporate training programmes and a well executed and integrated industrial policy (*Garvin*, 1984). This desire to unravel the 'secrets' of Japanese economic success in the applications of techniques which are used successfully in Japan is found in a wide variety of disciplines.

A Japanese example of this view is *Hasegawa's* (1986, p.156) statement that:

> There is much about the Japanese system to admire, much that top executives everywhere can put to their own use. With the spread of Japanese methods throughout the world, Japan will make a lasting contribution to mankind.

Similarly, in a foreword to *Japanese Management Accounting* (*Monden and Sakurai*, 1989), Howell, an American, asks 'Now with cost management, will the U.S. again find itself ten, fifteen or twenty years behind?' (p. xx)

Although this chapter focuses on Japan, much of what is said applies to a greater or lesser extent to the Eastern Asian newly industrialised countries of the Pacific Rim, including South Korea, Singapore and Malaysia, the Philippines and Hong Kong. Indeed, Korean vehicle manufacturers are beginning to challenge the Japanese industry. Some of these countries have already moved Japan out of some products and required Japanese firms to site some operations in other countries.

Some experts on Japan regard this wish to transfer Japanese methods and techniques without appropriate alterations as mistaken. *McMillan* (1985) believes that:

> the most common question foreigners ask about books on Japan is straightforward: what can we learn from that country? In a most fundamental way, this is the wrong question . . . . In reality, it is not a matter of learning the Japanese way and applying it to Western practice. Rather, the real questions are why the Japanese see the world as they do, what they intend to do about it and how their institutional arrangements fit their strategies (pp. v-vi).

It is in this spirit that this chapter is written. It is likewise difficult to disagree with *Aoki's* (1988) view that:

Western and Japanese firms can thus learn much from each other that will help make their industrial organisations more efficient and more humanitarian in spite of the cultural barrier. The hope is that the symbiotic development of human capacity and technology may help to fuse cultural differences into a new hybrid in the future. (p. 313)

Although almost every observation about Japan is controversial, there is general agreement that Japanese economic success cannot be traced just to a set of separate individual techniques and environmental factors. Rather, Japanese success is held to flow from mutually interacting institutional and cultural factors, objectives, organisational management practices and a set of interlinking techniques and practices. All of these factors build on and mutually reinforce each other.

Not all commentators subscribe to the view that Japan's longer-term cultural and historical roots play a predominant role in explaining its existing business mentality. However, Japanese management is today sufficiently distinct from that of the West to have led Western management thinkers to examine its characteristics and ponder on its usefulness in the Western business environment. Much literature has appeared in this vein attempting to describe the complexity and richness of Japanese management attributes but with differing degrees of success. There is, however, a consensus that some of the aspects which are central to Japanese-style management in their large companies include: enterprise unions, seniority-based payment/promotion systems, lifetime employment, consensus oriented bottom-up decision-making, lifetime in-company training, recruitment of workers directly from school/university for lifetime employment, and various company incentives and perks, including low-interest loans, company housing and special welfare schemes (*Gow*, 1986). Some industries and smaller companies seem not to fully share these characteristics and have many of the features of similar industries and firms in the West. Small firms of less than 100 employees employ over 50 percent of manufacturing labour force relative to about 18 percent in many Western countries. These small firms in Japan are well known to be substantially less efficient than large first division firms. Although certain of these features of Japanese management are specific to Japanese organisations, it can be argued that others are essentially variants of practices which also exist in the West (*Misawa*, 1987).

Thus the question is not just whether individual techniques are transferable: clearly many of them are being used by at least some companies. Just-in-time (JIT) supply and production methods have been used successfully in firms across the world as have quality circles (see Chapters 2 and 3). All such transfers have had to be adapted to the host environment and therefore utilised and organised in different ways from those encountered in Japan (*Schonberger*, 1982b; 1986). In many ways, this is no different from Japan where almost all the well known techniques are practised differently in different firms. In order to evaluate the transferability of Japanese management accounting, it is necessary to contrast the general environment of Japanese firms with that facing Western firms and similarly to contrast some of the characteristics of Japanese and Western firms. Here the contrasts will generally be between Japanese and UK firms.

6.3 Some Characteristics of Japanese Firms and their Environment

All that can be done here is to give a very succinct picture of the Japanese economic environment. It must be borne in mind that an understanding of management practice in Japanese firms is limited by Western conceptions of what management should constitute. The activities, processes and constituents perceived to comprise Japanese management are based upon what is understood by management in the Western context. Factors thus described as pertaining to Japanese management may actually be implicit aspects and reflections of a much wider array of social, economic and political practices. For instance, the success of Japanese techniques may rely on a process of informal interaction and communication between managers which is not always understood in the West. Each of the factors to be considered below may condition the ease of transfer of Japanese methods to a Western environment. Here we will concentrate on those factors which are especially relevant to Japanese management accounting.

The Japanese home market

The domestic market in Japan is regarded as immensely competitive between domestic suppliers. Market characteristics are usually held to be responsible for the desire of firms to introduce new products as quickly as possible, for providing products in a large number of variants to match the varying demand of consumers, and for the overwhelming objective of Japanese firms to achieve cost reduction relative to their competitors. The market environment in Japan also helps to explain why Japanese firms are seen as predominantly market driven and seek far more information concerning the market than in many Western companies (*Dahlgaard*, 1989).

The strength of home competition in the Japanese domestic market is supported by factors which seem to inhibit imports into Japan (*McMillan*, 1985), though these inhibitions have been relaxed recently. The Japanese distribution system is highly complex, and to Western eyes seems very inefficient. This system traditionally involves many thousands of local retailers of the 'corner shop' variety charging the same prices co-ordinated by trading associations. The market for many goods is highly segregated. Even if there are no non-tariff barriers to be overcome, most imports are handled by relatively few Japanese trading houses which are each part of one of the families of firms which form the large Japanese industrial groups. The above character of the home market helps to explain changes in Japanese production methods.

Production methods

Over time Japanese production methods have changed to better meet consumer demands, especially for product differentiation. This diversification among products has required firms in some industries, especially in electronics, to change their production methods away from mass production to a system of small lot sizes encompassing a wide range of product specifications. It has also required firms to adopt much shorter life cycles. 'Summer' and 'Winter' products are not unknown in some industries, though recent evidence suggests that these trends are being reversed somewhat.

Using data from a number of different samples of large companies, with a sample size varying from 400 to 700, *Tanaka* (1993) has shown that the number of firms claiming to produce a large variety of products has remained relatively stable from 1981 to 1990. The percentage of firms making this claim in 1990 was 73 percent. The switch to new products to meet new market demands is exemplified by the increased proportion of firms having products which have been in the market for less than three years (21 percent in 1986 and 26 percent by 1990).

The proportion of firms claiming to produce small quantities of individual products was 39 percent in 1981 and had risen to 43 percent by 1986 but had declined to 40 percent by 1990. The number of firms with a large variety of products but which can be produced in medium lot size is increasing. Assembly production was used by some 41 percent of firms in 1981 and had increased to some 44 percent by 1990. Mechanical process production similarly increased over this period from about 18 percent of firms for 1981 to 30 percent of firms in 1990. The other major production process, chemical process production, declined from 26 percent to 20 percent over the same period. Interestingly, *Bromwich and Inoue* (1993) found that the great majority of Japanese subsidiaries in the UK were involved only in assembly production. Not dissimilar findings have been obtained for the USA where some 60 percent of subsidiaries are assembly operations.

Tanaka (1993) also provides evidence concerning the automation of Japanese production in 1990. There is considerable use of computerised machines and computer aided techniques (CAD, CAE and CAM), though usage varies across the industry. Ninety percent of assembly firms used these techniques, but only about 50 percent of respondents in mechanical processing employed them. Assembly industries also employed robots and numerical control machines intensively (about 70 percent of respondents). Similarly, these industries used computerised methods for helping in other processes, such as automatic component distribution systems and computerised physical quality control systems. Such methods were used by over 50 percent of the sample in the assembly industry. His findings also confirm *Sakurai's* (1989) discovery of the relatively low use of flexible manufacturing systems and computer integrated manufacture. Such systems were reported as used by around 20 percent of his sample.

The large variety of products manufactured may be one reason why the Japanese are so attached to Just-in-time (JIT) methods. The spread of JIT methods in Japan is, however, much less than generally believed. Its use is focused on relatively few industries and products. Latest estimates suggest that the usage of this method is not greater than 15 percent across all Japanese industry (*Inoue*, 1992).

Management in adversity

The most important factors underlying Japanese success are held to be a society which seeks consensus and co-operation in achieving success, subject to a wide variety of constraints, such as resource scarcity and physical density, and economic shocks which need to be overcome in a way to lead to further success. Many scholars see the social structure of Japan historically and currently as centred around a wide range of social groups and mutually recognised social obligations. The starting point for such groups is the family, the spirit of which has now been extended to voluntary economic associations and groups of organisations. Each of these groups imposes responsibility and loyalty on the individual in return for rewards from the group (see *McMillan*, 1985; and *Nakane*, 1973).

With this view, the essence of conduct is not whether something is seen personally as right or wrong nor whether it is in a person's best interests. As *Uemura* (1989) says:

> In Japanese society the code of behaviour for every person is not whether his behaviour is right or wrong, but whether it is permitted by his circumstances. It is other-orientated behaviour. Permission by social circumstances means specifically the acceptance of a person's behaviour by the group to which he belongs (p. 15).

It is this value orientation which is seen as generating group-orientated thought, behaviour and values in Japanese organisations and is seen as determining the fundamental characteristics of personal conduct in organisations. The necessity to behave in a way acceptable to others may impose very substantial burdens on employees of all ranks. For example, by social convention, it is not infrequent for senior managers to offer personal guarantees to external parties in support of their firm's endeavours.

It may be expected if Japanese techniques are based in group-orientated behaviour that their transfer to at least some countries in the West may be difficult. In many countries, rewards are more geared to individual efficiency. Here, individual behaviour can be characterised by employees seeking to obtain control over their jobs and using this 'ownership' in their own interest, for example, by shirking and avoiding responsibility for their output, to the detriment of other employees and the firm (*Weisz et al.*, 1984). Similarly, in some Western regimes information remains private and is available to be exploited for the 'owner's' benefit, whereas in Japan work- orientated information should be shared.

Other commentators, while recognising the importance of culture, believe that Japanese behaviour can be seen more as a set of rational responses to the pressures of advanced industrial development (*Dore*, 1973). With this view, the late start in economic development by the Japanese means that they are freer of the constraints which inhibit change in 'older' economies. *Aoki* (1988) argues that group behaviour is not necessary for the transfer of Japanese methods. He puts much more weight on:

> the development of 'intellectual skills' in workers which will let them cope flexibly with usual local emergencies, frequent shifts in their tasks, and a new technology (p. 310).

He also emphasises the importance of the Japanese practice of long-term employment in a single company which allows the improvement and promotion of employee skills over a long time period and the long and relentless competition for promotion which motivates employees, and screens out less competent employees for promotion. He sees these factors as being rational responses to the environment of Japanese firms. In his view, such practices with suitable adaptations may well thrive in other countries which do not otherwise share all aspects of Japanese culture.

Overwhelmingly, studies have suggested that the predominant characteristic of Japanese organisations is their wish to harness group behaviour in order to overcome resource and other constraints and economic shocks, using skills gained over a long period in the firm to respond in a flexible manner to such problems.

Thus the Japanese response to the oil crises of the 1970s was not only to adopt energy saving approaches by reducing energy intensive sectors, and to reallocate resources to reduce oil consumption. The more important reaction was simply to become even more efficient in production thereby offsetting the effects of increased oil prices. This illustrates that Japanese firms can be seen as having flexible long-term strategies and as being willing and able to modify their strategies in the light of local and global economic change. This flexibility will be seen in both the characteristics of Japanese management practices and in Japanese management accounting.

Government Intervention And Support

Japanese governmental planning (and that of some other South East Asian countries) goes beyond the usual economic planning of governments in the West. In detailed co-operation with industry, government develops long-term industrial strategies geared towards maintaining raw material sources and increasing exports, both for the economy and for each industry. These plans provide resource support, guidance and information for export-orientated and sunrise industries and similarly support the rationalisation and reduction in size of sunset industries.

The aim is to provide strong direction for market and trade orientated endeavours in co-operation with industry concentrating on likely changes in technology, and to encourage very strong competition in each industry being focused upon. These activities are based on enormous amounts of information on individual industries on a worldwide basis. The relevant ministries are seen as major sources of information about global and technological trends and their detailed possible impact on Japanese industry (*McMillan*, 1985). The general availability of information from ministries has led to a common understanding of problems and of likely future developments within an industry. *Hasegawa* (1986) gives examples of how this planning system can still make mistakes.

Relationships between firms including banks

It is well known that large Japanese companies represent a 'family' of enterprises linked together by the group's trading company. On a formal level, this relationship is represented by interlinking directorships and shareholdings (generally, the directors of companies are line executives of companies in the group). At the informal level, the relationship is emphasised by the co-operation amongst firms in the same industrial family. This relationship between companies is strongly reinforced by the presidents of the firms within an industrial group meeting regularly to ensure that the group has shared goals, policies and information. The sub-contractors of the firms in the industrial group are also seen as (junior) members of the family, manifesting a very close relationship which includes helping sub-contractors to fulfil demands in a very efficient way. Major advantages claimed for this system of closely-knit industrial groups or families are the accumulation and transfer of information and decision making based on extensive discussion amongst the industrial group.

As suggested above, in addition to the interaction in an industrial group, there is substantial co-operation and interchange with government departments. These links are strengthened by senior government officials on retirement joining an industrial group, often in very senior positions.

This and the previous section suggest that one of the major roles of Japanese institutions is to accumulate very detailed and wide ranging information and to transfer this information across a wide range of organisations. Such a focus on the accumulation and distribution of information does not seem to be as manifest in Western economies. In the West, information might be said to be seen often as private to the generator of the information.

Associated with most industrial groups is a 'family' bank which provides both long-term and short-term funds to the companies in its industrial family, and tends to have the maximum allowed shareholdings in these companies (*Aoki*, 1985).

Japanese banks do not stand entirely at arm's length from their customers. There is extensive and frequent interchange of information. Japanese firms are much more heavily geared than Western firms. The average gearing ratio in Japan is about 70 percent debt and 30 percent equity.[1]

Much of equity (some 70 percent) is held by other firms and by financial institutions including banks. Corporate shareholdings represent some 25 percent of an enterprise's equity. These shareholdings are generally agreed to make Western style takeovers very difficult. The relatively high use of debt and the small

---

[1] There are a number of reasons for thinking that this gearing ratio is overstated. Historical cost reserves in Japanese accounting reports understate capital gains accruing to investors. Similarly, banks often require firms to borrow more than they wish in order to obtain credit. Finally, much of trade debts and creditors really represent internal transfers between firms in the same family.

proportion of individual equity holdings in a large Japanese company (some 25 percent) has been argued to mean that Japanese companies can borrow at low cost from banks. *Aoki* (1988, p.112) argues that this is not the case when the amount of debt is correctly evaluated and argues that the average return to stockholding in Japan is not obviously lower than elsewhere.

The great majority of the debt will be bank financed, though the major firms are now seeking to increase equity levels and the use of bonds, often internationally. Many firms are able to finance themselves almost entirely from self generated funds. Japanese banks because of their close co-operation with clients and their detailed understanding of their clients tend to take a much longer-term view of their lending and base their lending on security offered by the company as a whole and on the entire company's future prospects.

Characteristics of Japanese firms

Profit management

In the West, it is generally accepted that firms seek to maximise shareholder wealth and attempt to display a good short-term performance in terms of capital gains and dividends. The lesser importance of equity in Japanese financing, as well as the general desire to maximise economic growth and to increase exports, may help to explain why Japanese firms seem to place less emphasis on the objective of seeking shareholder gain.

A comparison between Japanese and USA firms shows that for American firms, shareholder gain is a joint first objective with return on investment (*Kagono*, 1984). In contrast, the priority objective of Japanese firms is market growth. This objective is given a very high priority in Japan relative to the next preferred objective (ROI). Reflecting this objective, return on sales (ROS) is used by an important minority of companies in Japan, especially in firms using Flexible Manufacturing Systems (*Sakurai and Huang*, 1989). This performance measure is hardly ever found in the West, perhaps because it basically treats investment as fixed or uncontrollable in the short run. Perhaps even more congruent with the underlying objectives of Japanese companies would be ROS based only on direct cost.

Sakurai and Huang (1989) give a large number of reasons for the popularity of ROS in Japan. ROS is very easy to calculate in an environment of high product variety whereas any ROI product figures would lack meaning because of arbitrariness in allocating investment. In 'high tech' factories (with large amounts of investment), ROI may not reflect the worthwhileness of promising products. Both Toyota and Matsushita use ROS to indicate target profits. They take capital investment into account in other ways. Basically, the aim of using ROS is to separate ROI into separate parts: return on sales and sales relative to investment.

Management/labour relations

It is well known that first division Japanese firms pursue a number of management practices which have come to be identified as Japanese. These include recruitment mainly at the entry stage after education, lifetime employment, training within the company and seniority pay and promotion. Lifetime employment is not founded in Japanese tradition, becoming established in the 1950s. It does however seem to fit well into the Japanese system of motivation.

These management practices probably only apply fully to some 10 percent of Japanese corporate employees. Even here, the above description is something of a caricature. Lifetime employment really reflects expected long-term job tenure at the firm and applies only to core employees. Firms also employ contract and temporary workers which give the firm flexibility in the face of changing demand. Also employees can be retired early and 'promoted' to jobs in subsidiaries or in suppliers.

It is equally well known that Japanese firms have what might be called 'in house' unions. These have considerable rights over conditions of service in return for being loyal to the company. This system reflects the fact that enterprises expect loyalty from their workers in return for the benefits offered. These benefits are often quite paternalistic and their receipt requires that the individual permit the firm to be involved with what would in the West be regarded as the employee's private life and that employees get involved in relationships off-the-job. The boundary between the employee's responsibility for relationships on and off the job in Japan is difficult to distinguish. Both help achieve group cohesiveness. Included in off-the-job activities are socialising with both colleagues and subordinates, often with the firm paying, and helping supervisors with their private affairs (see *Uemura*, 1989; and *McMillan*, 1985). All this adds up to a very trying lifestyle. For example, middle managers may have to travel for four hours a day to and from work and may return very late at night, to a home which is supported by company subsidies. In the literature, there are a number of statements that younger employees have more Western attitudes and will rebel against this lifestyle. However, there seems little evidence that this is the case. In effect, if reports are true that the 'hidden' unemployment figure is now 6.5 percent in contrast to the official 2.5 percent reported figure (*Pitman*, 1993, p.29) then any dissent may well be forestalled though firms are beginning to attack this problem.

Wages are based substantially on seniority and do not differ greatly between comparable white collar and blue collar workers of the same age. Increases in salary over a working life are fairly flat. Rather, small merit payments and accelerated promotion are possibly based on individual merit, assessed carefully over a number of years; first on a local office basis but then on a corporate basis, though union agreements restrict the ability to treat workers in asymmetrical ways. Thus, an ambitious employee has the difficult task of working wholeheartedly in support of the group of which he or she is a member while seeking also to demonstrate superiority over the rest of the group. Basically the major promotions may occur around every 10 years in a career, and at each stage a large number of employees are filtered and rejected for promotion. Demonstrated ability to learn and to respond flexibly are important for selection for more senior jobs.

Japanese management practices

Basically the above employment characteristics underline a number of production practices at the work place which have been argued to serve to identify a Japanese factory. These practices include:

(1) equal opportunities for using company facilities, generally only outside Japan;

(2) the wearing of a company uniform;

(3) the use of multi-skilled workers;

(4) management by walking (and talking) around;

(5) group-orientated decision making;

(6) the clean factory movement and

(7) quality control circles and suggestion schemes.

One theme running through this set of practices is a concern to maintain equity in treatment between employees (for example, items (1), (2) and (3)). A second is to obtain the maximum advantage from the groups of workers by allowing groups to have substantial control over their jobs, and by encouraging groups to use their members' skills in joint decision making in order to improve group efficiency (for example, items (5) and (7)).

Quality circles (which often meet outside working hours) are encouraged not only for improvements in operational terms (see Chapter 2) but also as a way of strengthening team work and motivation (*Ishikawa*, 1989). Suggestions by employees are seen as encouraging the taking of responsibility for the job, and as an important part of the worker's role. The number of suggestions made often figures in employee appraisals. It is not unusual for the number of suggestions made by an employee during the year to be very substantial. In 1980, Toyota received nearly 18 suggestions per employee (*Focus Japan*, 1981). Generally, the reward for a suggestion is small but the great majority of them are adopted even when their benefit may be marginal (*McMillan*, 1985).

Japanese decision making

Management by walking around is part of the informal system which allows a manager, as group leader, to obtain information about what is actually happening in his or her area of responsibility, and related areas, and about the views of the group. This is the part of the system whereby supervisors and subordinates are in very frequent informal contact. It is not unusual for local managers to call head office daily even when they seem to have little to say. Thus it can be said

> . . . that the corporate culture nurtures an atmosphere of mutual learning and camaraderie (*Tsurumi and Tsurumi*, 1985, p. 34).

As might be expected decision making in Japanese companies is consensus-orientated. The process for a specific decision commences with opinion seeking at *all* levels both formally and informally. The first step is to do the ground work in many informal discussions, not only to test the climate of opinion, seeing who may be affected and identifying areas of possible conflict, but also to determine likely quantitative and qualitative results and to share information. The objective of this process is to clear the ground for acceptance of the decision by the formal system.

The actual decision process involves the so called *Ringi* system where, after the above ground-clearing, a formal document is written at a relatively low staff level urging the acceptance of the decision. This proposal is passed through each level of management and involves all managers likely to have a view. It only proceeds further when consensus is reached at each level. In many ways what is happening is that the fit of the proposal with company policy and top management thinking is being considered using a bottom-up form of management very explicitly, and all levels of management are being committed to the proposal. Top management make the *actual* decision and explain it to affected groups. In Japan, the most important part of decision making is in defining the problem and in determining whether there is a problem which needs a decision. The formal acceptance of the decision is of far less importance as it follows from the problem formulation and its fit with corporate policy.

This system is difficult for Western managers to understand and it is very slow and cumbersome. It is, however, evolving and the emphasis put upon the system may vary especially where rapid action is required. *Hasegawa* (1986) gives examples where the system was not abandoned even in the face of major crises. Relative to Western decision-making, it helps to disseminate strategy, information and the shared assumptions agreed by top management throughout the organisation. It is meant to ensure commitment at all levels to the firm's strategy and to the corporate view. In contrast, in many Western companies knowledge of strategy and strategic assumptions is seen to be the private property of top management.

6.4 Accounting For Costs and Cost Control

The major trends in Japanese management accounting are fairly clear. One major role of accounting is to satisfy the requirements of financial accounting. Generally, the accounting principles used in financial accounting are imported into the management accounting system. This orientation towards fulfilling the needs of financial accounting is one reason that has been cited for the decline in using standard costing for cost reduction activities, because they are distorted by incorporating financial accounting principles. A major use of management accounting is cost management generally prior to production and the use of estimated costs in planning and cost reduction. Such systems may be separate from the normal cost control system and from the financial accounting system (*Makido*, 1989). A second major role of management accounting is to measure performance in a way congruent with strategy and to help to influence employees.

Overwhelming characteristics of Japanese management accounting are a desire to 'keep it simple', make sure it is understood by everyone, and a wish to use accounting techniques which only further the firm's objectives (*Bhimani and Bromwich*, 1992a). In this area, 'simple is beautiful.' The use of actual costing, and estimated costing (where cost book keeping is undertaken using estimated costs rather than actual costs) provides examples. Another is the use of payback for investment appraisal rather than more sophisticated discounted cash flow models. Though other reasons for this can be found in the Japanese finance system which have been argued to generate a lower cost of capital, the Japanese decision making system does not accord primacy to numerical calculation and encourages concerns about enterprise market growth, especially in an environment of short life cycles. Projects with a short payback period should have high market potential and are said to reduce the risk effects of short life cycles. Moreover, generally investments action an agreed strategy and therefore simple investment appraisal methods may be seen as quite appropriate.

The evidence from a large number of surveys and articles is that Japanese firms seem to use accounting figures much less in decision making than Western firms (see, for example, *Inoue*, 1988). Rather, the focus is on cost management, though it should be understood that relevant accounting figures are considered in the decision making process described earlier; they are just not given the primacy they seem to have in decision making in the West.

Enterprise cost structure in Japan is such that, on average, material and component costs account for some 60 percent of cost, direct labour some 14 percent and overheads some 24 percent (*Tanaka*,

1993), though these percentages vary very substantially across firms. On this evidence, it can be said that material costs are proportionally higher than in the West and that overheads are substantially lower. Similar figures from the USA are material and component costs 53 percent, direct labour 15 percent and overheads 32 percent. In Japan, it is expected that the material and labour cost percentages will remain stable and that overheads, especially fixed overheads, may increase. The higher proportion of material costs in Japanese cost structures reflects the assembly nature of many large Japanese firms.

The final assembly stage often takes place following receipt of material and bought-in parts produced by subcontractors who may at least help design the part and who in turn rely on other subcontractors lower down the chain for their inputs. In many organisations, between 80 and 90 percent of products are already processed by subcontractors (*Yoshikawa*, 1988b). Material cost control thus typically entails monitoring the labour and other overhead costs passed through the subcontractor pyramid to the final assembly plant. The manufacturing unit which heads the pyramid reduces its dependence on the managerial abilities of subcontracting suppliers, by itself playing an active role in evaluating and determining the operations, work standards, quality controls and cost containment practices of subcontracting firms. The corporate head office thus maintains control 'tentacles' throughout the pyramidal chain of suppliers.

Accounting for modern manufacture

There is no doubt that the introduction of JIT and many other modern production systems has substantial effects on accounting. The lack of inventories and the use of fixed and long-term contract prices mean that much of conventional material accounting is rendered redundant, as is much of the work of tracing materials.

The quality standards implemented under JIT mean that much of what is called quality accounting can also be abandoned. With modern operating processes including JIT, the supply of parts and logistic activities can be traced directly to either the production operation or the product batch which causes this activity. In Japan these costs are often encompassed in what are called *other direct costs* (to be discussed later) which, despite their name, may incorporate allocations. Moreover, JIT systems provide real time information in non-financial terms. Such non-financial information is used extensively in Japan. Here, information originating on the factory floor may be reported rapidly to highest managerial levels. Thus, much of traditional material cost accounting is rendered redundant by use of JIT and other modern operating techniques. These processes also reduce the amount of labour used in production. In Japan, these costs are therefore often included in variable overheads and called *conversion costs* (see *Monden*, 1988).

However, the use of methods such as JIT does not mean that accountants are excluded from considering material and components. Rather, they are expected to play a strong role in determining the target costs of material and components offered to suppliers.

Modern managerial flow techniques and accounting

Western views that modern management techniques, especially in the management of material and process flow, have rendered many conventional accounting techniques redundant (*Foster and Horngren*, 1988), may be very narrowly argued. In part, this is because the focus is on savings within the firm rather than over the whole material and supply chain. There is a considerable role for accounting expertise in negotiating with and helping suppliers, at least in a Japanese context. This, perhaps, illustrates a more general problem in Western management where except in some industries relationships outside the organisation tend to be often regulated by contracts rather than by forming relationships or partnerships with those external to the firm. With this Western approach the desired performance of suppliers is specified in detail. Performance is monitored by attempting to measure the impact on the purchasing firm. Extreme mis-performance is to be remedied by compensation, achieved, if necessary, through the courts.

Accounting reports reflect this approach by seeking in variance analysis to present the financial effects of those outside the firm failing to fulfil contracts. The accounting savings flowing from the implementation of JIT are generated in part by a reduced need to account for the effects of contractual performance.

With this contracting approach, which is frequently used in Anglo-Saxon countries, the dominant question is: can a supplier satisfy detailed specifications better than its competitors? Consideration may therefore not be given to whether the supplier is using optimal methods. Opportunities for co-operation in order to gain inter-organisational economies may not be exploited.

An alternative approach is for the firm to enter into more informal partnerships with relatively few supplying firms which are expected to continue in the long term. This is the Japanese practice where a large firm forms partnerships with relatively few first division suppliers who then sub-contract to other firms. These agreements allow the firms to co-operate in production and allow, at least, the purchasing partner access to supplying firms which permits the use of value engineering and engineering and production based control and monitoring systems.

Such a system is used by the Nissan company in the UK (*Truesdale and Carr*, 1991). Here suppliers are selected by inspecting the factory, plant and equipment, but more attention is given to management, people and attitudes and the discussion of possible products and the development, testing and costing of models and of prototypes. The supplier is expected to use dedicated plant and to adopt some aspects of Japanese management including placing more responsibility on operators for clearly defined tasks which are seen as 'owned' by the operator teams. Supplier development teams seek to improve the process and solve any problems encountered, with the emphasis on continual improvement.

Additional accounting requirements and indeed other additional resource requirements, especially involving engineering and planning, arise as such arrangements involve the firm and its partners in seeking to jointly optimise operations. Both parties to the arrangement gain information relative to the usual contracting procedures, experience learning effects, and gain from saving the transaction costs generated by conventional contracting arrangements involving a large number of organisations. They may also gain from exploiting any economies arising from long-term organisational economies and from an ability to enter into risk sharing arrangements better tailored to the risk preferences of the partners to any arrangement.

There are also many costs attached to such supplier partnerships. For example, they make it more difficult for either partner to diversify risk by having a large portfolio of customers or suppliers. They may cause management difficulties and, at least initially, high cost to suppliers and alter the conventional balance of authority, independence and information provision between the parties (*Sako*, 1992; and *Kawasaki and McMillan*, 1987). Little detailed analysis and empirical research exists on this and it is difficult to say whether these arrangements are better or worse than conventional contracting.

Labour costs

Labour costs are, perhaps surprisingly, variable to an appreciable extent over a fairly short period of time in Japan because the lifetime employment system is sufficiently flexible to allow output to be linked to labour input, for instance through adjustments to the allocation of the work force using multi-skilled workers, via 'forced demotions', release of contract and part-time workers, and some early retirement redundancies.

As we have seen labour costs constitute only a small percentage of total manufacturing costs in large Japanese industrial concerns and the causal relationship between labour costs and overhead costs is perceived to be tenuous. However, labour cost is often used as a base to allocate overheads. *Yoshikawa* (1988b) in his study states that '41.2 percent of the companies surveyed absorb overhead costs based on the direct labour hour rate' (p. 6). Japanese firms are said to believe that using direct labour to allocate overhead provides organisational sub-units with an incentive to use less labour (as well as other resources allocated on the basis of labour usage). Indeed, because of the technology used by Japanese firms, most of the parameters of production other than labour are fixed by the design of the product and of the planned structure of production processes. Changes in these parameters occur through product restructuring and the redesign of production processes. Thus, the Japanese justification for using labour costs as an allocation base, even though this base is known to be arbitrary and even though labour is becoming a proportionately smaller component of total manufacturing costs, arises from cost improvement objectives rather than as a means of determining product prices or enabling other types of managerial decisions (such as make-or-buy a product part and lease or purchase equipment).

Overhead costs in plants at the top of the manufacturing pyramid are as low as 5 percent to 10 percent of total product costs because these plants effectively only assemble parts. The level of overheads is largely determined by non-economic factors, such as the perceived need to, for instance, automate, advertise and maintain prestigious offices, so as to produce a desired image of the firm's stature in the business and wider community. It is thus argued that it would only be marginally useful to devise sophisticated control systems for managing overhead costs and 'Japanese managers and academics really prefer a simple method for allocating overhead' (*Sakurai*, 1989, p. 9). Nevertheless, records of a specific overhead category referred to as 'direct other costs' are kept by many firms (*Yoshikawa*, 1988b). These costs, which in spite of their name usually consist of allocated costs, relate to the production of particular products or particular phases of a production process (such as, for example, the use of a robot in packaging a specific product). These 'other direct costs' closely resemble costs which have been termed 'activity driven costs' by management accountants in the USA, though they portray the result of allocation procedures.

Thus, cost management is sometimes also facilitated by maintaining additional 'maintenance' and 'production' accounts to record particular categories of costs. These cost pools enable certain activities to be monitored, such as the expenses incurred in maintaining the productive capacity of new machinery or the level of desired work output per employee.

The usefulness of allocated overhead arises not from a need to satisfy costing objectives but in facilitating cost reduction. Using a particular application base to allocate costs is argued to automatically focus the attention of personnel on reducing the magnitude of the base both in planning and in operations (*Yoshikawa*, 1988a). The aim is to cast light on new opportunities yielded by manufacturing methodologies which provide equivalent or better output with lower resource utilisation. Costing exercises in large Japanese companies can be seen as a mechanism for encouraging innovation and the creation of novel means of production which enhance the optimal usage of available production factors. Costing also promotes the development of new capabilities, given the existence of constraints on input resources. This type of emphasis provides an important indication of the potential which production cost accounts may have for helping obtain new product designs which optimise manufacturing input/output relationships.

One important source of evidence of how cost information is actually used by Japanese managers comes from questionnaire surveys like that conducted by *Yoshikawa* (1988b) of 512 companies listed on the Tokyo Stock Exchange (the study also refers to some earlier surveys). The main industries covered by this study included food, chemicals, iron and steel, pulp and paper, electrical machinery, shipbuilding and transportation. The results indicated that 44.5 percent of Japanese firms use cost accounting for cost control and cost reduction, 25.8 percent for financial statement preparation and 13.5 percent for business planning and control. The emphasis was thus on using management accounting for cost control and reduction. There are a wide variety of accounting procedures for internal purposes that exist within different Japanese companies (*Kobayashi*, 1982; *Tanaka*, 1993).

On the surface, Japanese management accounting does not look dissimilar to Western accounting systems. Surveys suggest some 60 percent of firms use standard costing. Most integrate financial and management accounting systems though a substantial number of firms are developing free standing and specially designed management accounting systems. Budgetary control also figures strongly. One major difference is the use of actual costing where actual prices from previous periods are used instead of standard costs to simplify accounting. Direct costing is used for some purposes by about 50 percent of large firms though it is generally said to be disliked in Japan. This is somewhat surprising as it might be expected that enterprises that focus on increasing the size of their market might find direct costing to be attractive. The great majority of firms (over 80 percent) use absorption cost systems generally based on labour hours as the recovery base. Nearly 30 percent of firms use job costing and some 50 percent use process costing; about 30 percent use both systems. Process costing is especially used in the oil, glass, chemical and steel industries.

Although the number of products is often very large, generally product groups are used to simplify accounting. On average, firms will account for up to around 200 separate products. The number of cost centres seems to be based on the firm's organisation structure, though rather more cost centres will be used than the number of departments in the organisation, especially at lower levels of the firm. Generally, the aim is to try to ground accounting in the real operations of the organisation (*Nagamatsu and Tanaka*, 1988; and *Yoshikawa*, 1988b).

Budgetary control seems to be used more than standard costs for cost control. The role of standard costs seems to guide managers towards the regular cost reductions expected of them, though many firms calculate separate target costs for these purposes.

This emphasis on cost reduction and guiding management towards cost reduction is exemplified by how cost variances are used. Understanding the causes of variances is regarded as important in order to generate necessary improvements. Variances also generate information to be fed into the setting of goals for future cost reduction. Variances are thus seen as signals indicating the need for future improvements. Far less emphasis seems to be put on responsibility accounting and therefore on the responsibility for variances.

Much of the usual monitoring role of standard costing seems to be taken over by using at appropriate intervals non-financial measures or specially constructed cost data. The use of non-financial information for cost control spreads throughout the organisation though such information is utilised more by lower level management. However, it is not unusual for a substantial amount of this type of information to be received daily or very frequently by top management (*Garvin*, 1984).

Links between management accounting and corporate goals

The major role of management accounting in Japan can be considered to be that of aiding the pursuit of the enterprise's objectives especially in the area of cost reduction. Accountants play an important role in what is called 'target costing' which aims to set the cost for new products prior to their production. That is, cost targets are set for each stage of the product's life cycle (planning, design, purchasing and production) reflecting the fact that something like 80-90 percent of costs are set prior to production in some industries.

Targets determined in this way are then used when the product is in the manufacturing stage for budgetary control and for other means of cost control to indicate cost reduction targets of managers. Here, the emphasis is on seeking cost reduction, gathering information and generating additional improvements needed to meet the targets.

These targets embody the enterprise strategy. Top management set the overall target for the company and the enterprise's strategies (*Kato*, 1993) and these are encompassed within lower level targets.

Target costing

Because large Japanese firms deal in global markets with clear market prices, target costing is market orientated. It indicates for each product (and each cost element of that product) what cost reductions (over time) must be achieved by the firm and its suppliers in order to ensure that the company's strategy is realised throughout the product's life cycle.

A preliminary step in this process is for the enterprise to come to a view over the whole product life cycle as to their product strategy in terms of the product attributes to be offered relative to competitors, including options, quality and after sales services, the technology to be used and the desired profit and market share (as determined by senior management). A comparison with expected prices in the market over the product life cycle determines the price at which the product with the generally planned characteristics can be offered in the market and be expected to obtain their target profit and target market growth.

Target profit is often phrased in terms of a target return on sales or in terms of an absolute profit amount. Both of these measures are easy to calculate in a high variety product environment.

Difficulties in pricing using the market for a relatively new product is aided by 'pricing by functions' which is used by many Japanese firms. The product is decomposed into many elements or attributes and a price for each element is determined which reflects the amount the consumer is willing to pay for each element. Aggregating these attribute prices gives the estimated selling price (*Kato*, 1993).

This process requires a great deal of strategic information which often is not collected in the West or is, at least, not used for this type of decision. In order to set strategic targets, detailed information is required about competitors' strategies, their pricing policy, and likely changes over the product life cycle. This information is required in order to forecast the current state of the market and changes over time, and to estimate how successful the firm's strategy will be. Similarly, information concerning the product attributes which consumers value and for which they are willing to pay is required. Target costing thus links performance and strategy by incorporating the strategy of the organisation and communicating and forcing this down the organisation.

It is generally said that the contribution of target costing is in terms of cost management by planning cost reductions in the planning, design, development, purchasing and manufacturing stages of the product. It also plays an important role in satisfying consumer needs at the planning stage, in planning product quality and improving the time taken to introduce new products.

Target costing in Japan is seen as a cost reduction exercise which seeks to get 'cost down' in the pre-production stages. It seeks to force designers to reduce costs, though there is a substantial debate concerning how far target prices should seek to include strategy and how far it should be seen predominantly as a continuing cost reduction device. Such an approach may be supplemented by levying extra costs on non-standard parts, excessive tooling, non-standard or new machines and excessively long parts lists. The procedure contains a number of other lessons for Western firms. One is that prices are determined in the market and reflect competitors' strategies and customers' demands. Attempting to arrive at sensible prices relying substantially on cost plus pricing, however much these are adjusted for perceived market factors as is common in the West, is unlikely to arrive at prices which as fully reflect market characteristics. Target costing also requires that the firm collects and uses a great deal of information external to the organisation. Finally, it illustrates the possibility of incorporating strategy into accounting and performance measurement more generally.

This all suggests that target costing should, perhaps, be called in the West 'target pricing' to emphasise its connections with markets and the firm's strategic objectives.

The process of target costing

It is not intended to describe target costing in great detail. There are now a number of very good descriptions (see *Kato*, 1993; *Sakurai*, 1989; *Tani et al.*, 1993, *Yoshikawa et al.*, 1993). The stages of target costing are as follows:

(1) determine the target price for the product (as above);

(2) calculate the target cost of the product in manufacture after allowing for the desired profit;

(3) prior to production use value engineering teams and other techniques to reduce the expected cost of the product (so called drifting cost) to its target cost (allowable cost), thereby determining a target cost for each component and/or function, and

(4) set aggregate target costs for each production stage and monitor that these are met by using budgetary control and standard costing or a specially designed accounting system.

There are a number of ways of setting target costs. These include the following:

(1) determine the difference between allowable cost (selling prices – desired profit) minus forecast costs determined using current costs;

(2) determine the difference between allowable cost (using planned selling price net of the required return on sales) and current costs, and

(3) apply the desired cost reduction to current costs.

Tani et al., (1993) suggest that method (2) is the most popular in their sample of large firms. Nearly 40 percent of their respondents used this method whereas some 37 percent used method (1) and some 18 percent used method (3).

In the past, target costing has been predominantly used in assembly industries. However, there is now considerable evidence that process industries such as steel and chemicals also use this method.

One of the major difficulties associated with target costing is to decide on the tightness of the targets in terms of the effort required to obtain the target. *Tani et al.*, (1993) found that achieving allowable costs required considerable effort. Another problem is that of deciding at which level of the product hierarchy target costing should be applied in an environment of high product variety. The respondents to *Tani et al.'s* (1993) study indicated that 41 percent set a target cost for each level, 39 percent set this at the product level, and 16 percent used target costing at the product group level. The product level used varied substantially across industries, reflecting the degree of product variety.

The costs to which target costing is applied vary across industries. Generally all direct costs are included as are overheads and depreciation on incremental investments (often depreciation is set over the desired payback of the investment rather than over its economic life). The inclusion of incremental depreciation may reflect the wish of Japanese managers to ascertain as well as possible the incremental costs of products and activities. It might appear that including fixed overheads and depreciation brings uncontrollable costs into the calculation. However, the aim is to focus on feasible cost reductions in these items. It is possible to make suggestions to reduce fixed overheads by, for example, changing the production method to avoid using some fixed resources even though allocated costs are uncontrollable.

Much of the above process can be found in Western firms, though the emphasis seems almost entirely on reducing costs via value engineering rather than linking target cost reductions to market prices and with customer needs. *Kato* (1993) indicates that this method (which is called the 'adding-up method') is also widely used in Japan, where the target cost is obtained more generally by considering the possible cost reductions for each part and component. Target costs obtained in this way are added up to obtain the target costs for the product. This approach is regarded as less sophisticated in Japan as the target cost obtained is not connected to market prices and the firm's profit plans. However, some firms in Japan have moved towards this method because target costs derived from the market may be difficult to achieve following changes in factors beyond the control of managers. In contrast, the adding-up method deals only with factors within the control of managers.

The role of accounting in target costing

The accounting function in Japan (which will include a substantial number of non-accountants; none will be qualified accountants in the Western sense) plays a strong role in target costing and in a minority of cases is in charge of the function. It is generally more likely that this responsibility will reside with product planning, development or product engineering. Sometimes accountants are not included in the target costing team (in some 60 percent of firms, according to *Tani et al.*, 1993). In 20 percent of firms, the accounting department is in charge of preparing the information for target costs.

However, it is generally the accounting department's job to monitor the achievement of target costs especially at the purchasing and manufacturing stage.

Tools for target costing

In Japan, value engineering is an activity which helps to design products which meet customer needs at the lowest cost while assuring the required standard of quality and reliability. A number of tools are generally used in this activity. These include:

(1) Functional analysis

The aim here is to determine the functions of the product and indicate how far the design of these functions will satisfy the consumer (ascertained by market research) and at what cost relative to that part of the target cost allocated to that function. This allows the variance between the target cost per function and its current cost to be calculated. It also allows the contribution which a function makes to consumer needs to be ascertained relative to its cost, thereby leading to redesign where two items are not well matched (see *Yoshikawa et al.*, 1993; *Tanaka*, 1989).

Yoshikawa et al., (1993) make the point that with the widespread use of functional analysis in the firm 'a logical development is to incorporate costs by functions as well as parts' (p. 69), though they indicate that ideally the system would be set up to identify variable costs associated with each function.

(2) Cost tables

Cost tables are detailed simulated databases (generally, not yet computerised in Japan) of all the costs of producing a product, either for product functions or product components, based on a large variety of assumptions. Thus, they allow very quick answers to 'what if?' questions relating to decisions to change any aspect of the product. Such tables may well include simple mathematical versions of cost functions which, for example, show how changes in the material components of products will alter cost. Thus, a cost table will show the variety of cost performances when using different types of materials for a given component. The data in cost tables will be accepted by all members of the organisation, and therefore ensure common thinking throughout. There will be a cost table for each part of the product's life cycle. *Yoshikawa et al.*, (1993) see cost tables as the property of accountants. However, *Tani et al.*, (1993) suggest that the responsibility for these tables is spread around a number of departments in different firms, though accountants can make a substantial contribution to these tables wherever the responsibility for them is located. The use of cost tables does not seem well known in the West (*Yoshikawa et al.*, 1993).

(3) VE collections

These are libraries of case studies of the detailed experience from previous VE activity, the use of which is to improve future target costing and VE. Of course, all the other well known techniques used in Japan, such as JIT methods and quality circles, are utilised, where appropriate, in target costing exercises.

6.5 Conclusions

The adoption of any accounting technique from a foreign context is not a straightforward task because of associations with other factors, such as those discussed earlier, not fully understood by information systems designers and planners. One possibly important lesson for Western producers is the close link between corporate strategy and the organisational accounting policies, systems and processes evident in Japanese firms. For instance, reduced product costs may be achieved by tying design and the use of non-standard components to costs as noted earlier. This offers new possibilities for the design of information systems in Western firms. Western firms might find it fruitful to analyse with greater diligence how their cost accounting systems relate to their strategic objectives and find means of bridging any gap that is found to exist (*Bhimani and Bromwich*, 1991).

Likewise, it is important to appreciate the reasons why accounting numbers are de-emphasised by the Japanese in certain instances. The Japanese manufacturer's concern with quality is paramount and where accounting numbers cannot fully help, non-financial measures gain significance especially in the light of advanced manufacturing technologies being utilised which provide raw non-financial data. Many Japanese firms use measures, such as rates of unexpected equipment failures, ratios of preventive and corrective maintenance to total maintenance, reject rates and so forth to monitor quality

(*Schonberger*, 1982b). Western firms are only now beginning to appreciate the value of non-financial quantitative and qualitative data (*Bhimani*, 1993; 1994a). *Drury et al.*, (1993) indicate that many large firms in the UK often or always use non-financial measures, though it is unlikely that such measures are reconciled with the results produced by the accounting system or reported as part of the regular accounting package.

Bromwich and Inoue (1993) provide some insights into the ease of transfer of Japanese techniques into British and American Japanese subsidiaries. Generally, it was found that the most easily transferable techniques were the items which tend to identify a Japanese factory, such as equal use of facilities, company unions and group decision making. More difficulty surrounds the transfer of employment conditions such as using multi-skilled workers (even though some firms have been very successful here), because of the general labour/employment relations in the host country. Similarly, Japanese firms have had difficulty in introducing the Japanese contractor system. As yet, especially in Britain, few of the subsidiaries are strongly involved in planning and strategy, therefore their accounting departments are mainly involved in helping to seek cost reduction improvements imposed by head office.

Understanding how Japanese firms design and use management accounting information enables us to assess the potential benefits which can accrue if aspects of these information systems are adopted by UK firms, but such knowledge must be used with care, as many of the systems used in Japan seem especially tailored for Japanese use and rely on specific Japanese factors. However, a number of the approaches discussed here, such as cost tables, seem fairly context-free. Similarly, management accounting systems in Japanese firms are used more for motivating employees to act in accordance with long-term manufacturing strategies than to provide senior management with precise data on costs, variances and profits. The perceived need for accounting information in Japanese firms is different from that in the UK and USA where costing objectives often carry more weight, especially for financial reporting purposes. Cost data is not significant in determining product prices for a large segment of Japanese firms because target prices are based on the potential for marketability. However, if firms in the West place their emphases differently from the Japanese, this should not be taken automatically to mean that Western firms are at fault and ought to adopt the Japanese viewpoint. Nevertheless, Western firms may, as *McMillan* (1985) suggests, do as the Japanese do:

They study and learn from foreign techniques, selectively apply foreign ideas and adapt them to the domestic environment. Foreigners themselves would do well to 'copy' or 'imitate' this approach (p.v).

7

The North American
Perspective

7.1 Introduction

Some North American accounting scholars, consultants and
practitioners have over the past decade been most vociferous in
calling for management accounting reforms. Their concern, that
management accounting faces a state of crisis, is based on a
particular historical appreciation of changes in USA accounting
practices, as well as on the results of empirical studies and on
prognostications as to the future of management accounting if
changes are not implemented. Critics have, in certain instances,
been specific in their view of the problems by questioning whether
conventional accounting systems are able to capture, process and
convey data for both financial and operational decision making
within advanced manufacturing environments. For example, *Kaplan*
(1984, p.101) has indicated that:

> . . . an accounting model derived for the efficient production
> of a few standardised products with high direct labour content
> will not be appropriate for an automated production
> environment where factors critical to success are quality,
> flexibility, and the efficient use of expensive information
> workers and capital.

In effect, *Kaplan* (1983; 1985; 1986; 1988a; 1988b) sees management
accounting as lagging behind the times especially in view of
technological developments and as presently facing the important
challenge to devise new internal accounting systems supportive of
companies' changed manufacturing strategies. His view is that in
many instances, by the late 1980s:

> . . . companies had recognized the limitations of traditional
> cost accounting systems for measuring, motivating, and
> evaluating manufacturing performance (*Kaplan*, 1990a, p. 10).

This perspective is also echoed by *Neumann and Jaouen* (1986, p.132) who stress that:

> . . . traditional cost accounting data is obsolete in a repetitive manufacturing environment . . . cost accounting's dual purpose of planning and control must be redesigned.

Likewise, *Howell and Soucy* (1987a, p.27) reiterate that:

> Product oriented flow lines, automation, and information technology demand that management accountants reassess control and product cost determination.

The argument has largely centred on the view that managers faced with having to make decisions in complex technology driven situations are supplied with information by their firm's internal management systems which is inadequate. The general view of critics in North America is that traditional cost accounting systems 'are at odds with the realities of the new manufacturing environment' (*Lammert and Ehrsam*, 1987, p.32).

Much of this discontent stems from documented case studies and applied research. For instance, one empirical study of five USA manufacturing companies using flexible manufacturing technologies and novel modes of work organisation including JIT approaches, MRP systems and elements of CIM, has suggested that these companies recognised that their management accounting systems did not form 'a basis for adequate coordination and control in a modern environment' (*McNair and Mosconi*, 1986, p.30). More generally, *McNair, Mosconi and Norris* (1988, p. XVIII) have noted that:

> . . . the management accounting profession is following, not leading, the process of change and is often inhibiting rather than instigating productive manufacturing change.

Such criticisms levelled at accounting have continued to surface recurringly. Although some critics have viewed cost accounting as the major obstacle to making US manufacturing competitive (*Goldratt and Cox*, 1984), others have proposed alterations, if not an expansion, in the role of accounting. It is not clear however, that North American concerns over the state of management accounting are a purely logical reaction to the changing manufacturing environment. The adoption of flexible technologies and the transformation of markets globally may well affect the validity of accounting information. But, more importantly, these factors may have brought into clearer focus, certain pre-existing accounting and management problems. Thus, it has been argued that it is the short-term orientation of American managers that partly must bear the responsibility for the type of information which accountants supply (*Hayes and Abernathy*, 1980). Emphasising short-term returns and immediate profit yields has not been an accounting invention though accounting is strongly implicated with its stress on short-term control measures such as ROI and variances and the emphasis on ascribing responsibility for poor short-term performance. These characteristics of accounting must be seen as being linked to factors including the very ethos of American managerialism and the underlying spirit of business pursuits in general. Whereas short-termism may be appropriate behaviour in certain instances, within a climate of intense global competition, longer-term goals underscoring strategic positioning and sustainable profitability may have to take precedence. The 'problem' with accounting is thus not simply an inability to supply relevant information to managers in the face of a changing manufacturing environment, but the manner in which ideas about what constitutes accounting 'relevance' is changing.

Some accounting scholars and practitioners in the USA have adopted a proactive stance and are redesigning accounting systems and devising novel approaches to determining costs which attempt to provide information tied to newly emerging notions of critical success factors. For instance, at an early stage, *Kaplan* (1983) advocated the inclusion of non-financial and longer-term performance measures in accounting evaluations. Likewise, in the context of using discounted cash flows in evaluating AMT projects, *Hayes and Garvin* (1982) pointed out the inappropriateness of such techniques in appraising the long-term benefits of such investments given that the discounting process penalises distance returns. *Brimson* (1988) has similarly advocated activity and cost driver analysis as one approach to overcome the problem of near-sightedness. As such, much of the normative accounting literature attempts to deal with broader issues of managerial style including the presumed excessive emphasis on the short-term time horizon. Accounting can guide managers but cannot remedy poor management. A concern with the short term ultimately will translate into the development of short-term financial measures.

The concern with the short term would seem a root cause of much of the disquiet about accounting. Alternative accounting approaches to aid enterprise management have thereby been advanced. The source of short-termism has been linked to the demands and expectations of investors and shareholders, thereby indirectly affecting the nature of accounting information. The historical relationship between accounting information for external parties and managerial uses of accounting information has consequently recently become the focus of attention. *Johnson and Kaplan* (1987) have argued that until the early decades of this century, in USA, at least, management accounting evolved independently of the principles governing the preparation of financial accounting. However, from this time, the dominant concern with financial accounts hindered developments in internal costing techniques. Management accounting became subservient to financial accounting particularly after the Second World War when increased demands were being placed on financial reports. The increasing reliance on audited financial statements placed a premium on objective and verifiable figures. With this view, accounting information gave precedence to auditability rather than management needs. This perceived primacy of financial reporting over management accounts is held to lead to a number of problems. In particular, product costing in manufacturing companies was replaced with a form of internal accounting which failed to trace each product's consumption of resources for cost management purposes. *Johnson and Kaplan* acknowledge that nothing prevented managers fifty years ago from properly attributing product costs for internal purposes, rather than simply expressing these as a lump sum for financial and tax purposes. But they argue that:

> . . . given the costs, at that time, of operating multiple accounting systems, the benefits from a more accurate product costing procedure may not have exceeded the costs (*Johnson and Kaplan*, 1987, p.246).

In many companies still today, management accounting is said to primarily serve the needs of financial accounting. The valuation of inventory for external reports allocates indirect costs arbitrarily without tracing them to their cause. This allocation process may satisfactorily meet the objectives of financial reporting to portray overall profit figures and provides data for inventory valuation. But as discussed in Chapter 3, this approach is likely to be inappropriate for making decisions about, say, individual product prices and sales mixes. Product costs based on the principles of financial cost accounting are viewed as distorted, since in a multi-product firm, cross-subsidisation arising from the misallocation of overhead costs often exists. With this view effective strategic production decisions are consequently subordinated to financial accounting requirements. The budgeting system linking managerial rewards to departmental return on investment profit is said to further exacerbate the situation for enterprise segments. This problem occurs because internal decisions about product management are directly linked to financial reporting criteria.

All in all, the perceived malaise of management accounting has been attributed to its 'subservience' to financial reporting objectives. Although this line of argument has been found compelling in many quarters, it suggests lack of managerial ability, if not laxity, on the part of senior corporate executives for over five decades in allowing financial reporting obligations to determine internal management information priorities and distant enterprise strategies. *Johnson and Kaplan* (1987, p.246) believe that the treatment of many expenses as:

> . . . period rather than product costs has become so ingrained, few companies attempted to understand better the costs of their diverse . . . activities.

The idea that management accounting needs to dissociate itself from the dictates of financial accounting priorities and to return to late nineteenth century principles of cost management (i.e. independent of financial accounting concerns) has gained considerable currency among North American accounting commentators. Innovations in cost management are now attempting to reverse the 'fall of management accounting' (Ibid). Changes are taking place to respond to a variety of factors including a prioritisation of business strategy and global competitiveness, the primacy of the long term over the short, the changing face of manufacturing as well as the service and even the public sector and, finally, the challenge posed by oriental management philosophies. Over the past few years, sufficient empirical information has surfaced about North American companies' adoption of prescriptive accounting methodologies to enable initial observation of the nature and benefits of these changes to be made.

7.2 Accounting Innovations: the North American Experience

Much of the evidence concerning the propriety of altering cost management systems in American companies has emerged from case studies compiled at Harvard Business School in the USA (many of these are reproduced in *Cooper and Kaplan*, 1991b; see also *Cooper et al.*, 1992). The early focus was primarily on the impact of activity based costing on costing accuracy and the consequent uses of this product costing information. *Cooper and Kaplan* (1991a, p.130) see the evidence as suggesting that:

> ABC has emerged as a tremendously useful guide to management action that can translate directly into higher profits.

Ascribing increased profitability to the implementation of a costing technique such as ABC is a difficult if not foolhardy exercise. Problems arise in tracing changes in the 'bottom line' to managerial action associated with altered costing information. Moreover, the inability to isolate the effects of a single change such as the adoption of ABC *ceteris paribus* and to use another company as a 'control' for comparative purposes makes any assertion of a profitability link dubious. Perhaps the ultimate test of establishing whether a switch from a traditional cost system to ABC yields increased benefits is to ascertain whether such a switch becomes a permanent one for a sufficiently large number of companies adopting ABC. Given the relative novelty of this costing approach, however, it is probably too early to apply this test. Moreover if, as *Johnson and Kaplan* have suggested, inappropriate costing approaches can become 'ingrained' (1987, p.246) so as to prevent a better understanding of costs, then even the permanency of a switch to ABC by a large number of companies cannot be taken as conclusive of definite benefit stemming from ABC. One embedded system may be replaced by another which becomes equally ingrained. The profitability of altering costing mechanisms within an organisation should not be seen as an appropriate decision criterion, particularly over a short time frame since, given the relative infancy of the ABC approach, at this stage this would be tantamount to myopia.

It is significant that case studies in cost management often shed greater light on managerial perspectives and priorities than on the integrity of a costing approach. In examining the case studies supporting activity costing, it is difficult to escape the view that some of the documented problems of USA companies which have been the subject of ABC case study literature are more fundamental than can be solved by reforming their accounting systems. The companies reviewed sometimes seem, for example, to be wedded to providing a full range of products using cost dominated prices and appear to be willing to go to extraordinary lengths to provide spare parts for often long cancelled products. This may not be as sensible a policy as concentrating on a few high volume products. The large number of products also seems to force important strategic decisions down to very low levels in the managerial structure. Similarly, routine accounting workers are used to make important decisions which, at least ideally, need a consideration of future results. Pricing seems to exercise a great deal of management time and is often approached using routine methods resting largely on cost plus calculations. In many ways, these issues relate to business policy and management style rather than the efficacy of the cost management system in use.

Perhaps of equal significance is that investigations of internal costing practices and the potential impact of changing a costing approach illuminate the effectiveness of managerial priorities and attributes. By directing managers, accounting personnel and other employees' attention to operational and economic problems of an enterprise's functioning, knowledge about the wider aspects of the organisation beyond that provided by a simple change of accounting approach does not emerge. Most case studies offer little information capable of being generalised across a range of companies and industries except to show that altering cost management practices can unravel much about general management which may otherwise remain unarticulated. Indeed, many case studies implicitly generate the view that a main benefit of ABC is that it makes visible seemingly weak management strategies rather than directly influencing them.

In addition to case studies examining individual instances of altered accounting systems, a number of aggregate surveys to investigate cost management practices across a range of companies have been undertaken. Some surveys have focused on costing mechanisms which have only recently been documented in the accounting literature. For instance, product life cycle accounting offers one novel costing approach which has not yet found wide usage but which has been identified in companies as revealed by certain studies of cost management practices (see *Lammert and Ehrsam* (1987) for example). The following section discusses product life cycle costing, which is used by some American enterprises, and discusses a survey of companies using this costing approach.

The adoption of flexible production techniques and changes in the way in which products are manufactured have affected the production cost mix in many organisations. As discussed in Chapter 3, traditional costing systems emphasising the allocation of overhead costs on the basis of shrinking volume-related application bases have been criticised as being inadequate in capital-intensive technology-driven production environments. Likewise, standard costs have been seen as being inappropriate where standards need to be revised very frequently, where decision-making information has to be acted upon on a real-time basis and where continued improvement philosophies are being adopted. In addition to these problems with standard cost reporting in advanced manufacturing environments, a further drawback is the excessive focus on costs incurred during the production phase of a product rather than on other activities prior to and following manufacture where high levels of costs may be incurred. It has been reported that at least 80 percent to 85 percent of a product's total costs from inception to abandonment tend to be committed by decisions made early in the product's life cycle at least in some industries. Moreover, where cost management is a concern, it is notable that an outlay on pre-manufacturing activities such as product conception, design and testing, as well as market analysis, can render a ten-fold saving at the production and post-manufacturing stage (*Engwall*, 1988).

Perhaps of particular relevance to costing in the context of a hi-tech environment, is the fact that enhanced production capability and flexibility, increased competitiveness and greater product diversity potential, enable products to emerge swiftly in the marketplace and exit making way for new ones just as rapidly. Product life cycles in many industries are thus becoming much shorter. This is the case especially with certain products made by Japanese companies. The time frame over which a product is produced relative to the pre- and post-manufacturing stages is shrinking. Any cost system whose standards solely encompass production activities is unlikely to enable costings of organisational processes which increasingly represent a very high proportion of total product costs especially in the face of shortening product life cycles. As a consequence, many accounting commentators are now advocating product life cycle costing as an essential part of cost management strategies.

Life cycle costing

The US Department of Defence developed life cycle costing during the 1960s as part of an attempt to assess the effectiveness of government procurement. Since then, for the profit seeking enterprise, life cycle costing in general and as it relates to a firm's budgeting process in particular, has been seen to be an important means of enhancing profitability (*Czyzewski and Hall*, 1991).

The term product life cycle has been defined as:

> The period that starts with the initial product specification and ends with the withdrawal of the product from the market place. (*Raffish and Turney*, 1991, p.61.)

From a marketing perspective, a product's life cycle has been described in terms of different phases: introduction, growth, competitive turbulence, maturity and decline (*Wilson*, 1991). For costing purposes however, the production perspective is more relevant since it helps identify changes caused by the adoption of advanced technologies. *Susman* (1989) however has suggested that integrating the marketing perspective with the engineering approach offers important benefits. The various production related stages include product conception and design, product and process development, production and logistics (*Shields and Young*, 1991). Figure 7.1 indicates the stages over which funds are committed towards a product and the actual cash flows spent. A large portion of the funds commitment takes place during the product conception phase whilst 80 percent of expenditures are determined prior to the start of production, depending on the industry.

One survey of nine European and USA aerospace and electronics firms which have adopted product life cycle cost management systems (PLCCM) suggests that:

> Existing cost accounting systems are not effective for PLCCM (*Shields and Young*, 1991, p.44).

Partly this is because:

> Product manufacturing costs are emphasised at the expense of pre-manufacturing and post-manufacturing product activities (Ibid).

Figure 7.1 Life cycle costs from a production perspective

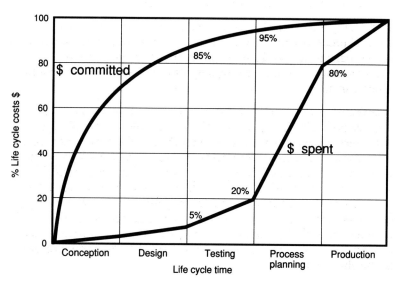

Adapted from Burnstein, 1988, p.261

Moreover, the authors of the study note that, in general, there is growing acknowledgement that the organisational structure adopted by most firms for product design and manufacturing is not effective. In many firms, individual functions or departments have an interest primarily in finishing their share of a project without considering how their work may affect the work of other departments or functions. For instance, the engineering department of a company may design a product as fast as possible in response to pressure from marketing and top management, but with little concern about the quality or producibility of the product. Manufacturing then takes over and decides how to make the product. Manufacturing consequently faces the added problem of having to build quality into the product since quality and producibility were not designed in by the engineering department. In spite of the general recognition of this problem, the survey results suggest that:

Existing cost systems tend to be oriented too much toward
reporting departmental or functional area costs rather than
product whole life costs by activity (Ibid).

In this respect, even where the structure of organisations and
internal processes are able to overcome certain problems caused by a
sequential and uncoordinated approach to engineering and
manufacturing, costing systems may still impede the management
process in an indirect way.

Shields and Young (1991) suggest on the basis of their survey that
organisations which implement PLCCM should use 'whole cycle
costs' rather than the more limited producer's life cycle costs only.
Whole life cycle costs offer a consumer's perspective which includes
purchase, operating, support, maintenance and disposal costs. These
are important to consider as the costs that a purchaser incurs after
buying a product are becoming a larger percentage of whole life
costs and therefore have a bearing on purchase decisions. The
producer must feel compelled to consider all product features that
concern the customer rather than just those that affect the producer
in the short run.

It has been noted that:

Actual formal applications of life-cycle costing are relatively
rare (*Seed*, 1990, p.29).

Whether cost management practices broaden to encompass some
notion of life-cycle accounting in the future remains to be seen. An
awareness that:

Products behave somewhat like biological organisms in that
they are born and eventually die (*Susman*, 1989, p.8)

has long been recognised. Accounting professionals have not
however shown an overwhelming concern to respect this view, and
in practice little seems to have been brought into operation by way
of product life-cycle cost management. With the advent of AMT
and the capacity to launch rival products flexibly and rapidly in
competitive markets, product life cycle accounting may be given a
more thorough consideration by many companies. In the USA, one
hurdle to be confronted is that:

Life-cycle accounting would require changes in the GAAP [Generally Accepted Accounting Principle] model (*Peavy*, 1990, p.32).

Others will no doubt surface but will likely be addressed if and once accountants perceive value in doing so.

General trends in cost management

Other studies have considered cost management practices more generally. For instance, in 1987 the National Association of Accountants (NAA) in the USA with Computer Aided Manufacturing International (CAM-I) commissioned a study on the state of the art in management accounting in automated factory environments (*Howell et al.*, 1987b). The study encompassed an examination of current practices in the areas of investment justification, cost accounting and performance measurement using questionnaires, interviews, literature reviews and the personal experiences of the researchers. The project consisted of a survey of 1000 management accountants and 1000 operations executives across a broad array of industries as well as interviews with over 150 executives from 17 leading manufacturing companies. The focus of the field interviews was on determining '. . . . how management accounting was adapting to specific initiatives on the plant floor' (Ibid., p.1), including automation, intensive quality controls and innovative inventory control practices.

The study revealed that capital investments were justified on the basis of both qualitative and quantitative factors. Qualitative factors relating to operating performance, market penetration and manufacturing efficiency were considered more important than strict financial projections. Quantitative measures emphasised material, labour, cost of quality and manufacturing efficiencies. The respondents believed that budget limitations and a short-term orientation were principal obstacles to investment making. They also placed importance on forecasting, quantification of opportunity costs (i.e. evaluating the implications of not undertaking the investment by comparing this outcome with that of the proposed investment) and on performing post-audits on investments undertaken.

The cost accounting systems used by respondents varied widely but emphasised standard costs and full cost determination using either job order or process costing. One third of respondents used a single manufacturing overhead rate for cost allocation and particular concern was expressed over finding bases for assigning overhead using means other than a single rate. However, management policies, habit and the lack of understanding of alternative methods were cited as barriers to improved cost accounting practices.

Financial indicators of performance were found in the study to stress sales, growth and income, whereas non-financial indicators stressed market share, labour productivity and delivery service. The companies had developed means of monitoring quality, delivery, throughput, scrap, yield, and machine performance. The authors of the study also reported that informal measures of vendor rating, product development, customer service and the cost of non-performance were also developed by the firms surveyed. Performance measures were said to be generally less satisfactory than investment appraisal methods or cost accounting techniques, particularly in view of their short-term orientation.

A smaller scale study undertaken by *Banker and Johnson* (1993), introduced a new approach to examining whether cost drivers other than volume help explain firm cost behaviour. The links examined were between the cost of complexity and diversity and certain organisational transactions in service industries. Their study lends support to the usefulness and effectiveness of using cost drivers as means of tracing costs to products as opposed to simple allocation using conventional methods. Specifically, the study investigated traffic statistics relating to the USA airline industry by estimating a system of cost functions with multiple cost drivers. The main conclusion was that

> . . . while output and volume are primary cost drivers, factors reflecting product diversity and production process complexity, which have been suggested as potential cost drivers in the manufacturing sector, are important secondary cost drivers (p. 29).

Another investigation by *Foster and Gupta* (1993) evaluated cross-sectional data from thirty-seven facilities of a USA multi-national electronics company. They likewise concluded that variables based on volume, complexity and efficiency were associated with actual manufacturing overhead costs but that volume based variables had the greatest level of influence. Both these studies suggest that cost driver analysis may be useful for product costing and lend support to calls for reforms in costing procedures. A number of other statistical studies of aggregate data have sought to test the hypothesis underlying ABC systems. *Datar et al.*, (1993) find that quality costs at a specific site are affected not only by volume. They find that a variety of measures of the complexity of products and of machines also significantly affect overhead resources. Importantly, they also indicate that the effects of a variety of cost drivers may interact and offset each other. Increase in scrap costs with product complexity is offset by activities aimed at preventing increases in quality costs and at managing complexity. To a degree this suggests that the independence of an activity from the level of other activities assumed with ABC needs to be reconsidered. Studies of this type may, like the more familiar case studies, generate different estimates of the firm's cost function. It has been argued that they cannot show that their estimates are better than others in terms of accuracy or in terms of the consequences of using their estimates in decisions (*Dopuch*, 1993). However, they can shed light on the form of cost functions by demonstrating whether their hypotheses fit well with the data. *Christensen and Demski* (1991) have suggested that these types of studies are likely to be prone to many different statistical problems especially that of measurement error stemming from omitted variables. Another thrust of recent statistical research is to investigate the effects of combining activities so as to use fewer cost drivers (*Babad and Balachandran*, 1993; *Hwang, Evans and Hegde*, 1993).

In Canada, a study of managers of plants supplying parts to General Motors of Canada focused specifically on the relationships between the adoption of flexible automation and aspects of accounting systems (*Dimnik*, 1988). The study revealed that the adoption of flexible technologies in the plants was, in the main, unrelated to financial criteria used in evaluating such projects. Moreover, difficulties in quantifying the potential benefits of automation were of little consequence in determining the adoption of the technology. The study also reported that managers who make use of labour related cost information even where labour amounts to no more than 5 percent to 10 percent of total manufacturing costs, do not use accounting systems naively. Indeed

> . . . because of their experience with their manufacturing process and an understanding of the relationship between the

process and accounting numbers, these managers make good use of their management accounting and control systems (*Dimnik*, 1988, p.180).

The results of this study pose a challenge to allegations against management accounting. *Dimnik and Kudar* (1989, p.16) reflecting on the results of this study are convinced that:

> . . . there is no crisis in management accounting and that managers should not abandon their current accounting systems.

Moreover, they affirm that:

> In opposition to those who suggest revolutionary changes in accounting, we argue for evolutionary development of the discipline (Ibid).

A study conducted in 1992 for the *Society of Management Accountants of Canada* by *Nicholson and Armitage* (1993) considered ABC adoption by 352 Canadian companies of which 88 percent had under 5,000 employees. The companies included manufacturing, life assurance, financial, retail, food and transportation among others. The survey results revealed that 67 percent of the companies had not considered ABC, 15 percent were currently assessing it, 4 percent had decided not to implement ABC after giving it consideration, and 14 per cent had implemented or were implementing it. Thirty percent of all responding organisations had not heard of ABC. The authors of the study suggest that the results indicate that:

> ABC is in the early stages of development in Canada and that the development in this country lags behind that of the United States (p.7).

Gosse's (1993) in-depth study of the role of cost accounting in a CIM environment drew on empirical information from field studies in eight USA plants. These factories produced a variety of fabricated metal products in large volumes with half the factories having implemented elements of CIM. The CIM sites had already implemented, or were in the process of implementing, MRP, manufacturing cells, 'pull-through' production flow systems, CAD, CAM and robotics equipment. The normative accounting view would predict that the CIM plants would have cost systems with more cost centres, that CIM plants would explicitly relate support costs through pools to relevant resource groups using appropriate assignment factors, and that the focus of accounting reports would be on strategic manufacturing objectives rather than the financial product-costing criteria as in a traditional factory.

The findings of the study however only provided 'weak support' for these expectations. *Gosse* (1993, p.15) notes that:

> In general, less change had occurred in the cost systems of the CIM sites than had been hypothesised.

The study also revealed that accountants in the CIM plants provided production managers with special cost reports for monitoring costs of materials, labour, tooling, maintenance, scrap and production waste. These reports were however produced informally with 'off-system' approaches rather than from the formal cost system. Moreover, engineers, product managers and other non-accounting officers prepared product cost estimates from 'non-system sources' such as telephone enquiry or manual calculations rather than relying on cost data available from the cost accounting system. In fact, although managers considered certain cost implications in their product decisions relating to lot size, lot sequence and frequency of set-ups, in general cost consequences were assessed on the basis of informal and intuitive analyses.

It is plausible that formal cost reporting at the CIM sites had not been adapted to better support cost management objectives and that once this has taken place heavier reliance on formal cost data would follow. As such, as *Gosse* (1993, p.20) suggests:

> Perhaps it simply takes more time to adapt cost systems to the changes in manufacturing that have been occurring; cost systems may be changing, but at a slower rate than expected.

Another survey by *Emore and Ness* (1991) of cost management practices in seventy Midwestern USA manufacturing companies from a variety of industries encompassing aerospace and defence, electronics, electrical equipment, food products, metal products, industrial machinery and instruments, and control products has also produced revealing findings. The survey included many companies which had implemented advanced automation and manufacturing techniques with 55 percent of these reporting the labour cost proportion of their products at under 10 percent and half having overhead costs exceeding 25 percent of product costs on average.

These companies were considered to have faced changed cost structures and the object of the study was to reveal the number of companies which had made corresponding changes in their cost accounting systems so as to provide more relevant information for decision making. The basic conclusion of the study was that:

> Traditional cost management systems based on direct labour are not only common but still well-accepted, and changing them does not seem to be a high priority (*Emore and Ness*, 1991, p.26).

The authors of the study express concern over the finding that as direct labour costs have shrunk and manufacturing overhead costs have increased, product costing systems remain largely unaffected. They specifically report that:

> Plant-wide overhead allocation methods (30 percent of the companies) are still common, and direct labour-based overhead allocation techniques (74 percent of the companies) predominate, even though direct labour accounts for less than 10 percent of total product costs for the majority of the firms responding (Ibid p. 38).

The authors stress, however, that 23 percent of the companies were using machine hours as well as material value and cycle time as methods of absorption in their product cost build-ups and note that:

> . . . the use of machine hours and alternative allocation bases indicates that some companies have begun to recognise the need to explore cost drivers other than those based on labor. (Ibid).

Emore and Ness (Ibid, p.39) suggest that the failure of so many firms to systematically collect cost information in enough detail to provide full product cost aggregates that include both manufacturing and non-manufacturing costs

> . . . implies that product profitability in its broadest sense is not well understood.

In effect, they see the failure of the companies to perceive a need for changing their cost systems as 'distressing', particularly in that managers

> . . . feel quite comfortable with continuing to compete by using product costing systems whose conceptual foundations are highly suspect (Ibid, p.45).

and maintain that:

> A 'new breed' of cost manager capable of challenging that status quo must emerge (Ibid).

Another major survey was undertaken by *Cohen and Paquette* (1991) to examine the cost practices of companies and the perceptions of plant and divisional controllers about the usefulness and timeliness of variance analysis for planning, control and evaluation given the changes occurring in manufacturing approaches. The survey was based on 244 responses to questionnaires represented mainly by companies in manufacturing (71 percent), as well as high-tech (9 percent) and the service sector (10 percent). Respondents had an average of seventeen years experience in accounting or finance. The survey revealed that 67 percent of the companies used a standard cost system with 62 percent using direct labour as

> . . . the *primary* basis for allocating overhead (*Cohen and Paquette*, 1991, p.75).

Small portions of the companies surveyed used machine hours (12 percent), production volume (5 percent) or direct material (8 percent) as the primary overhead allocation base.

The survey also revealed that only 13 percent of companies used different cost systems for internal reporting versus external reporting. The authors of the study interpret this as suggesting that

> . . . accountants have largely ignored the argument that . . . the long-run cost of modifying and maintaining different costing systems for different objectives is substantially less than the long-run benefits (i.e. from improved decision making) that would result from having more accurate and relevant information (Ibid, p.77).

In terms of variance analysis, 80 percent of the companies did not use a formal decision rule to prompt investigation of variances making it

> . . . evident that decisions about variance analysis are still primarily judgmental in nature (Ibid, p.78).

The authors of the survey generally conclude that:

Changes in management accounting practices occur slowly. This survey shows for the most part US companies continue to rely on traditional management accounting practices (Ibid, p.83).

Karmarkar, Lederer and Zimmerman's (1991) field studies of five manufacturing plants supplemented by a survey of a further 39 plants is concerned with the determinants of cost accounting systems and production control systems. Their central question is whether costing systems are dependent on the manufacturing process, the relative importance of overheads and the extent of product competition faced by a firm. Their empirical study reveals that:

Plant managers perceive their costing systems to be more useful in satisfying external reporting requirements than in serving internal managerial purposes (Ibid, p.375).

Moreover, the authors of this study conclude that

. . . in general, we found few empirical associations among costing and production control systems and the hypothesized independent variables (Ibid).

In interpreting their findings, the authors suggest that production controls and accounting systems may be slow to adapt to changes in production modes and that

. . . the reason that changes in the accounting systems lag production process changes is that the incremental benefits of changing the accounting system are less than the incremental costs (Ibid, p.376).

This and other empirical studies and aggregate surveys of current cost accounting practices indicate that emerging production technology, altering work organisation and management approaches, and perceived market and environmental changes do not have an immediate, straightforward and generalisable relationship to costing systems. Research results can readily be interpreted within narrow economic-based notions of whether the benefits of change surpass the costs. But, in effect, if the benefits cannot be ascertained *a priori* then this argument loses ground and needs to be further investigated. The lack of evidence of a comprehensive change of accounting practices among North American companies on a wide scale at this stage may be caused by a number of factors. At an abstract level, cost-benefit rationales may be brought to bear. Further, it is plausible that accounting change lags other organisational, technological and environmental changes and more time is required before more conclusive judgments can be made. Techniques such as activity based costing and product life cycle costing no doubt are reasoned on logical terms and it may be posited that once accountants, managers and other potential processors and users of accounting information comprehend more fully the implications and rationales underlying their use, increased application will follow. At least for now, aggregate surveys suggest otherwise. At the level of enterprise case studies however, the impact of accounting system changes tends to be cast in a favourable light at the technical level (see for instance *Clemens*, 1991; *Jones*, 1991; *Haedicke and Feil*, 1991), although such studies do not delve sufficiently into broader organisational and behavourial consequences. This is a necessary step before a thought out interpretation of cost accounting practices in North American companies can be made.

7.3 Field Studies: Organisational Implications

Just as only a small number of large scale empirical surveys of cost accounting practices have been undertaken, detailed enterprise case studies of the implementations of accounting techniques are also few. In this respect, *Cooper and Turney* (1990) have noted that they knew of less than ten fully documented activity based cost systems. Nevertheless, there are many analyses of changes in accounting practices at the company level in the literature though their descriptive content tends to be limited (see for examples *Borden*, 1990). The case studies discussed below focus on those that extend their coverage beyond a delineation of purely technical factors and shed light on broader organisational issues.

Changing costs and influencing behaviour

Lammert and Ehrsam (1987) have commented in the light of emerging cost management systems that at the implementation stage, attention must be paid to the 'human behavioural element' (p.36). Otherwise, they suggest that technical design will have been a 'tremendous waste of time and effort'. They recommend 're-education' of individuals not receptive to change given that many will have built their careers on traditional cost accounting systems. The contention effectively is to make organisational culture compatible with accounting innovation. *Shields and Young* (1989) elaborate on the resistance of organisations and employees to accounting change. They suggest that the implementation of a cost management system may be resisted on the grounds that it can adversely affect short-term profits and therefore the firm's performance in the capital markets as well as the compensation of executives. It may also yield unfavourable performance reports for certain employees and may create unrest among workers whose jobs may become altered given the new types of information generated by the cost management system and the consequent managerial actions. Their recommendations to counter resistance to change concentrate on educating workers and managers as to the rationales for altering cost practices and the propriety of attendant changes.

Certain case studies of alterations in costing practices document particular organisational consequences and behavioural reactions which may ensue and which shed light on a variety of fundamental issues worthy of consideration. For instance, the mode of costing may be seen as a means of altering behaviour by providing guidance on appropriate managerial action. *Cooper and Turney* (1990) as a case in point, report on changes in the production process at Zytec Corporation which were brought about by the implementation of a programme of continuous improvement. This was coupled with a general decrease in the labour content of products which was seen to render the cost system obsolete. However, the objective of a redesigned cost system at the company was not primarily to seek greater accuracy of costs. As the controller of the company explained:

> We wanted (these) drivers to capture the essence of our drive for continuous improvement. In particular we were convinced that the cost system could become a potent tool for behaviour modification (Ibid, p.297).

Likewise, *Cooper and Turney* (1990) co-report on the Portable Instrument Division (PID) at Tektronix which also implemented a continuous improvement programme consisting of just-in-time, total quality control and greater personal involvement by staff in the work process. A concomitant decrease in the direct labour content of the company's products led to the adoption of activity based costing. But as the management of this firm reported:

> Our objective with the cost system was to change the behaviour of the division management. We did not go to a more complex system, say an eight-driver system, immediately, because we wanted to take incremental steps and change behaviour permanently (Ibid, p.301).

One problem at PID had been the cost of excessive custom parts used in the assembled products. Activity based costing was used to send messages about the desirability of using common parts. As one PID manager commented:

> The number of parts will cease to be a useful behavioural cost driver when the design engineers see the value of common parts. When they come to believe that it hurts our competitive position to proliferate parts, they will naturally design the products with common parts, and we won't have to continually remind them to do so (Ibid, p.302).

To this he added:

> The cost system will be used to cause behavioural change in a series of steps. I can see that in a few years the system will use different cost drivers, for example, cycle time burdening (Ibid).

In the above examples, activity based costing systems were instrumental in educating managers about desirable operational actions by motivational means. This depended on the simplicity of the system. Managers who can understand a new costing mechanism will be influenced by it and learn from it, thereby making it an instructional tool. At stake is the primary purpose of the costing mechanism which in the case of the normative literature about activity based costing is supposed 'accuracy' of reported costs. As *Cooper and Turney* (Ibid, p.303) indicate:

> When the driver that sends the strongest message is not the one that most accurately reports product costs, designers will have to choose between the strength of the message and the accuracy of the reported product costs.

In effect a tense relationship may emerge between opting for simplicity, which makes possible the achievement of the organisation's immediate concerns (influencing managers to act in certain ways on the basis of less than accurate costings), and the reasoned principles on which sophisticated cost accounting techniques are advocated (to enable informed managerial action relying on cost accuracy).

Visualising cost changes

Some organisations see the availability of accurate and timely cost information as imperative (*Turney*, 1990). One such company is the Roseville Networks Division (RMD) of Hewlett-Packard whose managers were, during the mid-1980s, particularly concerned with finding products' 'real' costs. *Berlant, Browning and Foster* (1990) report that RND developed a new accounting system relying on measures of factors considered to drive costs with the result that:

> The cost-driver or activity-based system is more accurate, more timely, and ultimately more useful to its 'customers' – the manufacturing, R & D, and marketing people who rely on the information it provides (Ibid, p.178).

During the implementation of the new accounting system, which ultimately became a model for other Hewlett-Packard organisations to follow, it emerged that production managers had informally operated a 'private accounting system' (Ibid, p.179) for many years. This system attempted to view costs as constituting factors that reflected cost causation rather than as the result of a dubious allocation mechanism divorced from actual operations and lacking manufacturing insight. The 'private' system for costing served as 'the seed' for the new official accounting system. Implementing the cost driver approach was done by

> . . . talking to the people on the factory floor. The drivers were usually obvious to them (Ibid, p.182).

An unexpected but important result was that the new costing system

> . . . allows people to think in more physical terms – which is how engineers and designers like to think anyway (Ibid).

To an extent, the activity based system affirmed the engineering viewpoint which made its acceptability among production personnel easier. The new accounting system was not seen as a continuation of the accountants' previously perceived 'watchdog' (Ibid, p.176) role,

nor as an imposition from staff executives in widening the
management control function, but as an extension of the
manufacturing people's own decision-making tools in accounting
terms. The perceived appropriateness of the altered accounting
approach was reflected in the system's capture of the physicality of a
product's cost make-up:

> We understand that it costs a dollar and some change for a
> board to go through the start station because we can see the
> activity (Ibid, p.182).

Further the new accounting approach corroborated the beliefs of
production managers in manufacturing as well as in financial
language. Engineers, designers and accountants no longer argued
about how costs should come together (the manufacturing viewpoint
reigned) but focused on decision issues about how much a product
or process should cost. In essence, a common denominator was
identified through the development of a cost system which aligned
itself with production-based interpretations of resource
consumption:

> We speak the same language, and the emotionalism is gone
> (Ibid, p.182).

A significant but unanticipated organisational consequence of
implementing a novel costing approach is its effects at the
interpersonal level. Different functional managers develop
prejudices and adopt attitudes partly reflective of professionally
rooted perspectives. A communication mechanism which cuts across
functional boundaries is likely to be well received among
organisational personnel by dissolving much of the basis for conflict,
and novel accounting approaches are no exception. Thus, although
the installation of a novel costing system may be viewed as meeting
the need for more accurate information, its underlying effectiveness
may be derived as much from its conflict-resolving potential in a
broader organisational sense. A novel costing approach which forces
departmental interaction so as to produce information deemed
relevant also establishes lateral information channels. Such
information flows which sidestep arbitrarily defined functional
boundaries such as manufacturing, marketing, accounting and
R & D help integrate knowledge about enterprise activities and
enable a more comprehensive managerial outlook unimpeded by

departmental idiosyncrasies and parochialism. As *Drucker* (1990, p.99) states:

> In the traditional plant, each sector and department reports separately upstairs. And it reports what upstairs has asked for. In the factory of 1999, sectors and departments will have to think through what information they owe to whom and what information they need from whom. A good deal of this information will flow sideways and across department lines, not upstairs. The factory of 1999 will be an information network.

7.4 Conclusions

This chapter has reviewed recent studies of cost management practices among North American companies. The evidence suggests a level of diversity. At one level, certain enterprises seem to positively adopt altered accounting techniques for a variety of reasons including the changing manufacturing and service environments, altering market conditions and emerging philosophies. But likewise, many organisations do not perceive a need to shed their traditional view of the usefulness of accounting information, nor do they reveal any inclination to link accounting techniques to aspects of the changing business environment. The contrast between the direction of calls for reforming management accounting by North American commentators and the attitude of business managers and practising accountants is in many cases striking. Changes in practice appear to lag behind the views voiced by certain consultants, academics and practitioners. Exhortations favouring alterations in accounting techniques in many cases fall on deaf ears. Conversely, important accounting thinkers seem to be convinced of the appropriate steps that are to be taken and, more often than not, the adoption of approaches such as activity based costing, product life cycle costing, redefined performance measures, etc., are vociferously supported. Certainly, the theoretical rationales underlying such calls are often persuasive. But likewise, managers' practical wisdom sidestepping normative calls for change often prevails, remaining implicit in organisational endeavours and usually unexplained in surveys and case studies (*Bhimani*, 1994b). At times, it becomes evident also that unforeseen reasons emerge for an accounting systems change bestowing new light on the unspecified potential of specific accounting techniques (*Bhimani and Pigott*,

1992b; *Gietzmann*, 1991). It may well be that many of the alterations in services offered by accountants cannot be observed by looking for the formal accounting system which is often firmly embedded in the firm's organisational and management structure and therefore not easy to identify or change.

As many commentators have noted, it may be too early to judge the propriety of changes taking place (or failing to take place). In terms of the evidence available so far, however, what is clear is that the appropriateness for altered cost management approaches seems to be organisationally-defined rather than being of universal application. The decision to adopt novel costing methods within enterprises appears to be rooted partly in considerations of the technical benefits seen as potentially obtainable, as well as organisation-specific factors including management style, behaviour and priorities which are left undefined in economic terms.

The findings reviewed here do suggest that many firms have not felt it necessary to change their formal accounting systems. The empirical evidence for the take up of new accounting ideas is not yet substantial. A concern is that for many companies, this lack of a wish to change extends far beyond the formal accounting system. Research which considers *ad hoc* information generation by accountants and which seeks to see how far accounting innovations are being made outside the formal accounting reporting might be encouraged.

8
The View from the UK

8.1 Introduction

In contrast with the USA, commentators on British management accounting practices do not in the main perceive the field to be experiencing a crisis. Nevertheless, a substantial body of empirical research has emerged attempting to illuminate the state of management accounting in the UK. In part, this has been a reaction to the view that changing technologies in both manufacturing and service industries have altered the conditions under which enterprises must function and that such changes have implications for accounting practices. The question of whether such transformations in technology need to dictate a revision of traditional accounting approaches has, in the recent past, been posed with increasing frequency. The extent to which management accountants in the UK along with the users of their services have accepted that such links exist is the principal issue addressed in this chapter. It is to be noted that other reasons may exist to account for alterations in accounting practices. The nature of such underlying reasons and the lessons they offer for the management accounting profession more generally are also considered here.

At first glance, such questions may seem less than relevant at a time when British industry has been in the midst of a wide-ranging economic downturn which is also affecting other industrial nations. In a climate of economic slow-down, if not contraction, few firms undertake major capital investments, incur large business expenditures or apply significant new resources to stimulate growth. Consequently, the relevance of accounting innovations under stagnant economic circumstances may be seen as diminished. Such a view would be incorrect. Accounting activities, especially in supporting management tasks, are often aggressively mobilised during lean economic periods. Pressures on costs tend to increase managers' attention to accounting information. What is of interest is whether the accounting information is that used traditionally or whether it is obtained from innovative accounting systems.

One study of fifty companies from The Times 1000 index in early 1992 (*Business International*, 1992) revealed that 83 percent of these undertook a cost-cutting exercise over the previous year, 30 percent over 1990, 23 percent over 1989 and 6 percent in 1988. The primary objective of these companies was to create a process of on-going cost competitiveness. The suggestion is that over the time period management accounting was becoming more significant in the management process. This shift is of primary concern in this chapter. First, the chapter focuses on findings from studies exploring general changes taking place in UK industrial firms associated with the emergence of novel accounting techniques. Attention is then paid to the changing role of management accounting and management accountants in a new environment of information technology intensiveness. The subsequent section reviews the findings of some empirical studies of 'hi-tech' firms and the complex relationships between management accounting, costing and the process of organisational change within companies. This is followed by an examination of various surveys of British companies aimed at assessing the impact on investment appraisal in the new product environment. Finally, the chapter looks at evidence from certain other studies on activity based costing trends in the UK.

8.2 General Trends in Management Accounting Practices

In mid-1990 a major survey was carried out aimed at examining cost management techniques and practices in use and those being planned for introduction at UK manufacturing enterprises (*Davies and Sweeting*, 1991a; 1991b). The sample comprised 677 companies involved in the manufacture of metal goods, electrical/electronics, wood and paper products, food and drink, chemicals and pharmaceuticals among others. More than half of these companies employed over 500 people and had annual revenues exceeding £25 million.

This survey reveals that cost management information is most widely used for control, product pricing, investment justification and management performance. Respondents indicated that by introducing advanced costing techniques and practices into their organisations, they expected to obtain significant benefits, particularly to improve product profitability and cost reduction and obtain more timely and relevant management information. In terms of specific cost management techniques being used and planned, activity based costing was the most commonly cited and life cycle costing the least (see Table 8.1).

Table 8.1 Cost management techniques

	% Used or Planned for Introduction
Activity based costing	60%
Cost modelling	55%
Cost of quality	52%
Target cost planning	46%
Strategic management accounting	44%
Throughput accounting	40%
Back flushing	24%
Life cycle costing	11%

The survey also revealed that manufacturing resources planning was the most highly used (or planned) manufacturing technique and flexible manufacturing systems the least cited (see Table 8.2). The percentage in use however represented a much smaller portion than the percentage planned.

Table 8.2 Manufacturing techniques

	% Used or Planned for Introduction
Manufacturing resources planning	77%
Total quality management	69%
Just-in-time	48%
Computer integrated manufacturing	43%
Flexible manufacturing systems	23%

The emergence of novel management accounting practices did not, according to the authors, cause a revolution:

> Far from revolutionising practices in the manufacturing sector, the introduction of new costing techniques has caused confusion among management (*Davies and Sweeting*, 1991a, p.44).

The authors of the study suggest that in many companies accounting data was collected by costing systems but not reported to managers. Moreover, little planning appeared to be evident in the way in which many businesses build their cost management systems. Rather than critically analysing what the business and managers really required, an *ad hoc* and piecemeal approach was used by companies in developing their accounting systems. For instance, even though 32 percent of respondents reported using ABC, only 11 percent used cost drivers as a performance measure. Likewise, whereas 48 percent expected to adopt JIT manufacturing, only 24 percent intended to use backflush techniques. Thus the authors report that:

> We found a generally confused way forward adopted by managers to the way that new costing techniques and practices were introduced into manufacturing organisations (Ibid, p.45).

What is evident from the study is that along with changes in the manufacturing environment, companies are adopting novel accounting practices (or intend to) albeit not always with the desired level of success. *Murphy and Braund's* (1990) study of 263 UK management accountants also confirms the trend:

> New technology tends to reinforce the importance of management accounting for organisations, and often increases their reliance on it (p.40).

Their results suggest that increasingly companies are considering the implementation of more modern cost management techniques such as ABC, life cycle costing, throughput accounting, backflushing and strategic management accounting. Nevertheless, *Lyall, Okoh and Puxty's* (1990) study of 423 British companies indicates that:

> Reports of the demise of standard costing and budgetary control systems appear to be a little premature (p.45).

More generally, they note that their:

> . . . study suggests that the traditional financial control systems continue to be used extensively in industry and are probably

being adapted successfully to meet the challenges presented by recent developments in production and information technologies (Ibid).

Drury et al.'s (1993) study of management accounting practices in 303 UK manufacturing organisations provides a broad description of management accounting systems in use. This study covered a variety of areas in which accounting information is reported to management accounting including product costing, pricing, budgetary control, standard costing, capital investment appraisal, the impact of AMTs, divisional performance measures and transfer pricing. The aim of the study was to provide a comprehensive description of management accounting systems in use as well as reflect the perceptions of the experienced management accountants who generate them. The study reported that organisations use product cost information for decisions in a flexible manner, referring to both incremental and full cost constructions. Cost-plus methods are used selectively for pricing decisions. Simplistic methods are adopted to allocate overheads to products, including plant-wide rates and labour based methods for automated departments. Activity based costing (ABC) is not employed extensively but respondents report that it is being quite widely considered. There is no information to indicate that the degree of competition faced by organisations, the number of products produced or the proportion of overhead costs incurred, significantly influences the methods that are used to assign overhead costs to products. The authors state that of the companies surveyed, 13 percent have implemented or intend to implement ABC, and 37.6 percent are giving ABC some consideration.

In relation to budgetary planning and cost control, the separation of controllable and non-controllable costs in reports does not always take place. Additionally fixed and variable costs are not always distinguished. Standard costing is employed widely, especially for stock valuation, cost control and performance evaluation. *Drury et al.,* state that for capital investment decisions the payback method is popular, but this is frequently combined with a discounting method. The majority of respondents indicated that just-in-time (JIT) methods and advanced manufacturing techniques (AMTs) are not employed in their organisations.

Of particular relevance is that those organisations using just-in-time methods and advanced manufacturing techniques:

> . . . there is no indication that this has caused significant changes to be made to the management accounting information system (*Drury et al.*, 1993).

Conversely, greater emphasis was placed on non-financial performance measures (see also *Bhimani*, 1993, 1994a). The surveys revealed that the performance of divisionalised companies is measured most frequently by a target profit or return on investment (ROI) rather than residual income. Variable cost based methods were reported to be rarely used. The authors of the study reported that 'product costing and profitability analysis were areas of major concern to management accountants' (*Drury et al.*, 1993, p.3).

Cobb's 1993 survey of ten UK companies adopting JIT systems indicated that a portion of the companies had altered their cost accounting system, which became more complex. The trend in performance reporting was away from centralised, monthly reporting of results in mainly financial terms to a decentralised, daily or weekly reporting of operational indicators.

Overall in the UK, evidence is surfacing that the availability and uptake of AMTs and altered forms of work organisation are associated with a level of change in accounting practices in UK companies. The next section briefly discusses throughput costing which is a novel accounting technique finding increasing use in British companies. Thereafter, the chapter elaborates on management accounting trends and experiences vis-a-vis the adoption of IT, capital appraisal approaches and ABC.

Throughput accounting

Throughput accounting is a reaction against the traditional practice of direct and indirect allocation of costs, of adding value to inventory, and of adopting a conventional notion of economic batch size. The technique stems from ideas put forth by *Goldratt and Cox* (1984) but has been vociferously advocated in the UK by *Galloway and Waldron* (1988a; 1988b; 1989a, 1989b). Theirs is a call

> . . . for a new theory that welds together developments in our understanding of the true relationships between manufacturing response time, inventory, quality and profit with advances in the technology of manufacturing as encompassed by CIM (*Galloway and Waldron*, 1988a, p.34).

Their starting point is to develop concepts which enable managers to calculatively guide a manufacturing enterprise toward greater profitability. They suggest that in the short to medium term, the entire cost of a factory is fixed except for material costs. It is, therefore, acceptable to spurn decision-making based on conventional costing procedures which produce, for instance, cost per machine hour or per direct labour hour data. It is simpler and more appropriate to consider 'total factory cost'. Moreover, treating inventory as being comprised solely of material value rather than adding value to material to account for labour and overhead costs enables a focus on profitability tied to manufacturing activities. This is because the incentive to produce so as to absorb costs is removed. *Galloway and Waldron* (1988a, p.35) thus contend that:

> For all businesses, profit is a function of the time taken for manufacturing to respond to the needs of the market. This in turn means that profitability is inversely proportional to the level of inventory in the system, since the response time is itself a function of all inventory.

Another precept of the throughput accounting school is that it is not absolute product profitability which matters for a multi-product firm but relative product profitability. Profitability must be a measure of how quickly monetary returns can be obtained from manufacturing operations, which in turn is dependent on the volume of products produced. Thus, what is of essence is each product's contribution per production operation, where the object must be to maximise output of that product which returns the most based on the operation which has the least relative capacity. This logic leads *Galloway and Waldron* (Ibid) to assert that:

> It is the rate at which a product contributes money that determines relative product profitability. And it is the rate at which a product contributes money compared to the rate at which the factory spends it that determines absolute profitability.

The following example adapted from *Galloway and Waldron* (1988a and 1988b) illustrates the throughput accounting rationale together with some relevant ratios stemming from the concepts discussed above.

Consider two machined products, X and Y, with contribution margins (selling price less variable costs) of £0.825 and £8.82

respectively. Their production entails three operations with the following relative timings (in minutes):

Operations	1	2	3
Product X	0.2	0.3	0.20
Product Y	0.2	0.15	0.25
Capacity (minutes)	6,000	5,000	6,000

Since at operation 2, which has the least relative capacity, 16,666 units of X (5,000/0.3) can be manufactured whereas 33,333 units of Y (5,000/0.15) can be produced, it is in fact more profitable to produce Y rather than X. What the manager needs to ascertain is that the rate at which product Y earns money exceeds the rate at which money is spent making it. In other words, the return per factory minute (defined as (Selling Price – Material Cost)/Time on key resource) must exceed the cost per factory minute (defined as Total factory cost/Total time available on the key resource). Alternatively, the throughput accounting ratio (defined as Return per factory minute/ Cost per factory minute) must exceed one before a product can be considered as making money. Although the level of detail in analysing manufacturing operations can become more involved, the basic rationale of throughput accounting is to determine a product mix which makes the best use of resources whilst maximising the company's profits per unit time. In applying throughput accounting, a number of performance indicators linked to enterprise performance and strategy may be developed to suit the requirements of an organisation.

There is a lack of aggregate empirical studies on the ability of throughput accounting to provide better support for managers in comparison with more conventional approaches; even so, many British companies are expressing an interest in the technique. Although throughput accounting offers managers a different angle for viewing enterprise activities in comparison with activity based costing, it is a technique that is 'packaged' and 'publicised' in much the same way:

> . . . if you measure throughput, you get profit (*Waldron*, 1988, p.36).

and which also is aimed at a similar market:

Throughput accounting is about measuring manufacturing
performance in a way that is suited to modern manufacturing
philosophies (Ibid).

But *Darlington et al.*, (1992) are careful to point out that:

ABC is a technique which focuses primarily on overhead costs.
In contrast, the recent development of throughput accounting
provides an approach which takes overhead and labour costs as
given and concentrates on the flow of production through the
factory (p.32).

No doubt the extent to which throughput accounting focuses
managers' attention on internal processes and its perceived level of
complexity will, as with ABC, play a part in its viability in the
market for management ideas. What is to be noted is that, except for
the stress placed on profitability (which enables the technique to
have the label 'accounting' appended to it) throughput accounting
seems not to be a major departure from methods of optimising
resource capacity based on operations research. Whether it is likely
to be viewed as a means of addressing managerial concerns of over
costing, product pricing, overhead cost management and more
strategic organisational concerns remains to be seen given the
paucity of documented experiences with the technique. The next
part of the chapter resumes the focus on UK trends in management
accounting.

Management accounting and information technology

A research project of sixteen longitudinal case studies investigating
the management accounting and information technology (IT)
interface in companies over a three and a half year period until
August 1989 has been undertaken in the distribution, mineral
extraction, retailing and manufacturing industrial sectors (*King et al.*,
1991a). This research has been concerned with exploring the impact
of IT growth on organisational processes and the changing role of
the management accountant, with a particular focus on the manner
in which activities traditionally viewed to encompass management
accounting are being altered. The authors of this research report
suggest that management generally is undergoing a revolution in
that key aspects of organisation, strategy, structure, systems and
culture are in some enterprises being questioned and

> . . . the conventional wisdom of earlier years is being submerged within a wave of new ideas and practices (*King et al.*, 1991b, p.46).

Essentially, they see the increasing pace of competitive and market changes, technological development and economic forces as well as legal and political factors, as forcing good management to anticipate the future and be ready for it in advance. Concomitantly, they suggest that:

> Line managers will not be prepared to accept the management accountant as a passive historian or an autocratic controller or even an unhelpful watchdog (Ibid).

The approach taken in this set of empirical studies is to consider the different types of activities which management accounting has been seen to comprise. In terms of the scorekeeping function (i.e. the task of accumulating and reporting to all levels of management), most companies used a computerised accounting system but only a minority of companies were found to use computer-based systems which integrated financial and non-financial data, possibly because the prevailing accounting information systems were already partly computerised and full integration would entail a costly restructuring of the total system. In addition, computer systems in some firms did not allow the necessary compatibility for full integration. Information technology (IT) had thus not been used to design new systems but concentrated on making existing scorekeeping systems more efficient.

Some benefits appeared to have accrued from the implementation of IT in the firms. Significant improvements in routine scorekeeping and reporting activities were in evidence including higher labour productivity at all levels of the processes (for example data capture, processing, storage and retrieval), more rapid internal dissemination of accounting reports and enhanced ability to disaggregate information. The research, however, also revealed that the manufacturing sector, in comparison with retailing, distribution and extraction, had made less progress in adopting IT. Moreover, whilst IT had enabled a reduction in the amount of time the management accountant spent on operating the scorekeeping system, the time released became translated into a reduction of accounting staff or, at best, into coping with growth rather than permitting management accountants to pay greater attention to decision-support activities as might have been expected.

The attention-directing function which aims at explaining and interpreting reports thought to be relevant for the proper discharge of managerial duties was found not to be significantly enhanced by IT in the companies studied. However, problem-solving activities were affected by the use of IT, especially in providing analyses for decision-making and generating related reports.

With reference to the activities of management accounting, these case studies indicated that management accountants are oriented toward meeting the needs of senior managers rather than middle level managers. The studies also revealed a discrepancy between the role ascribed to management accountants by managers and the management accountants' own perception of their responsibility. Over the time period of the study there was a significant change in the orientation of management accountants:

> . . . with a reduction in the primary scorekeeping activity associated with historian and watchdog, and a movement towards the roles which combine decision support and scorekeeping, such as adviser and team member (Ibid, p.50).

This was based on the responses articulated by management accountants. The perception of managers using the services of management accountants differed. Indeed, a significant number of user managers did not perceive a significant improvement in the service received from management accountants. Even though a variety of issues concerning organisational change may explain such a discrepancy, the authors of the study warn that the management accounting profession must heed the need to improve end-user satisfaction.

In general terms, the research suggests that the focus and breadth of management accounting as a body of knowledge is changing and that traditional boundaries based around scorekeeping activities are being enlarged to include many more factors and processes. For instance, routine scorekeeping can be expanded to include graphics concerning sales and financial contributions, and broken down to products and customers to allow more decision-support and attention-directing information. This change is particularly accentuated by the accelerating pace of IT developments which is changing the nature of managerial activities and thus providing new challenges for management accounting. The case studies also suggest that the creation and operation of a management information system is not merely a technical issue but must be understood in the context of the interrelationships and dynamics existing between staff managers, line managers and other groups of individuals within the organisation. Moreover, the research reinforces the notion that management accounting and information management within organisations are utilised at levels well below the technical sophistication believed to be achievable in practice.

The studies also underscore a need for management accounting to develop an appreciation of marketing tasks, problems and objectives, so as to better integrate information systems which link production activities with market factors. The overall strategic plans of the organisation need to be more effectively integrated with the management accounting function and this requires the outward-looking orientation. In this light, management accountancy must emphasise 'managerial and strategic aspects' (*King et al.*, 1991a, p.5) rather than just technical aspects. The authors of the study conclude that:

> The research findings suggest a need for management accountants to take a more proactive, visionary and service-orientated approach to satisfying management information needs (Ibid).

Management accounting in 'hi-tech' organisations

In 1985, the Chartered Institute of Management Accountants in the UK commissioned three studies to assess the following hypothesis: growth businesses in high technology have adapted long-standing management accounting techniques and practices, and have created new ones, to cope with the demands of the new production environment. All three research groups carried out independent investigations choosing to conduct their empirical work largely through semi-structured interviews with various executives within a wide variety of companies.

Coates and Longden (1989) chose a group of twenty UK companies and five USA-based companies where rapid technological innovation was taking place. The firms investigated were spread across a number of sectors including new materials, semi-conductors, fibre optics, holograms and memory devices, software products, office automation, fine chemicals and pharmaceuticals and used CAD/ CAM robotics, CNC and CIM (see Chapter 2 for a discussion of these). The research methodology consisted mainly of interviews held with accounting, finance, marketing, production and general management executives.

The authors of the study reported that no evidence was found to support the thesis that firms operating in new/hi-tech growth industries developed new techniques of management accounting to cope with the new product environment. However, the view that traditional practices need to be adapted to provide information that is strategic and outward looking and which allows the anticipation of events, was held particularly strongly. For instance, efforts were being made by firms in the study to make absorption costing data more accurate through improved cost analysis with a view to enabling more efficacious studies of product profitability. In addition, the desire was expressed for developing means of attributing costs more precisely to individual production lines so as to allow the identification of the most profitable products and product areas and for dealing with changes in throughput times and work-in-process stock under JIT production systems. For the companies investigated by *Coates and Longden*, standard accounting techniques for performance measures, capital expenditure appraisal and learning curve analysis were not found to have been altered in practice, nor was there any evidence that future development in these directions was desired by these firms. Although the study did not support the hypothesis it set out to test, other issues which have considerable significance for the development of management accounting did emerge as outlined above. Technical options for dealing with some of these have been discussed in Chapter 3.

Littler and Sweeting (1989) carried out their study by examining the modes of operation of twenty UK and five USA new technology based businesses (NTBB) in the electronics, information technology, biotechnology and new materials sectors. Their survey was not confined to executives in the chosen firms but also extended to analysts and representatives of other NTBBs. The authors found that the firms examined formulated their business strategy largely on the basis of their technology and the need to keep abreast of technological development. Strategic objectives were thus stated in broad terms rather than as clear goals supported by quantitative targets of growth, turnover or productivity. As part of the decision making process, sensitivity analyses using quantified evaluations of different scenarios were often performed. In this regard, budgeting was undertaken to facilitate dialogue and explore assumptions about future factors affecting the business (which seems similar to Japanese practices). Qualitative information was used significantly to supplement traditional management accounting information usually represented in financial terms.

Littler and Sweeting's research shows that the rationales upon which the suitability of traditional accounting techniques for decision making purposes are established (e.g. maximising resource allocation and utilisation) were not readily identifiable in the firms they studied. In addition, they preferred not to rely solely on financial measures as there are areas which management accounting techniques are viewed as being able to penetrate only to a limited extent. For this reason:

> . . . the tendency was to develop and maintain a holistic view of the business, and thereby prevent a partitioning that might result in an easy focusing on financial measures (p.7).

Consequently, the authors of this study found that information flows which encompassed informal dialogues between executives and information exchange through impressions, innuendo, gossip and speculation was not discouraged in the companies investigated. It is interesting to note that this type of information exchange between managers is also reported to be an important part in the functioning of Japanese organisations (*Tsurumi and Tsurumi*, 1985). Likewise, the question of product pricing had interesting implications for management accounting in that similar to the Japanese approach to this problem (*British Chamber of Commerce in Japan*, 1988), the companies favoured setting prices according to perceived value of the product to the customer rather on the basis of cost-plus pricing.

According to *Littler and Sweeting*, the group of companies surveyed indicated the prevalence of a management philosophy which espouses flexibility, a lesser confidence in the value of quantitative information as an input to decision-making and greater emphasis on informal processes with important consequences for the role of the management accountant as an

> . . . *interpreter* of these often speculative and qualitative data, drawing out what it could mean for the performance of products and the business as a whole; a *counsellor*, in

articulating the rationale for advisable and nonadvisable courses; and as *guardian* of the business' financial integrity with external parties (p.58).

Their findings lead them to conclude that the firms studied had

> . . . unique features which in turn might compel or at least elicit, for reasons of practicality, modifications to existing, or even result in the development and adoption of novel, decision making aids and procedures (p.60).

These results have important implications for the role of management accounting in at least some types of firms because they suggest that unless management accounting mechanisms are devised for enhancing the efficacy of the functioning of organisations in an environment which is fast changing and turbulent, the significance and value of management accounting as a management function is likely to diminish. Such a view accords with *King et al.'s* (1991a) study discussed above. Moreover, it appears that novel forms of management accounting practices need to focus on the uniqueness of the firm's specific organisational processes. Further, account needs to be taken of the changing nature of corporate life with the increased use of advanced manufacturing technologies from a socio-technical perspective rather than relying on a needs-based financial framework without which it is assumed that the organisation cannot properly function. This assumption is often implicit in the application of conventional management accounting tools. An emphasis on socio-technical issues is especially important in the light of *Littler and Sweeting's* conclusions about the relevance of informal information exchange between organisational participants.

Innes and Mitchell (1989) carried out a survey of ten electronics companies in Central Scotland through interviews with senior management and general accounting executives. They supplemented their data using reviews of management accounting reports produced within the firms investigated. Their findings support the view that:

> The practices of management accounting have changed and are continuing to change and be adapted from the stereotypes provided particularly in the educational literature (p.39).

In reference to costing, they state that

. . . factors 'driving' costs such as quality, technical process and service activities were receiving increasing emphasis in the costing system (p.4).

In addition, simple actual costing systems were installed to help remove the complexities associated with establishing standard costs in a production environment which is fast changing and where product demand is not homogeneous.

Performance measurement techniques were also beginning to emphasise non-financial factors such as product quality, delivery performance, launch time for new products and customer satisfaction. Finally, attempts were made by the firms examined to incorporate outward looking strategic information on market conditions into budgets, decision information and performance measures to help monitor competitiveness.

Along with *Littler and Sweeting, Innes and Mitchell* (1989) found that informal communication between accountants and managers was not unimportant and that

. . . the accountants were expected to discuss the management accounting report informally with managers prior to any formal group meeting (p.14).

This type of inclusion of management accountants in multidisciplinary task teams dealing with competitive analysis, product design and cost evaluation enhances their direct involvement in the operational activities of firms and improves communication between operational managers and management accountants. Similar findings were noted with respect to Japanese management style in Chapter 5.

Management accounting and investment appraisal

Currie (1989a; 1989b; 1990; 1991) has reported the findings of a study of twenty British companies which aimed at examining managers' reasons for investing in computer aided design. The enterprises investigated were in the electronics, engineering, computing and shipbuilding industries, and the study involved interviewing individuals responsible for the selection and implementation of new technology. The results of the study suggest that:

. . . in contrast to the rational process described in some of the literature, decision-making was often *ad hoc* and sometimes initiated at the top of the organisation with little support from the shop floor (*Currie*, 1989a, p.87).

Partly, the problem in the companies studied was the rigid systems within which line managers operated to justify expenditure on new technology. Whereas engineers had to appeal to financial targets, such as return on investment and discounted cash flow measures, to obtain fund allocations, the returns typical of the proposed investments were primarily qualitative and operationally-specific (such as the ability to design new products, the quality of drawings and the achievable complexity and the detail of design) and were therefore not readily quantifiable let alone representable financially. The problem faced by line managers in adhering to organisational financial requirements ran deeper however. Whereas the majority of advanced manufacturing technologies implicitly require a long-term view, capital budgeting control systems focused on annual measures which in certain instances removed the benefits which AMT investments were adopted to attain (for instance by being unable to add advanced software in future years to take utmost advantage of hardware potential). Moreover, the lack of an enterprise-wide strategic frame of reference led to fragmentised AMT acquisition by individual organisational sub-units, which in turn reduced the possibility of systems interface. In this sense, the managerial infrastructure and protocol negated the underlying technological capabilities which, in theory, could be attained.

Perhaps of equal concern is that the study indicates ways in which accounting systems hindered and forestalled its very *raison d'être*. The tight financial procedures which line managers were forced to abide by directed their attention to developing ways of tactfully sidestepping their constraining elements:

> . . . the present formal budgetary control system invites a variety of informal and elaborate manipulation by decision-makers (in this case engineering managers), to circumvent its rigidity and short-term structure (*Currie*, 1989b, p. 20).

Rather than support and make visible the gains to be obtained from functional activities, the financial control practices created a preoccupation among line managers to seek ways of overcoming accounting hurdles so as to enable investments to proceed which would positively contribute to organisational change and growth. The difficulties faced by the companies surveyed may not have been fully representative of British firms in general, but they do raise important issues. Whilst the problem may be 'cultural, organisational and technical' (*Currie*, 1991, p.28) in nature rather than functionally-specific, management accounting probably contributed to it. Understanding the nature of its role in given enterprises is likely to be a fruitful exercise to be engaged in before shedding past accounting practices and replacing them with emerging cost management innovations without due consideration. Indeed, *Currie* (Ibid) contends that:

> . . . problems in managing AMT are better understood by a knowledge of the historical development of particular management styles than merely by promoting the latest management fact as a panacea of organisational ills.

Another study of nine large companies (including British Airways, ICI, Shell and Rank Xerox) by *Sheppard* (1990) suggested similar conclusions. The researcher interviewed key managers on their information technology (IT) investment appraisal process including the relevance of strategic thinking. One finding was that the large size of IT expenditure led companies to desire the application of normal capital investment appraisal methods so as to fulfil the normal rate of return criteria:

> . . . yet the more innovative applications of IT, involving much uncertainty, defy such quantifications (Ibid, p.174).

The author of the study asserts that investments require monetary and non-monetary assessments and

> ROCE and payback appraisals cannot be used in isolation because of the high uncertainty associated with those investments which may yield a potential for competitive advantage (Ibid, p.179).

Further, *Sheppard* (1990, p.171) noted that '. . . decisions are based on more informal processes' than that suggested in the normative literature which recommends more sophisticated and rational decision-making models. A proper balance must therefore be achieved between emphasising quantitative versus qualitative benefits.

Woods et al. (1985) carried out a survey of 101 mechanical engineering firms in the UK to identify the investment appraisal methods most commonly used in practice. In particular, the survey was aimed at firms considering the acquisition of new production technology in the form of computer aided design and manufacturing equipment, including computerised numerical control machines. For those firms making substantial investments in CAD/CAM systems (47 firms in total), the survey revealed that a large number of firms opted to use no formal appraisal system (see Table 8.3). This signifies a recognition of the limited practical use of formal appraisal methods when considering the acquisition of advanced manufacturing technology.

Table 8.3 Investment appraisal method used by firms

	Major Users of CAD/CAM Systems Sample Size: 47 %	Non-Users Sample Size: 29 %
Payback	34.00	34.48
DCF	12.70	10.34
Both	2.12	10.34
Non-financial	6.38	13.79
Other	8.50	20.68
None	37.17	—

Adapted from Woods et al., 1985, p.42

The authors of the study concluded that the survey shows a widespread acknowledgement that risk cannot be dealt with objectively in the context of a capital budgeting system. Instead, certain firms are more in favour of subjective judgement and the assessment of investment decisions abandoning formal investment appraisal altogether. The results of the survey point to the need to reassess the propriety of conventional investment appraisal techniques for AMT acquisition decisions. The potential exists for incorporating informal variables into project evaluation analyses along the lines of strategic investment appraisal techniques (see Chapter 5).

Another study to assess the relative influence of management accounting practices on decisions to invest in new technology has been carried out by *Nixon and Lonie* (1991). These researchers studied the investment decision process of thirteen technology-dependent companies (ten in the UK and three in the USA). The findings of this study broadly accord with those discussed above in that they suggest that:

> . . . information which is impounded in competitive strategy decisions but which is presently informal and outside the formal management accounting system (and MIS) can be identified and brought, at least, into the semi-structured domain (Ibid, p.41).

This, the authors maintain, will entail exploring more forward looking information in order to evaluate the technological, commercial and financial risks and benefits of both activities, of speed of progress, and of procrastination. Effectively, the study illustrates ways in which perceptions of strategic significance are influenced by internal organisational arrangements. Consequently, the design of management accounting systems has an important role to play in that there is:

> . . . a need to develop, both at the conceptual and management accounting practice levels, closer links between the manufacturing, technology and competitive strategies (Ibid).

The view which emerges from these empirical studies about AMT investment appraisal is that alterations in evaluation techniques and the adoption of more sophisticated models of assessing capital investments are unlikely to resolve problems on their own. AMT investments must certainly fit in with an enterprise's strategy and practical ways of doing this are available (see Chapter 5), but the right balance must be reached between quantitative and qualitative factors to be evaluated. Moreover, integration of financial evaluations within a perspective which takes account of other elements of organisational concerns is desirable. Management accounting practices must exist and interact alongside an enterprise's operations, rather than simply exert controls to monitor organisational activities.

ABC in British companies

Activity based costing has received much publicity in the UK over the past five years. Indeed, *Davies and Sweeting* (1991, p.29) have reported that 60 percent of respondents in their survey of 677 companies expected to have ABC in place by 1994 and noted that:

> It is not surprising, given all the exposure which it has received in recent years, to find that Activity Based Costing (ABC) will be by then the front runner. Is this then becoming a one horse race?

Today a small but not insignificant number of British companies have actually implemented ABC. *Bailey* (1991) has documented the experiences of ten companies having adopted the technique, whilst *Innes and Mitchell* (1990) have reported on three. In a major survey on ABC carried out in late 1990, *Innes and Mitchell* (1991) revealed that out of 187 usable replies from management accountants, 11 respondents indicated that their organisations had decided to implement ABC although:

> Only two of these claimed that full systems of ABC had been implemented, the other nine having only partial implementation (p.28).

This contrasts with 62 respondents who stated that they were still at a stage of assessing ABC. Of possible concern is the lengthy period of deliberation which companies considering the adoption of ABC are engaging in. *Cobb, Innes and Mitchell's* (1992) study of thirty companies which were considering implementing ABC in 1990 revealed that one year later twenty of these were still considering it. The delay was:

> . . . commonly attributed to the perceived problems of the amount of work in installing an ABC system, the existence of higher work priorities than ABC, lack of time and resource (accountants, computer staff and managers) and the difficulty of selecting appropriate cost drivers.

Given that many companies are considering activity based costing it is likely that more information will surface over the next few years about the benefits, problems and issues which its use entails. The existing literature on ABC in the UK nevertheless already offers important insights into ABC in the UK.

Innes and Mitchell's (1991) survey uncovers important issues which are worthy of consideration at this stage. Of the 187 responses to their questionnaires, slightly over half had seriously considered ABC, around one-third were vetting it, six percent (11) had commenced implementation and nine percent had rejected it. Half of the companies assessing ABC were seeking to improve the accuracy of product costs for pricing, product line profit analysis and overcoming other perceived deficiencies of their accounting systems. Other companies were concerned with improving their understanding of cost structure and cost incursion as well as with obtaining new information which could help in improving performance in an increasingly competitive environment. Some respondents thought that the changing structure of costs and the absolute and relative magnitude of overheads was relevant in instigating their interest.

The assessment of ABC by these companies brought a clearer focus on the likely costs of implementing ABC which led to a considerable level of reservation in going ahead with the accounting systems change. Others were concerned especially with the apparent level of complexity, with many management accountants expressing difficulty in fully comprehending ABC. Generally, some concern existed about how far managers would accept this new costing methodology not only because of questions as to whether it would be intelligible to those using ABC data, but also in terms of the repercussions of revised selling prices given new costings. Some respondents wondered whether marginal costing would not be better suited to their needs.

There were several cases of companies deciding against adopting ABC prior to any implementation having taken place (fifteen respondents) whereas only two companies rejected the technique following first hand practical experience. The desire for more accurate product costings, improved cost control, and a wish

> . . . to obtain for the directors a different view of the firm's cost structure, one which 'cut across departmental boundaries' (*Innes and Mitchell*, 1991, p.30)

were expressed as objectives which had been sought by those companies which had rejected ABC. Conversely, those firms which had implemented ABC fully or partially were all positive about the benefits. These enterprises were content with

. . . the availability of new information and insights within the organisation and . . . the use of information in managerial decision making (Ibid, p.28).

A smaller scale study by *Nicholls* (1992) echoes some of these findings. Nicholls's study obtained 62 replies to a questionnaire on ABC from a sample of 179 companies covering a wide cross section of British industries. These companies employed from 150 to more than 1,000 workers and had from less than £15m turnover to more than £100m.

The survey revealed that over 80 percent of respondents used traditional methods of cost recovery based on labour content, unit volumes, machine hours or a combination (55 percent using direct labour content). Ten percent of these companies indicated that they had implemented ABC. Sixty-two percent were investigating ABC techniques and eighteen percent were piloting ABC techniques. The initial interest in ABC was driven by a number of factors. Sixty-five percent sought to understand 'true' product costs, 50 percent were not entirely satisfied with their current system and 45 percent were concerned to identify and reduce product costs.

Problems with ABC implementation included the unavailability of adequate detailed data, lack of resources and reluctance to change traditional accounting methods. Those companies which had implemented ABC, or were piloting the technique, indicated that:

. . . the task of implementing ABC was more involved and consumed more management time than first anticipated (p.23).

One company which had implemented ABC commented that:

. . . companies who implement ABC without fully understanding the behavioural issues of new performance measures or cost drivers may underestimate the impact of changes internally (Ibid).

Such unforeseen consequences arising from ABC implementation have been noted elsewhere (*Bhimani and Pigott*, 1992; *Gietzmann*, 1991).

Nicholls (1992, p.28) suggests that:

Without doubt any company able to identify true product costs will have a tactical advantage over a competitor who is unable to do so.

Whilst no product costing system can ever provide 'true' costs, Nicholls's study does suggest that some companies are adopting ABC in pursuit of such an ideal.

8.3 Conclusions

Some important conclusions may be drawn from the findings of the UK based research studies reviewed in this chapter. One strain of argument which arises in most of the observations cited in the research about the relationship of the management accountants and the rest of the organisation is that their expertise cannot be applied independently of knowledge about the operational activities specific to their organisation. A link must exist between the particular processes considered to be required for organisational success and the technicalities of the management accounting task.

Management accounting, on the basis of the results of the studies undertaken, appears to have a need to become embedded within operational activities to enhance their effectiveness. For this to take place, the management accountant possibly needs to develop a language which reduces the distance between the contribution he or she can make in the form of attention-directing or decision-making information and what is understood by the line manager. In this sense, the value of communicating management accounting information through informal channels must not be underestimated. The evidence for this stems not only from UK companies but also from Japan (see Chapter 6) and some USA enterprises (see Chapter 7). Moreover, most of the empirical studies reviewed reveal the growing importance of qualitative information which arises because of the changing product environment.

Greater stress is being put on quality, delivery performance, customer satisfaction etc. and the development of measures to account for such factors appears to be desirable. In addition, these empirical studies point to the need for management accounting to cultivate an understanding of marketing problems and processes, as well as to become increasingly integrated with the strategic components of organisational activities. A concern with strategic priorities is undoubtedly shaping and guiding accounting information suitability and decision-making needs in many British companies.

Some of the studies reviewed indicated that the utilisation of AMTs in manufacturing settings results in traditional accounting techniques being viewed as failing to serve the costing information requirements of the firm. They considered the adoption of novel ways of viewing the accumulation, tracing and allocation of costs as arising from changes taking place on the factory floor. It is thought desirable for the management accountant to remain informed about the nature of such changes. Additionally, the growing dissatisfaction with traditional investment appraisal techniques in certain companies indicates the presence of factors encompassing the decision to acquire AMT equipment which are not assessable. Perhaps strategic investment appraisal, which offers a method of incorporating informal analysis alongside the formal, can help to overcome this concern.

It cannot be doubted that many British companies have taken note of the normative calls for reforms in management accounting practices and that some of these have found the rhetoric of advocates of change persuasive. The number of enterprises which appear to have made a permanent switch to novel internal accounting practices remains small but is not negligible. At the same time, many of those aware of new ideas on offer remain uncommitted or unconvinced. What is of interest is the variance between expectations and reality. Many firms have reported unanticipated difficulties at the implementation phase, others have had to confront resistance to change on the part of some line managers, which some accountants have deemed constructive and useful. Yet others have reported changes of a behavioural type which have altered the organisational status quo in unintended ways. Such observations highlight not only the impact of techniques such as throughput accounting or ABC on enterprises but also the intricate web within which such approaches can come to operate in different organisational contexts. One lesson for the practising management accountant must be that novel accounting ideas offer many possibilities for action. Some of these may also engender change beyond that presumed by their advocates.

9

The Future of Management Accounting

9.1 Introduction

In the recent past, commentators on management accounting have appealed for change more than at any other time in the history of the field. No doubt, concerns by accounting practitioners, academics and consultants parallel wider questions being asked about correct approaches to management generally, which in turn reflect an array of important changes in the business and economic environment. These latter changes include altering forms of technology and the fast pace of changes in consumer markets, as well as intensifying worldwide competition and the emergence of a more receptive attitude on the part of Western enterprises towards foreign management philosophies.

Advocates of reform in management accounting are aware of such factors and therefore vociferously call for significant changes. What must be borne in mind in reflecting on their exhortations is that management accounting itself has a rich past which has been subject to much thought as to how particular enterprise problems can be addressed by designing new accounting techniques. Management accounting as it stands today is the product of historical forces of change which cannot be ignored in conceiving novel pathways leading to further transformations. This concluding chapter seeks to bring to the fore issues covered in earlier chapters which are relevant to those considering ways in which management accounting could change. If management accounting can be viewed as amenable to progress, then what is attempted here is to outline some pathways to progress. Prior to this, however, a discussion of organisational, managerial and technical issues is offered to provide a perspective on future directions in management accounting. The chapter closes by summarising some of the more technical accounting changes considered in this report.

9.2 *Organisational and Managerial Concerns*

The advent of advanced forms of manufacturing technologies and automated systems of production has given rise to a variety of concerns for management accountants. Some of these are technical in nature, but equally a variety of organisational and more broadly managerial concerns have also emerged:

(1) It has been suggested that the installation of a NC machine, or a CAD/CAM system or some other flexible manufacturing system, cannot be considered to be an isolated event to be judged on its own merits given the wide effect on inputs, departments and products that are directly and immediately affected as a consequence. Thus it is not sufficient to consider the cost of the particular AMT vis-à-vis its merits (financial or otherwise). What is essential is to question whether the expected benefits are able to accrue given the specific organisational and managerial structure of the enterprise. If, for instance, a reduction in labour is deemed a benefit, it needs to be asked whether releasing labour is a viable proposition in the context of the enterprise and whether those making the decision to purchase the machine are able also to effect labour resource allocation decisions.

(2) A more fundamental problem is whether a capital acquisition decision can be formulated in terms which embed factors at play in the utilisation of the AMT in question. Effectively, what needs to be considered is whether those who stand to gain from an acquisition need to 'massage the figures' to see the decision go through.

(3) In terms of implementing a management philosophy such as just-in-time or total quality management, which have a variety of accounting implications (see Chapters 2 and 3), it is widely held that such management programmes can ultimately affect most, if not all, areas of organisational activities. Yet it is often not clear that management accounting encompasses the financial implications in such wide terms. This is of particular relevance in organisations which have a diverse product base requiring sophisticated manufacturing technologies and processes and which operate within a complex supply and marketing infrastructure. Moreover, organisations tend to develop particular characteristics over time which become an ingrained part of their functioning. Accounting changes deemed desirable cannot overlook employee attitudes and

organisational culture which can in large part determine the 'success/ failure' of an accounting information system implementation irrespective of technical merits.

(4) There is evidence that in many Western organisations (see Chapters 3, 7 and 8) accounting information systems often collect and process information which is not ultimately reported or where the intended manager does not use it. Whilst such instances are not new, they ought to raise questions about whether such information should be collected and whether it addresses managerial needs. It is not implausible that organisational changes precede accounting alterations with a time lag that is unjustifiably long. For example, a related problem is that of the accounting information systems designer often creating accounting needs in the absence of managerial needs for such data. It might be argued that, ideally, accounting information should reflect a managerial 'pull' rather than an accountant's 'push' view. This does not however preclude accountants from perceiving managerial situations where an accounting innovation may be appropriate.

(5) In considering the installation of AMTs or the adoption of novel work organisation philosophies, it is difficult to escape the view that changing methods of production will affect the manner in which and to whom information is communicated aside from technical considerations. Altering channels of communication as well as the substance of information is likely to affect accounting information needs and uses. It is for the management accountant to understand specific enterprise situations where such changes are occurring and ideally to alter the provision of accounting information accordingly. Associated with this are the more fundamental changes in operational workers' responsibilities and controls caused by production changes. An accounting system must attempt to match controllability and responsibility given work circumstances with the accounting information collected and reported.

(6) Finally, accounting information intended for decision making does not always shape the decision. Rather, in many instances, once the decision is taken, appeal is made to accounting to lend support to it. Although this is not necessarily an undesirable role for accounting, as it can facilitate the managerial process, especially its informal processes, it is essential that the management accounting professional is aware of the way in which accounting is likely to be used. This is especially significant where the organisation adopts

alternative accounting mechanisms since resistance to their adoption may be reflective of accounting's latent functions.

Effectively, what is evident from the studies reviewed in this report irrespective of context, is that only in very limited instances does a change in one aspect of the functioning of the enterprise not have consequences for others. Altering technology or work methods can be seen to implicate accounting change, though not necessarily in an isolated way. Moreover, accounting processes affect an array of enterprise activities indirectly which cannot be disregarded in environments where a systems change is being considered. Given the above observations on organisation and management it is now sought to consider the implications of changes in management accounting for those with an interest in the field.

9.3 Pathways to Progress

This report has covered a wide literature stemming from theory, practice and learned commentaries. It has addressed both technical and organisational and wider managerial issues in exploring existing concerns and challenges in management accounting. Any attempt to distil the variety of issues covered into a set of techniques giving surefire success cannot be fruitful. What is sought, however, is to indicate possible ways in which the management accountant can assess specific enterprise situations in the context of current developments in the field. The following are suggested as offering potential for enhancing accounting's advance toward becoming involved in, if not tackling, certain enterprise concerns, which directly or indirectly impinge on management accounting activities.

(1) The ensemble of emerging work organisation philosophies and advanced manufacturing technologies affect ways in which cost management can take place. The implementation of JIT, TQM or MRP as well as the installation of AMTs have been accompanied in many enterprises by the adoption or consideration of novel accounting perspectives. These include activity based costing, target costing, throughput accounting, life cycle costing, backflush accounting and others (see Chapter 3). There is no recorded instance of any of these techniques fully resolving the problems they set out to tackle. But likewise, many companies using such approaches decidedly continue to do so. Clearly certain benefits are perceived and learning about accounting's potential continues to

take place. Ultimately, no cost management approach can be deemed good or bad in generalised terms. Organisational context and managerial ethos play a large part in determining the worthwhileness of accounting approaches. What is clear is that many companies are experimenting with novel accounting approaches and others are well beyond that stage. Novelty has become convention in many cases and the change is irreversible. Our conclusions cannot therefore dwell on assessing go/no-go judgements on particular techniques and approaches but must highlight what has been learned. What can be said is that any one novel technique or even a combination of such techniques can neither shore up a poorly managed organisation or convert badly managed firms into leading edge firms. Such problems require more than a change in accounting technique. By the same token, one lesson has been that experimenting with novel approaches in management accounting can be of much value as long as more traditional accounting tools are not jettisoned prematurely.

(2) The evidence suggests that accounting mechanisms do not operate in isolation of organisational or managerial factors. Thus in exploring the potential of novel techniques in management accounting, attention must be paid to interrelationships between accounting activities and other enterprise processes. Moreover, innovative cost management techniques often create novel communication channels and information links between accountants and operational line managers. Such changes in the organisational infrastructure cannot be ignored and must comprise part of any effort to redesign an accounting information system.

(3) Trends in altering management philosophy in the functioning of organisations affect cost management systems. Accounting can thus be viewed as reactive to enterprise changes. However, it is not always clear what potential an innovation in management accounting has for enhancing the managerial process until it is in phase and experience with its workings has been gained. The management accountant has a duty to go beyond a watchdog function and to positively develop mechanisms of likely use to the manager or management team. The fast pace of developments in the field allows him or her to satisfy such a role more so than ever before. Ultimately, management accounting can seek to proactively mobilise managerial attention and action in ways which may be neglected in the absence of the accountant's initiative.

(4) More focused pathways must entail some technical issues, including the following:

- Accounting's role is expanding as enterprise activities grow. For example, manufacturer-supplier relationships are in many industries becoming more intricate and purchasers and suppliers interface to a more significant extent. This requires an expansion of the role of accounting in channelling information effectively and in ways seen as relevant to managers. Certainly, extending a system of backflush accounting may be appropriate if just-in-time approaches are in place. But, likewise, where activity based costing is utilised, monitoring trends in cost driver measures can offer insights on experience effects.

- It is clear that activity based costing offers attractions to some companies and not others which have considered its permanent adoption. Certainly, ABC's organisational 'fit' is an issue. But more generally, it remains to be more fully acknowledged that ABC requires certain quite stringent preconditions to be met. It is largely a technique which depends on the ability to trace costs to the point where they become instrumental vis-a-vis the product or the enterprise's hierarchy. Such traceability is not always conceptually, let alone operationally, possible. Problems exist with the manner in which costs are shared by different facilities or departments or products. It has been suggested that the incremental contribution table approach (see Chapter 4) offers one avenue to resolving some of the problems. Again, the extent to which such an approach can provide a viable solution is associated with the managerial ethos of the company.

- It has been pointed out that a financial evaluation of managerial options is appropriate in different contexts but has its limits. It is sometimes desirable to quantify in non-financial terms the specifics of a project or the priorities for the organisation. For example, in considering strategy as a relevent issue in appraising investments, quantification of significant variables may be possible (see Chapter 5). It remains a reality of managerial decision making, nevertheless, that decisions cannot and need not take place purely on the basis of numbers. Not all organisational complexities are amenable to expression within a quantified frame of reference. For this reason, it is not undesirable for a company to consider financial and non-financial measures of performance in tandem with qualitative information. Cost management innovations must therefore not be seen as precluding the worthwhileness of unquantified information.

- Ultimately, enterprise problems entailing the use of accounting information can be aided by a particular technique such as ABC or target costing or life cycle costing depending on circumstances. But no enterprise can tackle all its accounting challenges through any one such technique. ABC or any other such accounting tool cannot be a universal panacea for enterprise ills.

(5) This report has attempted to place cost management practices in the context of countries in which they are found to exist. Certain techniques may seem so innocuous as not to require a specific cultural context. For instance, activity based costing, throughput accounting and life cycle costing may at first appear to be able to yield anticipated effects in whatever cultural context in which they are applied. Conversely, target costing, benchmarking and backflush accounting might be expected to be dependent on an acceptance of their underpinnings. Yet it has been suggested that different countries focus on very different technical accounting approaches. Thought must be given to the array of organisational practices which are in some sense reflective of wider cultural characteristics before any attempt is made to transplant these mechanisms into a foreign environment. No doubt attempts can be made to mould any technique or philosophy to a given context, but expectations as to what they might contribute must likewise be reassessed. It is not here suggested that the Japanese approach to cost tables, or the French *tableau de bord* or the German capacity usage focus is not to be adopted outside these countries, but that emphasis on these practices may rely on a variety of factors which may not be present in all contexts. Thus, experimentation is desirable so long as an awareness of enterprise-specific complexities and possibly relevant social factors is present.

Reforming management accounting

Many possibilities for maintaining the continued relevance of management accounting in organisations adopting advanced manufacturing technologies have been considered in this book. It is believed that the arguments mounted for any one technique or set of techniques are not sufficient to suggest that management accounting in the UK overall should change in any one particular direction or set of directions. Calls have been made for altering management accounting practice in the name of theoretical ideas about its true role in advanced manufacturing environments. New approaches to the better practice of management accounting have been articulated relying on relatively limited empirical evidence. As indicated above, much ground remains to be covered, however, to achieve an understanding of the relevant factors in manufacturing environments adopting innovative production systems and workflow organisation techniques before management accounting reforms can be fully considered.

This report has indicated certain possible repercussions from the adoption of AMT. There are implications for information systems and information flows, including changes in the forms of information seen as relevant (for instance, whether financial, quantitative or qualitative data is appropriate). AMT necessitates use of a shifting time-frame (incorporating the short term and the long term). Management attitudes can affect management accounting practices. An outward-looking management team may, for example, focus on target product prices as opposed to predetermining product costs in order to formulate prices. Likewise, shifting relationships between suppliers, producers and assemblers may alter the areas which information systems and management controls need to encompass suggesting that associated changes in reporting practices, accounting decision-making and control systems should accompany such shifts in relationships. Further, if links are forged using strategic management accounting between corporate strategy and operational processes within manufacturing or service organisations, such ties may also point to the need for new forms of accounting data and the use of new communication channels for financial information.

This report has attempted to highlight a number of opportunities represented by novel accounting methods. However, many challenges and opportunities remain for still further exploring possibilities in management accounting as changes take place in the manufacturing environment and other sectors of industry. One important element of the new manufacturing environment which appears to have been neglected in the literature is the accounting and control of material and bought-in parts as well as the evaluation of subcontractors. The use of purchaser/supplier partnerships (see Chapter 6) as producers, suppliers and assemblers become increasingly integrated, allows the accountant to introduce altered controls and management accounting techniques suitable for this approach. This is equally true of the service sector and of the financial services industry in particular. This is a fast changing sector within which firms are rapidly diversifying their portfolio of activities; because of the lack of space, it has been generally ignored here.

Other challenges will continue to compete for attention. For example, an increasingly market orientated emphasis on product costing and its relation to strategy rather than an internally focused pursuit of accurate product costing seems not only to hold prospects for new management accounting developments in this area but very possibly represents a desirable avenue for change. The management accounting profession continues to be faced with the opportunity of integrating and co-ordinating the output of non-financial data emanating from corporate activities in both advanced manufacturing environments and service industries, into management accounting systems. The relevance of considering qualitative and non-financial quantitative information encompassing the management of strategic and operational organisational processes cannot be overemphasised. Empirical evidence suggests a growing role for this type of information in enterprise management and management accountants cannot ignore calls for their involvement in this respect.

Boundaries of individual entities have become blurred in chains of organisations, such as subcontractor chains, as well as within organisations adopting increasingly flexible, informal and less regimented styles of management. Management accounting can position itself so as to play a more important role in the management of such organisations by gaining an appreciation of new forms of information requirements and the changing nature of information exchange processes. In this respect it has been possible to comment on some possible developments in the more technical accounting sphere. Some arguments made in this book are briefly reiterated below to help make the case for these observations.

Technical concerns

The shift to changed production technology or to novel forms of work organisation is a managerial decision, sometimes strategic and proactive, and at other times a survival tactic. The repercussions are far-reaching, ranging from organisational and managerial effects as discussed above to those involving important technical considerations in accounting terms. This part of the chapter discusses some of the technical concerns.

(1) A major problem has always been that of allocating costs in an acceptable and rational manner. Yet usefulness and the cost of information must be viewed as imposing limits to the search for accuracy. Today, it may be argued that information technology has removed many of the logistical and financial barriers to the pursuit of cost accuracy. The set-up and processing costs of an accounting system producing what is considered accurate data are no more expensive than one producing inaccurate data. Yet there are still limits to cost accuracy. In part, this is because the old dictum 'different costs for different purposes' continues to have relevance. Accuracy is not an independent notion. True costs do not exist though costs that are viewed as of sufficient utility in particular situations can be obtained. Thus, as the cost of obtaining accuracy in technological terms has diminished, ideas about the attainability of accuracy have also changed. Relevant accuracy must be judgemental rather than objective.

(2) Likewise, alterations in production complexity and automated technology have caused shifts in ideas about what ought to be measured. Thus, the adoption of AMT, where it is accompanied by a reduction in labour usage, as is often intended, can result in direct labour usage no longer being correlated in any reasonable way with changes in overheads. This difficulty is compounded by reductions in direct labour input being accompanied by large increases in overhead costs. These stem in part from the actual investment in AMT but also from associated support costs such as additional maintenance, training and software costs.

Where direct labour is reduced as a result of AMT and other investments, machine utilisation measures such as machine hours or power input provides an appropriate alternative determinant of overhead costs. But this is again subject to difficulties. The reasoning is based on the rejection of any volume based measure as a determinant of overhead. Clearly, if certain costs referred to as overheads are not in any way tied to volume changes then measures of scale cannot be thought appropriate for costing purposes. This has led to a body of literature appealing for cost drivers reflective of scope as well as scale. Certainly, activity based costing has been adopted by some enterprises as an alternative to the use of traditional, simple volume based determinants of overheads.

(3) The empirical literature on activity based costing is limited but nevertheless indicates that whereas the use of cost drivers relating to scope is deemed useful in certain instances, in others scale continues to be seen as the more relevant. This does not discredit the value of activity based costing. Indeed, it confirms its role albeit in perhaps quite limited circumstances (see Chapter 3). What is of concern is the question of why companies which could seemingly benefit from the application of cost driver analysis are averse to it. The response to this question may certainly relate to organisational and managerial factors as suggested above. Resistance to change does not need to be justified by only economic logic. Organisational structure and enterprise culture can combine to impede attempts to instil accounting rationality. In such cases, the problem with activity based costing is not that certain enterprises are unwilling to partake in it; it is that activity based costing is itself inappropriate for the enterprises in question.

(4) Perhaps more fundamentally, activity based accounting cannot ensure the comprehensive traceability of costs to products. This is simply because certain costs are not amenable to such a search. A resource may be categorised into one of three classes: that which is traceable to specific final goods outputs or to process outputs; that which is not traceable in this manner because resources and their outputs are generally available throughout the organisation; and that which produces outputs which are common to more than one cost object and which may fall into either of the other two classes. ABC attempts to strip out of overheads the resources in the first class and treat them as traceable. The second class of resources which simultaneously provide the same service throughout the organisation is viewed here as requiring a very different accounting treatment.

It is also to be noted that the effects of a given driver of costs may not be generally independent of the chosen levels of other drivers. It has been suggested in this report that the volume of output in a period cannot be treated as independent of production scheduling unless all scheduling decisions are frozen. The conditions that have to be placed on the interaction of resources in order to yield independent resource pools are very restrictive and more constraining when cost pools are considered. This view suggests that volume related factors are far more important than some ABC advocates believe.

(5) It is thus suggested that the use of ABC may help us understand some costs which are presently treated as fixed overheads but this use of ABC is limited because ideally it requires an empirically based exercise to ascertain how costs vary with activities. The use of ABC also requires certain very stringent conditions to be met. There are costs which ABC cannot address. This arises where resources and therefore costs serve more than one facility, product or department.

The cost of the resources which manifest jointness between products or organisational units cannot be traced to the consumption of their outputs only by any organisational constituent except where they are fully dedicated to a given organisational unit, such as a cost centre, plant or division and are excluded from use by other parts of the organisation. Thus, the costs of joint outputs and resources may be difficult to trace other than to the set of all organisational units which require their use and which cannot be excluded from their use. Many resources of this type are sited at the division, group and corporate level and cannot therefore be further traced down the organisation. That joint resources involve providing capacity rather than variable inputs used up directly in production leads to a major suggestion in this report. This is that capacity resources and their associated costs should be accounted for in a way that reflects both capacity provision and the public or joint characteristics of such resources.

(6) It has been noted that, in principle, an economically sensible transfer price can be ascertained for the use of joint resources where exclusion is possible or where opting out is permitted, especially where equivalent services are available on the market. Firms may have a larger number of tools to enforce exclusion than the market. Thus, accountants should seek to distinguish between those joint resources which are excludable and those which are not.

(7) It has also been suggested that levying a charge for capacity normally in the form of a total 'rental' charge on the users of that capacity distinguishing between unused capacity and utilised capacity can be considered. This type of fixed charge for the capacity provided in a period reflects the pattern of resource usage of capacity resources. Separating this charge into the part relating to utilised capacity and that relating to unused capacity should help decision-making. This charge is not an allocated cost; rather, it is the contribution required to fund the resource in accordance with plans

made to finance the resource at the time of its acquisition. Ideally, the charge for utilised capacity should be based on the price of obtaining this service on the market as is frequently done for floor space in hotels and departmental stores. If this is not possible, any charge should be based not on allocated costs but on seeking a contribution to joint costs based on what products or organisational units can bear. Such charges are not allocations because they reflect the characteristics of the markets faced by firms.

(8) Finally, it has been suggested that a revised form of accounting report which may be more helpful in dealing with costs in dynamic and unstable environments and which has a long history of use in Germany can be implemented. This report incorporates the suggestion that many of the problems with overheads can be overcome by using a contribution approach for each element of the organisation and the product hierarchy. Such a statement shows an ascending set of contributions either for organisational elements or for parts of the product hierarchy. The actual format of the statement depends on the technology of the firm, the organisational hierarchy of the company and the responsibility of the various managers. The actual arrangement will thus be firm-specific. Such an approach has been recommended where resources are not traceable to lower levels in the product or organisational hierarchy. In order to make sense of the contribution of each product or organisational category, it is necessary to deduct from the unit's revenue all the incremental costs of the unit. A greater use of contribution analysis as defined than is normal in Anglo-Saxon accounting is thus being suggested.

9.4 Concluding Remarks

Organisations should be encouraged to react to challenges to management accounting arising from the installation of modern production systems and other factors using ideas discussed in this report and in other ways considered innovative. Management accountants have an important role to play here. There is an urgent need to commission further empirical studies concerning not only the manufacturing sector but also the service sector, to identify and evaluate new management accounting systems and to evaluate the reasons for some companies' reluctance to change their accounting systems in any fundamental way. Certainly, that students are being educated and examined on new techniques and concepts in a critical way is desirable. Practising management accountants should continue to be encouraged both to attend professional development courses exploring theoretical techniques in the face of changes in the manufacturing and service environments and especially to participate in discussion networks. The management accounting profession should continue to keenly monitor the results of changes and continue its research efforts in the areas covered in this book. The Chartered Institute of Management Accountants needs to continue to encourage its members to participate in developing innovative ways of maintaining their important role in aiding the management of enterprises. The Institute might enhance its role of becoming a principal repository of information concerning the 'new' management accounting and establishing itself further as a leading authority on these matters.

A number of challenges and opportunities for management accounting have been identified in this report. The Institute can take the lead in their further growth and is well positioned to play a major role in financial management in the twenty-first century. Journeys along at least some of the pathways to progress identified here offer considerable promise for continued growth of the profession of management accounting. Equally, ignoring the challenges listed here and those which will arise in the future are likely to harm the profession substantially.

As management accounting moves into the twenty-first century, what happens in this last decade of the millennium will be crucial. Management accounting has already undergone a period of trials and tribulations and will no doubt continue to do so. Alterations, in many cases irreversible, have taken place whereas instances of resistance to change also continue to emerge, and with good reasons. What is essential is for management accounting to continue its self-inspection, and to do so by heeding transformations external to the field. Certainly shifts in management philosophies will continue to occur, trends will come and go and new realisations will emerge as technological advances and other societal changes take place. Within such a context of dynamic change, management accounting cannot afford to be inward oriented. Its continued development must rest on its rich history side by side with an appreciation of pressures, constraints and opportunities that enable it to maintain a proactive edge.

Glossary

Activity based accounting

Examination of activities across the entire chain of value-adding organisational processes underlying causes (drivers) of cost and profit.

Backflush accounting

A cost accounting system which focuses on the output of the organisation and then works backwards to allocate costs between cost of goods sold and inventory.

Computer aided design (CAD)

Computer-based technology allowing interactive design and testing of a manufacturing component on a visual display terminal.

Computer aided manufacturing (CAM)

Computer-based technology to permit the programming and control of production equipment in the manufacturing task.

Computer integrated manufacturing (CIM)

The use of computers and other advanced manufacturing techniques to monitor and perform manufacturing tasks.

Cost driver

An activity or factor which generates costs.

Cost tables

Databases of all costs involved in production incorporating cost-based knowledge of sub-components.

Economic order quantity (EOQ)

A mathematically derived optimal quantity of stock which should be ordered so as to minimise both holding and ordering costs.

Functional analysis

An activity aimed at linking product functions and perceived value to customers with the cost of designing functions.

Flexible manufacturing system (FMS)

An integrated production system which is computer controlled to produce a family of parts in a flexible manner.

Islands of automation (IA)

Stand alone advanced manufacturing technology not fully integrating the total manufacturing process.

Just-in-time (JIT)

Workflow organisation technique to allow rapid, high quality, flexible production whilst minimising stock levels and manufacturing waste.

Life cycle costing

Accumulation of costs for activities that occur over the entire life cycle of a product, from inception to abandonment.

Materials requirements planning (MRP)

A system which maximises the efficiency in the timing of raw material orders through to the manufacture and assembly of the final product.

Numerical control machine (NC machine)

A manufacturing tool which can be programmed within predefined performance criteria to perform required production activities. It can be computer controlled (Computer NC) or centrally controlled (Direct NC).

Set-up

Process of preparing a machine or manufacturing cell for production.

Strategic investment appraisal (SIA)

Linking corporate strategy to costs and benefits associated with AMT adoption by combining both formal and informal evaluation procedures.

Strategic management accounting

Accounting procedures which stress extra-organisational variables as well as value-added results of internal activities and non-financial data evaluation.

Target cost

A product cost estimate derived from a competitive market price. Used to reduce costs through continuous improvement and replacement of technologies and processes.

Throughput accounting

A method of performance measurement which relates production and other costs to throughput. Throughput accounting product costs relate to usage of key resources by various products.

Transactions

Physical and electronic documentation of any production activity.

Value engineering

An activity which helps to design products which meet customer needs at the lowest cost whilst assuring the required standard of quality and reliability.

Work cell

Grouping of individual or machines to perform a manufacturing task.

Bibliography

Adler, P.S. (1987), 'A Plant Productivity Measure for "Hi-Tech" Manufacturing', *Interfaces* (November/December).

Aggarwal, S.C. (1985), 'MRP, JIT, OPT, FMS?', *Harvard Business Review* (September/October).

Albright, T. and Roth, H. (1994), 'Managing Quality Through the Quality Loss Function', *Journal of Cost Management* (Winter).

Allen, D. (1986), 'Strategic Financial Management', in M. Bromwich and A. G. Hopwood (eds.), *Research and Current Issues in Management Accounting*, Pitman.

Allen, D. (1991), 'Management of Quality', *Management Accounting* (UK) (October).

Anderson, J.R. (1988), 'Unit Manufacturing Cost Tracking Systems at Xerox' in *Cost Accounting for the 90's: The Challenge of Technological Change*, Montvale, New Jersey: NAA, 1988.

Ansari, A. and Modaress, B. (1986), 'Just-In-Time Purchasing: Problems and Solutions', *Journal of Purchasing and Materials Management* (Summer).

Aoki, M. (1985), *Information, incentives and bargaining in the Japanese Economy*, Cambridge: Cambridge University Press.

Archer, G. (1991), 'MRP: A Review of Failure and a Proposal for Recovery Using CBS', *BPICS Control* (January).

Ardoin, J.L., Michel, D. and Schmidt, J. (1986), *Le Controle de Gestion*, Paris: Publi-Union.

Argyris, C. and Kaplan, R.S. (1993) 'Implementing New Knowledge: The Case of Activity Based Costing', Harvard Business School Working Paper No. 93-043.

Armstrong, P. (1985), 'Competition Between the Organisational Professions and the Evolution of Management Control Strategies', *Accounting, Organizations and Society*, 10/2.

Armstrong, P. (1987), 'The Rise of Accounting Controls in British Capitalist Enterprises', *Accounting, Organizations and Society*, 12/5.

Armstrong, P. (1990), 'The Bromwich and Bhimani Report – A Lay Person's Reaction', *Management Accounting Research* (June).

Ashton, J.E. and Cook, F.X. (1989), 'Time to Reform Job Shop Manufacturing', *Harvard Business Review* (March/April).

Ashton, D., Hopper, T., and Scapens, R. W., (eds.) (1991), *Issues in Management Accounting*, London: Prentice Hall.

Astebro, T., 'Computer Aided Design', in R.U. Ayres, W. Haywood, M.E. Merchant, J. Ranta and H-J Warnecke (eds.) (1992), *Computer Integrated Manufacturing (Volume II): The Past, the Present and the Future*, London: Chapman and Hall.

Atkinson, A.A. (1987a), *Intraform Cost and Resource Allocation: Theory and Practice*, Society of Canadian Management Accounting and Canadian Academic Accounting Association Research Monograph.

Atkinson, A.A. (1987b), *Cost Estimation in Management Accounting – Six Case Studies*, Toronto: SMA.

Atkinson, A.B. and Stiglitz, J.E. (1980), *Lectures on Public Economics*, Maidenhead Berks: McGraw–Hill.

Ayers, J.B. (1988), 'Understanding your Cost Drivers – the Key to Disciplined Planning', *Journal of Cost Management for the Manufacturing Industry* (Fall).

Ayres, R.U. (1991), *Computer Integrated Manufacturing* (Vol.1): *Revolution in Progress*, London: Chapman & Hall.

Azzone, G. and Bertelé, U. (1990), 'Idle Capacity and Timeliness in Mix Change Decisions', *Engineering Costs and Production Economics*.

Babad, Y.M. and Balachandran, B.V. (1993) 'Cost Driver Optimisation in Activity-Based Costing', *The Accounting Review* (July).

Bailey, J. (1991) 'Implementation of ABC Systems by U.K. Companies', *Management Accounting* (UK) (February).

Banker, R.D. and Johnston, H.H. (1993), 'An Empirical Study of Cost Drivers in the US Airline Industry', *The Accounting Review* (July).

Banker, R.D. and Potter, G. (1993), 'Economic Implications of Single Cost Driver Systems', *Journal of Management Accounting Research*.

Banker, R.D., Potter, G. and Schroeder, R.G.(1993), 'Reporting Manufacturing Performance Measures to Workers: An Empirical Study', *Journal of Management Accounting Research*.

Barekat, M. (1991), 'The Painless Route to Successful MRP II Implementation', *Logistics* (May).

Barratt, M. (1990), 'Making MRP and JIT Work', *Purchasing and Supply Management* (August).

Baumol, W.J. and Ordover, J.A. (1986), 'On the Optimality of Public Goods Pricing with Exclusion Devices', in Baumol, W.J. (ed.) *Microtheory: Applications and Origins*, Brighton: Wheatsheaf.

Baumol, W.J., Panzar, J.C. and Willig, R.D. (1988), *Contestable Markets and the Theory of Industry Structure*, (revised edition), New York: Harcourt Brace Jovanovich.

Bennett, R.E., Hendricks, J.A., Keys, D.E. and Rudnicki, E.J. (1987), *Cost Accounting for Factory Automation*, Montvale, New Jersey: NAA.

Berlant, D., Browning, R. and Foster, G. (1990), 'How Hewlett-Packard Gets Numbers it can Trust', *Harvard Business Review* (Jan./Feb.).

Berliner, C. and Brimson, J. (1988), *Cost Management in Today's Advanced Manufacturing: The CAM-I Conceptual Design*, Boston: Harvard Business School Press.

Bescos, P., Dobler, P., Mendoza, C. and Maulleau, G. (1993), *Controle de Gestion et Management*, Paris: Montchrestien.

Bhimani, A. (1993), 'Performance Measures in UK Manufacturing Companies: The State of Play', *Management Accounting* (UK) (December).

Bhimani, A. (1994a), 'Monitoring Performance Measures in U.K. Manufacturing Companies', *Management Accounting* (UK) (January).

Bhimani, A. (1994b), 'Modern Cost Management: Beyond Functionalism', paper presented at the Management Accounting Symposium of the European Accounting Association Conference, Venice (6–8 April).

Bhimani, A. (forthcoming), 'Modern Cost Management: Putting the Organisation before the Technique', *International Journal of Production Economics*.

Bhimani, A. and Bromwich, M. (1989), 'Advanced Manufacturing Technology and Strategic Perspectives in Management Accounting', *European Accounting News*, (January).

Bhimani, A. and Bromwich, M. (1991), 'Accounting for Just-In-Time Manufacturing Systems', *CMA: The Management Accounting Magazine*, (February).

Bhimani, A. and Bromwich, M. (1992a), 'Management Accounting: Evolution in Progress', in C. Drury (ed.), *Management Accounting Handbook*, (London: CIMA).

Bhimani, A. and Bromwich, M. (1992b), 'Advanced Manufacturing Technology and Accounting: A Renewed Alliance' *Computer Integrated Manufacturing Systems*.

Bhimani, A. and Pigott, D. (1992a), 'ABC in a Pharmaceuticals Company: A Remedy?', *Management Accounting* (UK) (December).

Bhimani, A. and Pigott, D. (1992b), 'Implementing ABC: A Case Study of Organizational and Behavioural Consequences,' *Management Accounting Research* (June).

Bicheno, J. (1991), *Implementing JIT*, Bedford, UK.: IFS Publications.

Biddle, G.C. and Steinberg, R. (1984), 'Allocation of Joint and Common Costs', *Journal of Accounting Literature* (Vol.3).

Boons, A.A.M., Roberts, H.J.E. and Roozen, F.A. (1992), 'Contrasting Activity-Based Costing with the German/Dutch Cost Pool Method', *Management Accounting Research*, (June).

Borden, J.P. (1990), 'Review of Literature on Activity-Based Costing', *Journal of Cost Management for the Manufacturing Industry* (Spring).

Bright, J., Davies, R.E., Downes, C.A. and Sweeting, R.C. (1992), 'The Deployment of Costing Techniques and Practices: A UK Study', *Management Accounting Research* (3).

Brimson, J.A. (1988), 'High-Tech Cost Accounting', *Journal of Cost Management for the Manufacturing Industry* (Winter).

Brimson, J.A. (1991), *Activity Accounting: An Activity-Based Costing Approach*, New York: John Wiley.

Brinker, B. J. (1993), 'Theme Issues on Business Process Reengineering'. *Journal of Cost Management* (Fall).

British Chamber of Commerce in Japan (1988), *Seihin-ka How Japan Brings R & D to the Market* (Tokyo, Japan: BCCJ).

Bromwich, M. (1988), 'Managerial Accounting Definition and Scope – from a Managerial View', *Management Accounting* (UK) (September).

Bromwich, M. (1989), 'The Revolution in Management Accounting?', R. J. Chambers Research Lecture, delivered at University of Sydney.

Bromwich, M. (1990), 'The Case for Strategic Management Accounting: The Role of Accounting Information for Strategy in Competitive Markets', *Accounting, Organizations and Society*, 1.

Bromwich, M. (1991), 'Accounting Information for Strategic Excellence' in Lars Vedso (ed.), *Management Accounting and Strategy: New Ideas, New Experiences* (in Danish), Herning, Denmark: Systime.

Bromwich, M. (1993), The Economic Foundations of Activity Based Costing (ABC) in Dellman, K. and Franz, K. P. (eds.) *Neuere Entwicklungen ims Kostenmanagment*, Paul Haupt Verlag.

Bromwich, M. (1989), and Bhimani, A., *Management Accounting: Evolution not Revolution*, London: CIMA.

Bromwich, M., and Bhimani, A. (1991), 'Strategic Investment Appraisal', *Management Accounting* (USA) (March).

Bromwich, M., and Inoue, S. (1994), *Management Practices and Cost Management Problems in Japanese-Affiliated Companies in the United Kingdom*, Research Report, London: CIMA.

Bromwich, M., and Wang, Q. (forthcoming), 'Accounting for Overheads Critiques and Reforms', *Research Report*, CIMA, 1993.

Bruns, Jr., W.J. (1987), 'A Field Study of an Attempt to Change an Embedded Cost Accounting System', in Bruns and Kaplan.

Bruns, Jr., W.J. and Kaplan, R. (1987), (eds.) *Accounting and Management: Field Study Perspectives*, Boston, Mass.: Harvard Business School Press.

Brunsson, N. (1990), 'Deciding for Responsibility and Legitimation: Alternative Interpretations of Organisational Decision-Making', *Accounting, Organisations and Society*, Vol.15, No.1/2.

Burchell, S., Clubb, C., Hopwood, A.G., Hughes, J. and Nahapiet, J. (1980), 'The Role of Accounting in Organisations and Society', *Accounting, Organizations and Society*, Vol.5, No.1.

Burstein, M.C. (1988), 'Life-Cycle Costing' in *Cost Accounting for the '90s: Responding to Technological Change*, Montvale, New Jersey: National Association of Accountants.

Business International, *Cost Reduction Programmes in the United Kingdom*, London: KPMG Management Consulting, 1992.

CAM-I, *Glossary of Activity-Based Management*, CAM-I, 1990.

CIMA, *Performance Measurement in the Manufacturing Sector*, London: CIMA, 1993.

Campbell, A., Currie, W., and Warner, M. (1989), 'Innovation, Skills and Training: Micro-electronics and Manpower in the UK and W. Germany' in Hirst, P. and Zeitlin, J. (eds.), *Reversing Industrial Decline?* Oxford: Berg.

Campbell, R.J. and Porcano, T.M. (1979), 'The Contribution of Materials Requirements Planning (MRP) to Budgeting and Cost Control', *Cost and Management* (January/February).

Choi, F.D.S. and Hiramatsu, K. (1987), *Accounting and Financial Reporting in Japan*, Berks, UK: Van Nostrand Reinhold.

Christensen, J. and Demski, J.S. (1991), 'The Classical Foundation of "Modern" Costing', Working Paper, Yale University.

Clemens, J.D. (1991), 'How we Changed our Accounting System', *Management Accounting* (USA) (February).

Coates, J.B. and Longden, S.G. (1989), '*Management Accounting: The Challenge of Technological Innovation*', London: CIMA.

Cobb, I. (1991), 'Just-in-Time and the Management Accountant', University of Dundee Research Survey.

Cobb, I. (1993), *JIT and the Management Accountant: A Study of Current UK Practice*, London: CIMA.

Cobb, I., Innes, J. and Mitchell, F. (1992), *Activity-Based Costing: Problems in Practice*, London: CIMA.

Cohen, J.R. and Paquette, L. (1991), 'Management Accounting Practices: Perceptions of Controllers', *Journal of Cost Management for the Manufacturing Industry* (Fall).

Cohen, S.I. and Loeb, M. (1982), 'Public Goods, Common Inputs and the Efficiency of Full Cost Allocation', *The Accounting Review*, (April).

Cokins, G., Stratton, A., and Helbling, J. (1992), *An ABC Manager's Primer*, Montvale, N.J.: IMA.

Cole, R.E. (1993), 'Improving Product Quality through Continuous Feedback', *Management Review* (October).

Collins, F. and Werner, M.L. (1990), 'Improving Performance with Cost Drivers', *Journal of Accountancy* (June).

Cooper, R. (1987), 'The Two-Stage Procedure in Cost Accounting – Part 2', *Journal of Cost Management for the Manufacturing Industry* (Summer).

Cooper, R. (1988), 'The Rise of Activity Based Costing – Part I' *Journal of Cost Management for the Manufacturing Industry* (Summer).

Cooper, R. (1989a), 'You Need a New Cost System When ...', *Harvard Business Review*, (January/February).

Cooper, R. (1989b), 'The Rise of Activity Based Costing: Part Three', *Journal of Cost Management for the Manufacturing Industry* (Fall).

Cooper, R. (1990a), 'Implementing an Activity-Based Costing System', *Journal of Cost Management for the Manufacturing Industry* (Spring).

Cooper, R. (1990b), 'Cost Classification in Unit-Based and Activity-Based Manufacturing Cost Systems', *Journal of Cost Management for the Manufacturing Industry* (Fall).

Cooper, R., and Kaplan, R. S. (1987), 'How Cost Accounting Systematically Distorts Product Costs', in Bruns, W. J. and Kaplan,

R. S. (eds.), *Accounting and Management: Field Study Perspectives*, Boston: Harvard Business School Press.

Cooper, R. and Kaplan, R.S. (1991a), 'Profit Priorities from Activity-Based Costing', *Harvard Business Review* (May/June).

Cooper, R. and Kaplan, R. S. (1991b), *The Design of Cost Management Systems: Text Cases and Readings*, Englewood Cliffs, N.J.: Prentice Hall.

Cooper, R. and Kaplan, R. S. (1992), 'Activity-Based Systems: Measuring the Cost of Resource Usage', *Accounting Horizons* (September).

Cooper, R., Kaplan, R. S., Maisel, L.S., Morrissey, E., and Oehn, R. N. (1992), *Implementing Activity-Based Management: Moving from Analysis to Action*, Montvale, NJ.: IMA.

Cooper, R., and Turney, P. B. (1990), 'Internally Focused Activity-Based Cost Systems', in R. S. Kaplan (ed.), *Measures for Manufacturing Excellence*, Cambridge, Mass.: Harvard Business School Press.

Coulthurst, N. (1989a), 'The New Factory', *Management Accounting* (UK) (March).

Coulthurst, N. (1989b), 'Organising and Accounting for the New Factory', *Management Accounting* (UK) (May).

Crosby, P.B. (1979), *Quality is Free*, New York: McGraw Hill.

Crosby, P.B. (1984), 'The Just-in-Time Manufacturing Process: Control of Quality and Quantity', *Production and Inventory Management* (Fourth Quarter).

Currie, W. L. (1989a), 'Investing in CAD: A Case of Ad Hoc Decision-Making', *Long Range Planning*.

Currie, W. L.(1989b), 'The Art of Justifying New Technology to Top Management', Paper presented at the Organisational and Strategic Decision-Making Workshop, Bradford Management Centre (January).

Currie, W. L. (1990), 'Strategic Management of Advanced Manufacturing Technology', *Management Accounting* (UK).

Currie, W. L. (1991), 'Managing Technology: A Crisis in Management Accounting', *Management Accounting* (UK).

Czyzewski, A.B. and Hull, R.P. (1991), 'Improving Profitability with Life Cycle Costing', *Journal of Cost Management for the Manufacturing Industry* (Summer).

D'Amore, R. and Miller, R. (1988), 'Revving the Motors at Harley-Davidson: New Manufacturing Technology Requires New Accounting Philosophy' in *Cost Accounting for the 90's: Responding to Technological Change*, Montvale, New Jersey: NAA.

Dahlgaard, J. J., Karijc, G. K., Kristensen, K., and Norreklit, L. (1989), *A Comparative Study of Quality Control Methods and Principles in Japan, South Korea and Denmark* (Aarhus, Denmark: Institute for Informations Behandling).

Dale, R.G. Lascelles, D.M. and Plunkett, J.J. (1990), 'The Process of Total Quality Management', in B.G. Dale and J.J. Plunkett (eds.) *Managing Quality*, London: Philip Allan.

Darlington, J., Innes, J., Mitchell, F. and Woodward, J. (1992), 'Throughput Accounting: The Garrett Automotive Experience', *Management Accounting* (UK) (April).

Datar, S.M., Kekre, S., Mukhopadhyay, T. and Srinvasen, K. (1993), 'Simultaneous Estimates of Cost Drivers', *The Accounting Review*, (July).

Davies, R., and Sweeting, R. C. (1991a), 'Surmount Major Barriers and Establish New Techniques', *Management Consultancy* (January).

Davies, R. and Sweeting, R. C. (1991b), 'Industrial Revolution'?, *Certified Accountant* (May).

Davis, H. and Kramer, S. (1991), 'QRP Route Will Consolidate Grip of Giants', *Materials Handling News* (September).

Deming, W.E. (1982), *Quality, Productivity and Competitive Position*, Cambridge, Mass.: MIT Press.

Develin and Partners (1988), *The Effectiveness of the Corporate Overhead in British Business – 1988 Report*, London: Develin and Partners.

Dilts, M.D. and Grabski, S.V. (1990), 'Advanced Manufacturing Technologies: What They Can Offer Management Accountants', *Management Accounting* (USA) (February).

Dimnik, A.P. (1988), 'Management Accounting and the Adoption of Flexible Automation', Ph.D. Dissertation (University of Western Ontario).

Dimnik, T. and Kudar, R. (1989), 'Don't Throw Out the Baby with the Bathwater', *CMA The Management Accounting Magazine* (July-August).

Dopuch, N. (1993), 'A Perspective on Cost Drivers', *The Accounting Review* (68).

Dore, R. (1973), *British Factory – Japanese Factory: The Origins of National Diversity in Industrial Relations*, University of California Press.

Drucker, P. (1990), *The New Realities*, New York: Harper and Row.

Drury, C. (1989), 'Activity-Based Costing', *Management Accounting* (UK) (Sept.).

Drury, C. (1990), 'Product Costing in the 1990's', *Accountancy* (May).

Drury, C. (1992), (ed.), *Management Accounting Handbook*, Butterworth Heinemann in association with CIMA.

Drury, C., Braund, S., Osborne, P. and Tayles, M. (1993), *A Survey of Management Accounting Practices in UK Manufacturing Companies*, London: ACCA.

Dugdale, D. (1990), 'Costing Systems in Transition: A Review of Recent Developments', *Management Accounting* (UK) (January).

Ellis, J., and Williams, D. (1993), '*Corporate Strategy and Financial Analysis*', London: Pitman.

Emore, J.R. and Ness, J.A. (1991), 'The Slow Pace of Meaningful Change in Cost Systems', *Journal of Cost Management for the Manufacturing Industry* (Winter).

Engwall, R.L. (1988), 'Cost Management Systems for Defence Contractors', in *Cost Accounting for the '90's: Responding to Technological Change*, Montvale, N.J.: National Association of Accountants.

Faulhaber, G.R. (1975), 'Cross Subsidization: Pricing in Public Enterprise', *American Economic Review* (65).

Feigenbaum, A.V. (1983), *Total Quality Control*, New York: McGraw-Hill.

Ferguson, P. (1988), 'Accounting for Just-in-Time: Sorting out the Conflicting Advice', *Management Accounting* (UK) (December).

Fern, R. H., and Tipgos, M. (1988), 'Controllers as Business Strategists: A Progress Report', *Management Accounting* (USA) (March).

Finnie, J. (1986), 'Financial Evaluation of Advanced Manufacturing Systems' in Voss, C.A. (ed.), *Managing Advanced Manufacturing Technology: Proceedings of the UK Operations Management Association Conference, 2-3 January 1986*, Kempston, Beds: IFS Publications.

Fitzgerald, L., Johnston, R., Brignall, T. J., Silvestro, R. and Voss, C. (1992), *Performance Measurement in Service Businesses*, London: CIMA.

Foster, G., and Horngren, C. T. (1987), 'JIT: Cost Accounting and Cost Management Issues', *Management Accounting* (USA) (June).

Foster, G. and Horngren, C.T. (1988), 'Cost Accounting and Cost Management in a JIT Environment', *Journal of Cost Management for the Manufacturing Industry* (Winter).

Foster, G. and Gupta, M. (1993), 'Manufacturing Overhead Cost Driver Analysis', *Journal of Accounting and Economics* (January).

Fox, R. (1991), 'ABC: A Comment on the Logic', *Management Accounting* (UK) (October).

Fremgen, J.M. and Liao, S.S. (1981), *The Allocation of Corporate Indirect Costs*, Montvale N.J.: National Association of Accountants.

Galloway, D. and Waldron, D. (1988a), 'Throughput Accounting: The Need for a New Language for Manufacturing', *Management Accounting* (UK) (November).

Galloway, D. and Waldron, D. (1988b), 'Throughput Accounting Part 2: Ranking Products Profitably', *Management Accounting* (UK) (December).

Galloway, D. and Waldron, D. (1989a), 'Throughput Accounting Part 3: A Better Way to Control Labour Costs', *Management Accounting* (UK) (January).

Galloway, D. and Waldron, D. (1989b), 'Throughput Accounting Part 4: Moving on to Complex Products', *Management Accounting* (UK) (February).

Garvin, D.A. (1983), 'Quality on the Line', *Harvard Business Review* (Sept./Oct.).

Garvin, D.A. (1984), 'Japanese Quality Management', *Columbia Journal of World Business* (Fall).

Gietzmann, M. (1991), 'Implementation Issues Associated with the Construction of an Activity-Based Costing System in an Engineering Components Manufacturer', *Management Accounting Research* (2, No. 3).

Goldratt, E. and Cox, J. (1984), *The Goal*, London: Gower.

Goold, M. C. (1986), 'Accounting and Strategy', in M. Bromwich and A. G. Hopwood (eds.), *Research and Current Issues in Management Accounting*, London: Pitman.

Gosse, D.I. (1993), 'The Role of Cost Accounting in a Computer-Integrated Manufacturing Environment: An Empirical Field Study', *Journal of Management Accounting Research*.

Gow, I. (1986), 'Raiders, Invaders or Simply Good Traders?', *Accountancy* (March).

Grant, R. M. (1991), *Contemporary Strategy Analysis: Concepts Techniques and Applications*, Oxford: Basil Blackwell.

Green, F.B. (1991), Amenkhienan, F. and Johnson, G., 'Performance Measures and JIT', *Management Accounting* (USA) (February).

Guin, M. (1990), 'Focus the Factory with Activity-Based Costing', *Management Accounting* (USA) (February).

Gupta, M. (1993), 'Heterogeneity Issues in Aggregated Costing Systems', *Journal of Management Accounting Research*.

Haas, E.A. (1988), 'Breakthrough Manufacturing' in *Cost Accounting for the 90's: Responding to Technological Change*, Montvale, New Jersey: NAA.

Haedicke, J. and Feil, D. (1991), 'Hughes Aircrafts set the Standard for ABC', *Management Accounting* (USA) (February).

Hand, M. (1991), 'Designing Quality into Business Process', *Management Accounting* (UK) (January).

Harris, E. (1990), 'The Impact of JIT Production on Product Costing Information Systems', *Production and Inventory Management Journal.*

Harris Research Centre (1990), *Information for Strategic Management: A Survey of Leading Companies 1990*, KPMG Peat Marwick Management Consultants.

Harrison, M. (1990), 'MRP – Dead or Alive?', Paper presented at the IPS Conference (30 January).

Harvey, M. (1991a), 'A New Era in Costing', *Certified Accountant* (May).

Harvey, M. (1991b), 'Waste Control', *Certified Accountant* (September).

Hasegawa, K. (1986), *Japanese Style Management – An Insider's Analysis*, Tokyo: Kodasha International.

Hayes, R. H., and Abernathy, W. J. (1980), 'Managing Our Way to Economic Decline', *Harvard Business Review* (Winter).

Hayes, R.H. and Garvin, D.A. (1982), 'Managing as if Tomorrow Mattered', *Harvard Business Review* (May/June).

Heagy, C.D. (1991), 'Determining Optimal Quality Costs by Considering Cost of Lost Sales', *Journal of Cost Management for the Manufacturing Industry* (Fall).

Hegtler, P.G. (1984), 'The Industrial Robot: 1985-1995', in S.N. Dwikedi (ed.) *Robotics and Factories of the Future*, N.Y.: Springer-Verlag.

Hendricks, J.A. (1988), 'Applying Cost Accounting to Factory Automation', *Management Accounting* (USA) (December).

Hiromoto, T. (1988), 'Another Hidden Edge – Japanese Management Accounting', *Harvard Business Review* (July/August).

Hirst, P. and Zeitlin, J. (1989), Introduction in Hirst, P. and Zeitlin, J. (eds.), *Reversing Industrial Decline?*, Oxford: Berg.

Hollander, A.S. and Roth, H.P. (1991), 'Statistical Process Control that Minimises Wasteful Production', *Financial and Accounting Systems* (Spring).

Hopwood, A.G. (1980), 'Organisational and Behavioural Aspects of Budgeting and Control', in Arnold, J., Carsberg, B. and Scapens, R. (eds.), *Topics in Management Accounting*, Oxford: Philip Allan.

Horngren, C.T. and Foster, G. (1991), *Cost Accounting: A Managerial Emphasis*, Englewood Cliffs, NJ: Prentice-Hall.

Horngren, C. T., Foster, G., and Datar, S. (1994), *Cost Accounting: A Managerial Emphasis*, Englewood Cliffs, NJ: Prentice-Hall.

Horovitz, J. and Panak, M. (1992), *Total Customer Satisfaction*, London: Pitman.

Hounshell, D.A. (1988), 'The Same Old Principles in the New Manufacturing Environment', *Harvard Business Review* (November/December).

Howell, R. A., Brown, J. D., Soucy, G. R., and Seed, A. H. (1987), *Management Accounting in the New Manufacturing Environment*, Montvale: New Jersey: NAA.

Howell, R. A., and Soucy, G. R. (1987a), 'The New Manufacturing Environment: Major Trends for Management Accounting', *Management Accounting* (USA) (July).

Howell, R.A. and Soucy, G.R. (1987b), 'Cost Accounting in the New Manufacturing Environment', *Management Accounting* (USA) (August).

Hutchins, D. (1989), 'Having a Hard Time', *Fortune*.

Hwang, J., Evans, J.H. and Hegde, V.G. (1993), 'Product Cost Bias and Selection of an Allocation Base', *Journal of Management Accounting Research*.

Inman, R.A. and Mehra, S. (1991), 'The Transferability of Just-in-Time Concepts to American Small Businesses', *Interfaces* (March/April).

Innes, J. and Mitchell, F. (1989), *Management Accounting: The Challenge of Technological Innovation: Electronics Firms*, London: CIMA.

Innes, J. and Mitchell, F. (1990), *Activity-Based Costing: A Review with Case Studies*, London: CIMA.

Innes, J. and Mitchell, F. (1991), 'ABC: A Survey of CIMA Members' *Management Accounting* (UK) (October).

Inoue, S. (1988), 'Recent Development of Cost Management Problems Under Technological Change in Japan', *Research Paper No. 30*, Department of Information Science, Kawaga University.

Inoue, S. (1992), 'A Comparative Study of Cost Management Problems: JUSs (Japanese Affiliates in the USA) and JUKs (Japanese Affiliates in the UK)', *Research Paper No. 46*, Department of Information Science, Kagawa University.

Ishikawa, A. (1989), 'Principles of QC Circle Activities and their Effects on Productivity in Japan: A Corporate Analysis', *Management International Review*, Vol. 25.3, 1985, reprinted in Monden, Y. and Sakurai, M. (eds.), *Japanese Management Accounting: A World Class Approach to Profit Management*, Cambridge,Mass.: Productivity Press.

Jaikumar, R. (1986), 'Post-Industrial Manufacturing', *Harvard Business Review* (November/December).

Jeans, M., and Morrow, M. (1989a), 'Management Accounting in AMT Environments', *Management Accounting* (UK) (April).

Jeans, M. and Morrow, M. (1989b), 'The Practicalities of Using Activity-Based Costing', *Management Accounting* (UK) (November).

Johansson, H.J., Vollman, T.E. and Wright, V. (1986), 'The Effect of Zero Inventory on Cost (Just-In-Time)', in *Cost Accounting for the 90s: The Challenges of Technological Change Proceedings*, Montvale, New Jersey: NAA.

Johnson, H. T. (1987), 'Organisational Design Versus Strategic Information Procedures for Managing Corporate Overhead Cost: Weyerhauser Company 1972-1986,' in Bruns, W. J. and Kaplan, R. S. (eds.), *Accounting and Management: Field Study Perspectives*, Boston, Mass.: Harvard Business School Press.

Johnson, H.T. (1988), 'Activity-Based Information: A Blueprint for World-Class Management Accounting', *Management Accounting* (USA) (June)

Johnson, H. T. (1992), *Relevance Regained*, New York: Free Press.

Johnson, H.T. and Kaplan, R.S. (1987), *Relevance Lost: The Rise and Fall of Management Accounting*, Boston, Mass.: Harvard Business School Press.

Jones, B. (1989), 'Flexible Automation and Factory Politics: The United Kingdom in comparative Perspective', in Hirst, P. and Zeitlin, J. (eds.), *Reversing Industrial Decline?*, Oxford: Berg.

Jones, L.F. (1991), 'Product Costing at Caterpillar', *Management Accounting* (USA) (February).

Jonsson, S. and Gronlund, A. (1988), 'Life with a Subcontractor: New Technology and Management Accounting', *Accounting, Organization and Society*, 13/5.

Juran, J.M. (1988), *Quality Control Handbook*, New York: McGraw Hill.

Kagono, T. and Kansai Productivity Centre (1984), *How Japanese Companies Work?*, Nippon Keizai Shinbun-sha.

Kaplan, R. S. (1983), 'Measuring Manufacturing Performance: A New Challenge for Managerial Accounting Research', *The Accounting Review* (October).

Kaplan, R. S. (1984), 'Yesterday's Accounting Undermines Production', *Harvard Business Review* (July/August).

Kaplan, R. S. (1985), 'Accounting Lag: The Obsolescence of Cost Accounting Systems', in Clark, K. and Lorenze, C., (eds.), *Technology and Productivity: The Uneasy Alliance*, Boston: Harvard Business School Press.

Kaplan, R. S. (1986a), 'Introduction', *Cost Accounting for the 90s: The Challenges of Technological Change Proceedings*, Montvale, New Jersey: NAA.

Kaplan, R.S. (1986b), 'Must CIM Be Justified by Faith Alone?', *Harvard Business Review* (March/April).

Kaplan, R. S. (1988a), 'Relevance Regained', *Management Accounting* (UK) (September).

Kaplan, R.S. (1988b), 'One Cost System Isn't Enough', *Harvard Business Review* (January/February).

Kaplan, R.S. (1990a), 'Introduction', in R.S. Kaplan (ed.) *Measures for Manufacturing Excellence*, Mass., USA: Harvard Business School Press.

Kaplan, R.S. (1990b), 'The Four-Stage Model of Cost Systems Design', *Management Accounting* (USA) (February).

Kaplan, R. S. and Atkinson, A. A. (1989), *Advanced Management Accounting* (Englewood Cliffs, N.J.: Prentice Hall).

Kaplan, R. S., Shank, J. K., Horngren, C. T., Boer, G., Ferrara, W. L., and Robinson, M. P. (1990), 'Contribution Margin Analysis: No Longer Relevant/Strategic Cost Management: The New Paradigm', A Debate edited by M. Robinson, *Journal of Management Accounting Research* (Fall).

Karmarkar, U. (1989), 'Getting Control of Just-in-Time', *Harvard Business Review* (Sept./Oct.).

Karmarkar, U.S., Lederer, P.J. and Zimmerman, J.L. (1991), 'Choosing Manufacturing Production Control and Cost Accounting Systems', in R.S. Kaplan (ed.), *Measures for Manufacturing Excellence* (Cambridge, Mass.: Harvard Business School Press).

Kato, Y. (1993), 'Target Costing Support Systems: Lessons from Leading Japanese Companies', *Management Accounting Research*, (March).

Kawasaki, S. and McMillan, J. (1987), 'The Design of Contracts: Evidence from Japanese Subcontracting', *Journal of the Japanese and International Economies* (I).

Keating, P. J., and Jablowsky, S. P. (1990), *Changing Roles of Financial Management – Getting Close to Business* (Financial Executives Research Foundation).

Kilger, W. (1990), 'Contribution Costing' in Grochla, E., Gangler, E. *et al* (eds.), *Handbook of German Business Management* (Stuttgart: Poeschel Verlag and Springer Verlag).

Kin, I., Park, H.G. and Besser, L.J. (1988), 'Are You Ready for JIT?', *CMA Magazine* (July/August).

King, M., Lee, B., Piper, J. and Whittaker, J. (1991a), *Information Technology and the Working Environment of the Management Accountant*, London: CIMA.

King, M., Lee, R. A., Piper, J. A., and Whittaker, J. (1991b), 'W(h)ither Management Accounting?' *Management Accounting*, (UK), (March).

Kingcott, T. (1991), 'Opportunity Based Accounting: Better than ABC?', *Management Accounting* (USA) (October).

Kobayashi, K. (1982), 'Direct Costing for Pricing Custom-Made Products in Japan's Industries', in Sato, S., Sakate, K., Mueller, G.G. and Radebaugh, L.H. (eds.), *A Compendium of Research on Information and Accounting for Managerial Decision and Control in Japan*, Florida: AAA.

Lammert, T.B. and Ehrsam, R. (1987), 'The Human Element: The Real Challenge in Modernising Cost Systems', *Management Accounting* (USA) (July).

Lancaster, K. S. (1979), '*Variety, Equity and Efficiency: Product Variety in an Industrial Society*', Columbia University Press.

Lebas, M. (1993), 'Tableau de Bord and Performance Measurement', Paper presented at the Management Accounting Research Group Conference, LSE, London, 22nd April.

Leonard, R. (1988), 'Elements of Effective CIM' in *Robotics and Factories of the Future* 1987, N.Y.: Springer-Verlag.

Lewis, C., and McFadyen, K. (1993), 'World Class Finance - 2', *Management Accounting* (UK) (October).

Lillrank, P. and Kano, N. (1989), *Continuous Improvement: Quality Control Circles in Japanese Industry*, Ann Arbour, Mi.: University of Michigan.

Lind, R. (1993), 'Productivity: What are the Prospects?', *Accountancy* (November).

Littler, D. A., and Sweeting, R. C. (1989), *Management Accounting: The Challenge of Technological Innovation: High Technology Industries*, London: CIMA.

Loft, A. (1991), 'The History of Management Accounting: Relevance Found', in D. Ashton, T. Hopper and R.W. Scapens (eds.), *Issues in Management Accounting*, London: Prentice-Hall.

Lorenz, E.H. (1984), 'The Search for Flexibility: Subcontracting Networks in French and British Engineering', in Hirst, P. and Zeitlin, J. (eds.), *Reversing Industrial Decline?*, Oxford: Berg.

Lyall, D., Okah, K. and Puxty, A. (1990), 'Cost Control into the 1990's' *Management Acounting* (UK) (February).

MacArthur, J.B. (1992), 'ABC/JIT Costing', *Journal of Cost Management for the Manufacturing Industry* (Winter).

Mackay, J.T. (1987), 'Eleven Key Issues in Manufacturing Accounting', *Management Accounting* (USA) (January).

Main, J. (1984), 'The Trouble with Managing Japanese Style', *Fortune*, 2/4.

Makido, T. (1989), 'Recent Trends in Japan's Cost Management Practices', in Monden, Y. and Sakurai, M., (eds.) *Japanese Management Accounting: A World Class Approach to Profit Management*, Cam., Mass: Productivity Press.

Manes, R.P. and Cheng, C.S. (1988), 'The Marginal Approach to Joint Cost Allocation: Theory and Application', *Studies in Accounting Research # 29*, Sarasota, Flo: American Accounting Association.

Manoocheri, G.H. (1984), 'Suppliers and the Just-in-Time Concept', *Journal of Purchasing and Materials Management* (Winter).

Maskell, B. (1986), 'Management Accounting and Just-in-Time', *Management Accounting* (UK) (September).

Maskell, B. (1989a), 'Performance Measurement for World Class Manufacturing', *Management Accounting* (UK) (July/August).

Maskell, B. (1989b), 'Performance Measurement for World Class Manufacturing', *Management Accounting*, (UK), (September).

Maskell, B. (1993), 'Why MRP II hasn't created world class manufacturing ... where do we go from here?', *Management Accounting* (UK).

Maurice, M. (1980), Sorge, A. and Warner, M., 'Societal Differences in Organising Manufacturing Units: A Comparison of France, West Germany and Great Britain', *Organization Studies*.

Mayhew, K. (1985), 'Reforming the Labour Market', *Oxford Review of Economic Policy* (Summer).

McHilhattan, R.D. (1987), 'How Cost Management Systems Can Support the JIT Philosophy', *Management Accounting* (USA) (September).

McMillan, C.J. (1985), *The Japanese Industrial System* (Berlin: de Gruyter, 2nd revised edition).

McNair, C. J., and Mosconi, W. (1987), 'Measuring Performance in an Advanced Manufacturing Environment', *Management Accounting* (USA) (July).

McNair, C.J., Mosconi, W. and Norris, T. (1988), *Meeting the Technology Challenge: Cost Accounting in a JIT Environment* (Montvale, New Jersey: NAA).

Mecimore, C.D. (1988), 'Product Costing in a High-Tech Environment, *Journal of Cost Management for the Manufacturing Industry* (Winter).

Merchant, M.E. (1984), 'World Trends in the Automation of Manufacturing', in S.N. Dwivedi (ed.), *Robotics and Factories of the Future*, N.Y.: Springer-Verlag.

Merkle, J.A. (1980), *Managment and Ideology: The Legacy of the International Scientific Management Movement*, Berkeley, Cal.: CUP.

Miles, R. W., and Snow, C. C. (1978), *Organisational Strategy, Structure, and Process*, N.Y.: McGraw Hill.

Miller, J.G. and Vollmann, T.E. (1985), 'The Hidden Factory', *Harvard Business Review* (September/October).

Miltenburg, G.J. (1990), 'Changing MRP's Costing Procedures to suit JIT', *Production and Inventory Management*.

Mintzberg, H. (1978), *'Mintzberg on Management Inside our Strange World of Organisations'* (NY.: Free Press).

Mintzberg, H. (1987), 'Crafting Strategy', *Harvard Business Review* (July/August).

Misawa, M. (1987), 'New Japanese Style Management in a Changing Era', *Columbia Journal of World Business* (Winter).

Molyneux, N. and Davies, R. (1988), 'Machiavelli and the Art of Cost Management', *Leading Edge* (Spring).

Monden, Y. (1989), 'Cost Accounting and Control in Just-in-Time Production Systems: The Daihatsu Kogyo Experience', *Kigyo Kaikei* 40, No. 5, 1988, translated and reprinted in Monden, Y. and Sakurai, M. (eds.), *Japanese Management Accounting: A World Class Approach to Profit Management*, Cam. Mass.: Productivity Press.

Monden, Y., and Sakurai, M. (eds.) (1989), *Japanese Management Accounting: A World Class Approach to Profit Management* (Productivity Press).

Morgan, M. (1990), 'Quality Circles: Management Accounting Applications': *Management Accounting* (UK) (November).

Morgan, M.J. and Weerakoon, P.S.H. (1989), 'Japanese Management Accounting: Its Contribution to the Japanese Economic Miracle', *Management Accounting* (UK) (June).

Morrow, M. (1992), *Activity-Based Management*, Hertfordshire, UK.: Woodhead-Faulkner.

Morrow, M. and Ashworth, G. (1994), 'An Evolving Framework for Activity-Based Approaches', *Management Accounting* (UK) (February).

Moxon, B. (1987), 'Sensor Fusion: The Quest for Autonomous Robots' in R. Radharamann (ed.), *Robotics and Factories of the Future '87*, London: Springer-Verlag.

Moyes, J. (1988), 'The Dangers of JIT', *Managerial Accounting* (UK) (February).

Muellbauer, J. (1986), 'Productivity and Competitiveness in British Manufacturing', *Oxford Review of Economic Policy* (Vol. 2, No. 3).

Mueller, D.C. (1989), *Public Choice II*, Cambridge: Cambridge University Press.

Munro, R. (1987), 'From Just-In-Case to Just-In-Time', *The Accountants' Magazine* (August).

Murphy, J. and Braund, S. L. (1990), 'Management Accounting and New Manufacturing Technology', *Management Accounting* (UK) (February).

Musgrave, R.A. and Musgrave, P. (1980), *Public Finance in Theory and Practice*, N.Y.: McGraw-Hill.

Musgrove, C.L. and Fox, M.J. (1991), *Quality Costs*, Hertfordshire, UK.: Technical Communications.

Nagamatsu, H. and Tanaka, T. (1988), *Management Accounting in the Advanced Manufacturing Surrounding - Comparative Study on Surveys in Japan and USA*, Tokyo, Japan: NAA.

Nakane, C. (1973), *Japanese Society*, Middlesex: Penguin.

Nanni, A.J., Miller, J.G. and Vollmann, T.E. (1988), 'What Shall We Account For?' *Management Accounting* (USA) (January).

New, C.C. and Myers, A. (1987), *Management Manufacturing Operations in the UK 1975-85*, London: British Institute of Management.

Newmann, B.R., and Jaouen, P.R. (1986), 'Kanban, Zips and Cost Accounting: A Case Study', *Journal of Accountancy* (August).

Nicholls, B. (1992), 'ABC in the U.K. - A Status Report *Management Accounting* (UK) (May).

Nixon, B., and Lonie, A.A. (1991), 'A Strategic Approach to Management Accounting: Preliminary Evidence from 13 Case Studies'. (Paper presented for the BAA Scottish Conference, Aberdeen).

Noreen, E. (1991), 'Conditions Under Which Activity-Based Costing Systems Provide Relevant Costs', *Journal of Management Accounting Research* (Fall).

O'Neal, C.R. (1987), 'The Buyer-Seller Linkage in a Just-In-Time Environment', *Journal of Purchasing and Materials Management* (Spring).

Ohno, T. (1988), *Toyota Production System: Beyond Larger-Scale Production*, Cambridge, Mass.: Productivity Press.

Ostranga, M.R. (1990), 'Activities: The Focal Point of Total Cost Management', *Management Accounting* (USA) (February).

Ostranga, M.R. (1991), 'Return on Investment Through the Cost of Quality', *Journal of Cost Management for the Manufacturing Industry* (Summer).

Panzar, J.C. and Willig, R.D. (1981), 'Economies of Scope', *American Economic Association, Papers and Proceedings* (May).

Parker, T. and Lettes, T. (1991), 'Is Accounting Standing in the Way of Flexible Computer-Integrated Manufacturing?', *Management Accounting* (USA) (February).

Pasework, W.R. (1991), 'The Evolution of Quality Control Costs in American Manufacturing', *Journal of Cost Management for the Manufacturing Industry* (Spring).

Pearson, G. (1986), 'The Strategic Discount—Protecting New Business Against DCF', *Long Range Planning*.

Peavey, D. E. (1990), 'Battle at the GAAP? It's Time For a Change', *Management Accounting* (USA) (February).

Philips, A. and Collins, D.E. (1990), 'How Borg-Warner made the Transition from Pile Accounting to JIT', *Management Accounting* (USA) (October).

Pitman, J. (1993), 'Japan is Sailing Towards An Unemployment Iceberg' *The Times* (22 October).

Plunkett, J.J. and Dale, B.G. (1990), 'Quality Costing' in B.G. Dale and J.J. Plunkett (eds.) *Managing Quality*, London: Philip Allan.

Plunkett, J.J., Dale, B.G. and Tyrrell, R.W. (1985), *Quality Costs*, London: DTI.

Ponemon, L.A. (1990), 'Accounting for Quality Costs', *Journal of Cost Management for the Manufacturing Industry* (Fall).

Porter, M. E. (1985), *Competitive Advantage: Creating and Sustaining Superior Performance*, New York: The Free Press.

Price, F. (1990), 'TQM "Cocklestalls" Build a Firm Quality Muscle', *Management Consultancy* (July/August).

Primrose, P.L. (1988), 'AMT Investment and Costing Systems', *Management Accounting* (UK) (October).

Primrose, L., Creamer, G.D. and Leonard, R. (1985), 'Identifying and Quantifying the Company-Wide Benefits of CAD Within the Structure of a Comprehensive Investment Programme', *Computer Aided Design*.

Raffish, N. and Turney, P.B.B. (1991), 'Glossary of Activity-Based Management', *Journal of Cost Management for the Manufacturing Industry* (Fall).

Ramasech, R.V. (1990), 'Recasting the Traditional Inventory Model to Implement Just-in-Time Purchasing', *Production and Inventory Management Journal*.

Rickwood, C. P., Coates, J. B., and Stacey, R. S. (1990), 'Stapylton: Strategic Management Accounting to Gain Competitive Advantage', *Management Accounting Research* (March).

Robinson, M.A. and Timmerman, J.E. (1987), 'How Vendor Analysis Supports JIT', *Management Accounting* (USA) (December).

Robson, M. (1988), *Quality Circles: A Practical Guide*, Hants., UK.: Gower.

Romano, P. L. (1987), 'Manufacturing in Transition', *Management Accounting* (USA) (November).

Romano, P.L. (1989), 'Advanced Manufacturing: US vs. Japan', *Management Accounting* (USA) (February).

Roth, H.P. and Borthick, A.F. (1989), 'Getting Closer to Real Product Costs', *Management Accounting* (USA) (May).

Russell, G.W., and Dilts, D.M. (1986), 'Are Accountants Delaying the Automation of America?', in *Cost Accounting for the 90's: The Challenge of Technological Change Proceedings*, Montvale, N.J.: NAA).

Russell, J.P. (1991), *Quality Management Benchmark Assessment*, New York: Quality Resources.

Sabel, C.F. (1989), 'Flexible Specialization and the Re-emergence of Regional Economies', in Hirst, P. and Zeitlin, J. (eds.), *Reversing Industrial Decline?*, Oxford: Berg.

Sako, M. (1992), *Prices, Quality and Trust: How Japanese and British Companies Manage Buyer- Supplier Relations*, Cambridge: Cambridge University Press.

Sakurai, M. (1989), 'Target Costing and How to Use It', *Journal of Cost Management for Manufacturing Industry* (Summer).

Sakurai, M. and Huang, P.Y. (1989), 'A Japanese Survey of Factory Automation and its Impact on Management Control Systems', in Monden, Y. and Sakurai, M., (eds.), *Japanese Management Accounting: A World Class Approach to Profit Management*, Cambridge, Mass.: Productivity Press.

Scapens, R.W. and Roberts, J. (1993), 'Accounting and Control: A Case Study of Resistance to Accounting Change', *Management Accounting Research* (March).

Schiff, J.B. (ed.) (1991), *Cost Management Update*, National Association of Accountants (September).

Schniederjans, M.J. (1993), *Topics in Just-In-Time Management*, Mass; USA: Allyn and Bacon.

Schoenfeld, H-M.W. (1974), *Cost Terminology and Cost Theory: A Study of its Development and Present State in Central Europe*, Urbana: Center for International Education and Research in Accounting.

Schoenfeld, H-M.W. (1990), 'The Development of Cost Theory in Germany: A Historical Survey', *Management Accounting Research* (Vol.1 No.4).

Schonberger, R.I. (1982a), 'The Transfer of Japanese Manufacturing Management Approaches to US Industry', *Academy of Management Review*.

Schonberger, R. I. (1982b), *Japanese Manufacturing Techniques: Nine Hidden Lessons in Simplicity*, New York: Free Press.

Schonberger, R.I. (1986), *World Class Manufacturing*, New York: Free Press.

Seddon, J. and Jackson, S. (1990), 'TQM and Culture Change', *The TQM Magazine* (August).

Seed, A.H. (1988), *Adapting Management Accounting Practice to an Advanced Manufacturing Environment*, Montvale, New Jersey: NAA.

Seed, A. H. (1990), 'Improving Cost Management', *Management Accounting* (USA) (February).

Seicht, G. (1990), 'Cost Accounting' in Grochla, E., Gangler, E. *et al* (eds.), *Handbook of German Business Management*, Poeschel Verlag and Springer Verlag.

Shank, J. K. (1989), 'Strategic Cost Management: New Wine or Just New Bottles?', *Journal of Management Accounting Research*, 1.

Shank, J. K., and Govindarajan, V. (1988), 'Transaction-Based Costing for the Complex Product Line: A Field Study', *Journal of Cost Management for the Manufacturing Industry* (Summer).

Shank, J. K., and Govindarajan, V. (1989a), 'Making Strategy Explicit in Cost Analysis: A Case Study', *Sloan Management Review* (Spring 1988) reprinted in Shank and Govindarajan, 1989b.

Shank, J. K., and Govindarajan, V. (1989b), '*Strategic Cost Analysis: The Evolution from Managerial to Strategic Accounting*', Homewood Il.: Irwin.

Sharkey, W.W. (1989), *The Theory of Natural Monopoly*, Cambridge: Cambridge University Press.

Sheppard, J. (1990), 'The Strategic Management of IT Investment Decisions: A Research Note', *British Journal of Management*.

Shields, M.D. and Young, S.M. (1989), 'A Behavioural Model for Implementing Cost Management Systems', *Journal of Cost Management for the Manufacturing Industry* (Winter).

Shields, M.D. and Young, S.M. (1991), 'Managing Product Life Cycle Costs: An Organisational Model' *Journal of Cost Management for the Manufacturing Industry* (Fall).

Simmonds, K. (1981A), 'Strategic Management Accounting', *Management Accounting* (UK) (April).

Simmonds, K. (1981b), 'The Fundamentals of Strategic Management Accounting', ICMA Occasional Paper Series, London: ICMA.

Singhal, K. (1987), 'Introduction: The Design and Implementation of Automated Manufacturing Systems', *Interfaces* (November/ December).

Smith, M. (1994), 'Improving Management Accounting Reporting Practices: A Total Quality Management Approach Part I, *Journal of Cost Management* (Winter).

Society of Management Accountants of Canada (1993), *Activity Based Costing* (Management Accounting Issues Paper 3).

Spicer, B.H. (1992), 'The Resurgence of Cost and Management Accounting: A Review of Some Recent Developments in Practice, Theories and Case Research Methods', *Management Accounting Research* (March).

Stamm, C.L. and Golbar, D.Y. (1991), 'Customer and Supplier Linkages for Small JIT Manufacturing Firms', *Journal of Small Business Management* (July).

Staubus, G.J. (1990), 'Activity Costing: Twenty Years On', *Management Accounting Research* (December).

Stec, S. (1989), 'Costing for the 90's', *Management Accounting* (USA) (September).

Stokes, C.R. (1989), 'JIT: Will Suppliers Embrace their New Roles?', *Business* (June).

Strange, N.P.J. (1991), *Accounting for Decline: Management Accounting in Large Engineering Companies in Germany and Great Britain* INSEAD.

Susman, G. I. (1989), 'Product Life Cycle Management', *Journal of Cost Management for the Manufacturing Industry*, (Summer).

Tagushi, G. (1986), *Introduction to Quality Engineering*, New York: Asian Productivity Organisation.

Tanaka, M. (1989), 'Cost Planning and Control in the Design Phase of a Product', in Monden, Y. and Sakurai, M. (eds.), *Japanese Management Accounting: A World Class Approach to Profit Management*, Cambridge, Mass.: Productivity Press.

Tanaka, Y. (1993), *Problems in Manufacturing and Cost Management in Japan: The Situation in 1990*, Working Paper, Kagawa University.

Tani, A. (1992), 'Diffusion of Numerically Controlled Machine Tools in Japan and the USA', in R.U. Ayres, W. Haywood and I. Tchijov (eds.), *Computer Integrated Manufacturing (Volume III): Models, Case Studies and Forecasts of Diffusion*, London: Chapman and Hall.

Tani, T., Okano, H., Shimizu, N., Iwabuchi, Y., Fukuda, J., Cooray, S., Kobayashi, T. and Kata, Y. (1993), 'Genka Kikaku in Japanese Firms: Current State of the Art', Kobe University Working Paper.

Tatikonda, M.V. (1988), 'Just-in-Time and Modern Manufacturing Environments: Implications for Cost Accounting', *Production and Inventory Management*.

Tatikonda, L.U. and Tatikonda, R.J. (1989), 'Success in MRP', *Management Accounting* (USA) (May).

Tchijov, I. (1992), 'International Diffusion Forecasts', in R.U. Ayres, W. Haywood and I. Tchijov (eds.), *Computer Integrated Manufacturing (Volume III): Models, Case Studies and Forecasts of Diffusion*, London: Chapman and Hall.

Teece, D.J. (1980), 'Economies of Scope and the Scope of the Enterprise', *Journal of Economic Behaviour and Organisation* (September).

Teece, D.J. (1982), 'Towards an Economic Theory of the Multi product Firm', *Journal of Economic Behaviour and Organisation* (March).

Thackray, P. (1990), 'The Issue is Quality', *Management Accounting* (UK) (September).

Truesdale, T.A. and Carr, C. (1991), *The Experience of Nissan Suppliers: Lessons for the United Kingdom Engineering Industry*, National Economic Development Office.

Tsurumi, Y. and Tsurumi, H. (1985), 'Value-Added Maximising Behaviour of Japanese Firms and Roles of Corporate Investment and Finance', *Columbia Journal of World Business* (Spring).

Turney, P.B.B. (1990), 'Ten Myths About Implementing an Activity-Based Cost System', *Journal of Cost Management for the Manufacturing Industry* (Spring).

Uemura, S. (1989), 'The Japanese Way Of Management: Its Characteristics, Current Practices And Future Perspectives', *Business Review* (No. 2).

Vangermeersh, R. (1986), 'Milestones in the History of Management Accounting', in *Cost Accounting for the 90s: The Challenges of Technological Change Proceedings*, Montvale, New Jersey: NAA.

Vor, J.A., Saraph, J.V. and Petersen, D.L. (1990), 'JIT Implementation Practices', *Production and Inventory Management Journal*.

Voss, C.A. and Robinson, S.J. (1987), 'Application of Just-in-Time Manufacturing Techniques in the United Kingdom', *International Journal of Operations and Production Management* (Number 4).

Waldron, D. (1988), 'Measure Your Way to Profit', *Certified Accountant* (May).

Walkin, L. (1991), 'ABC-Key Players and their Tools', *Management Accounting* (USA) (February).

Weisz, R., Rothbaum, F. and Blackburn, T.C. (1984), 'Standing Out and Standing In - The Psychology of Control in America and Japan', *American Psychologist* (39).

Wilson, G. E. (1983), 'Theory Z: Implications for Management Accountants', *Management Accounting* (USA) (November).

Wilson, R.M.S. (1991), 'Strategic Management Accounting', in D. Ashton, T. Hopper and R.W. Scapens (eds.), *Issues in Management Accounting*, London: Prentice-Hall.

Woods, M.D. (1989), 'How We Changed Our Accounting', *Management Accounting* (USA) (February).

Woods, M., Pokorny, M., Lintner, V. and Blinkhorn, M. (1985), 'Appraising Investment in New Technology: The Approach in Practice', *Management Accounting* (UK) (October).

World Competitiveness Report (1993), IMD International and World Economic Forum.

Worthy, F.S. (1991), 'Japan's ... Secret Weapon', *Fortune*, August 12.

Yoshikawa, T. (1988a), Report of Meeting on March 14, Edinburgh University.

Yoshikawa, T. (1988b), 'Characteristics of Cost Accounting Systems and their Practical Applications in Japan', unpublished paper, Yokohama University.

Yoshikawa, T., Innes, J. and Mitchell, F. (1989), 'Japanese Management Accounting: A Comparative Survey', *Management Accounting* (UK) (November).

Yoshikawa, T., Innes, J., Mitchell, F. and Tanaka, M. (1993), *Contemporary Cost Management*, London: Chapman and Hall.

Young, S.M. and Selto, F.H. (1991), 'New Manufacturing Practices and Cost Management: A Review of the Literature and Directions for Research', *Journal of Accounting Literature* (10).